Children's Book Collecting

Carolyn
Clugston
Michaels

Children's

Book

Collecting

Decorations by William Michaels

Library Professional Publications 1993

First published 1993 as a
Library Professional Publication, an imprint of
The Shoe String Press, Inc.,
Hamden, Connecticut 06514

Library of Congress Cataloging-in-Publication Data

Michaels, Carolyn Clugston.
Children's book collecting
by Carolyn Clugston Michaels
p.   cm.
Includes bibliographical references and index.
1. Book collecting—United States.
2. Book collecting—Great Britain.   3. Children's literature,
English—Collectors and collecting—United States.
4. Children's literature, English—Collectors and
collecting—Great Britain.   I. Title.
Z987.5U6M53   1993   92-35088   002′.074′73—dc20
ISBN 0-208-02267-8 (alk. paper)

Excerpt from "One Moment" by Vesle
Fenstermaker is reprinted with the author's
permission.

Excerpts from "The Osborne Collection of
Early Children's Books" by Judith St. John
in *The Horn Book Magazine*, September/October
1984, pp. 652–660, are reprinted by permission
of The Horn Book, Inc., 14 Beacon St., Boston,
Massachusetts 02108.

The paper used in this publication meets the minimum
requirements of American National Standard for
Information Sciences—Permanence of Paper for Printed
Library Materials, ANSI Z39.48-1984. ∞

Printed in the United States of America

Think what a book is. It is a portion of the eternal mind, caught in its process through the world, stamped in an instant, and preserved for eternity.

—Lord Houghton
The Life and Letters of John Keats

To three patches of my storybook, with love:

Where I came from—
my parents, Alice Madelyn Beck Clugston
        Charles Dennett Clugston

Where I am now—
my husband, William Manly Michaels
and
my children, Bruce Carl Leopold
        Madelyn Dennette Leopold

Where I hope my spirit will find a continuing home—
my grandchildren, Clare Evett Kazanski, 1985
        Christopher Joseph Leopold Kazanski, 1990

Contents

Preface

A preface functions as a rearview mirror of the completed text. Written last, it permits the author a personal reprise after enough time has elapsed for a sense of the whole to emerge. *The Bookman's Glossary* suggests such preface topics as "Why write this particular book?" and "What, if any, wisdom grew from the reading and research—library and human?"

The answer to "why" is Virginia Mathews, who asked if I would like to write a reference book on collecting children's books. So I began—by shopping for a word processor. Two years, much learning, and 2,000 miles of toting computer and reference library between Washington, D.C., and Charleston, South Carolina have now come and gone.

My professional experience preceding this book doesn't represent a straight line to anything. I term it "patchwork"—created by fitting ability and opportunity into a design determined by marriage and motherhood. Patches relevant to this book include a master's in library science from the Catholic University of America, school librarianship in Washington, D.C., a position as curriculum librarian to the Montgomery County, Maryland, Board of Education, public library reference librarianship, authorship on librarianship, children's book reviewing, desultory dealership in antiquarian children's books, and fifty years of active personal collecting. All the patches show a lifetime of reading children's books. Being paid to read and evaluate them was fun, but having one on my bedside table to compose my spirit for sleep is necessary. I truly believe that America's current ability to co-exist with our overwhelming social ills is the direct result of the need to develop a mental skin thick enough to watch the eleven o'clock television news and then go to sleep.

As for what I learned from writing this book, my author's rearview mirror reflects a clearer understanding of the development of that special adult who is addicted to children's books. What distinguishes the work of these writers, publishers, illustrators, librarians, collectors, and booksellers from their peers is an orientation toward service, not profit. Except for collectors, all of us operate with a bottom line, but it acts as our servant, not our master. Our greatest enthusiasm is for form and content—books of spiritual and physical quality to serve the highest needs of children. We view childhood as a human resource for whose welfare we are responsible, not as a gold reserve to fill our pockets. As nurturers we believe in the existence of a right and a wrong way to "grow" children—and the right way demands positive literature to foster and sustain growth.

How does children's literature operate to shape the adult values that distinguish the people of the children's book world? How does the intensity of its first impact endure? How did childhood stimuli "grow into" mental guideposts capable of directing adult thinking? In the title essay of *Climb into a Bell Tower*, the author, teacher and poet Myra Cohn Livingston gives one person's answer, based on her childhood exposure to Hans Christian Andersen's *The Snow Queen*:

> It would be tempting for me to have reread this story long before now, but I won't, for it remains . . . one of the few keys I have to books as I remember them—not what they *are* to the adult in me, but what they *were* to the child in me that lives. I speak now of the important difference between comprehension, the complete understanding, and apprehension, the almost unconscious awareness of what is rumbling beneath the words, the intuitive understanding, if you will. *The Snow Queen*, then as now, is about the friendship of a boy and girl for each other, interrupted by something evil, a glass sliver in Kay's eye, a painful separation, but something to make everything all right in the end . . . I tend to view literature and art in terms of apprehension, and I suspect children do too . . . Literature, in my terms, deals in symbols broad enough to reach beyond the specific, to engage the reader in a dialogue not only with universals but with himself, as part of that universe. So, if the sliver in Kay's eye appeared to me as an apprehension of evil, I was able then, and now, to put a hundred names to that evil in other forms. (p. 208)

Livingston's explanation of how the power of "fairy" can be internalized in childhood describes the development of the mind-set that distinguishes those adults for whom children's books are important. Because we early feel comfortable in "calling a spade a spade"—naming the white witch evil—we continue to connect to literature that makes these calls. Because we do not hide from naming and being named, we acknowledge standards of conduct. As adults we must live with situational ethics, but for children's book people "right" comes first to mind, whether the standard it directs can always be applied or not.

My *Snow Queen* is George MacDonald's *The Princess and Curdie*. It showed me evil—conquered by trust and hope. The princess and her father the king trusted a young miner, Curdie, who trusted the "great, great, great grandmother, Queen Irene" enough to plunge his hand into her rose-petal fire where he receives the gift of knowing character. Queen Irene speaks to Curdie:

> Now here is what the rose-fire has done for you; it has made your hands so knowing and wise, it has brought your real hands so near the outside of your flesh gloves, that you will henceforth be able to know at once the hand of a man who is growing into a beast; nay, more—you will at once feel the foot of the beast he is growing, just as if there were no glove made like a man's hand between you and it . . . According then to your knowledge of that beast, will be your knowledge of the man you have to deal with. (p. 69–70)

Magic adds the power of hope to Curdie's native abilities, allowing him to complete his charge of rescuing Gwyntystorm. Though my character-reading ability comes from the magic of life and love, I still believe in the message of hands. But what about the grim in Grimm that Bruno Bettelheim, Betsy Hearne, and many others believe to be the other side of "fairy"—the back without which there cannot be a front?

That precisely is the connection I wish to make. Angels we people of the children's book are not. We are human beings whose childhood experiences with literature shaped our characters, producing adults with value systems never deaf to morality. A determining characteristic of our chosen literature is its presentation of the bare bones of life—the evil and the good—in a story that includes the requisite power of hope provided either by some magic word or by a wise being. That is my rearview mirror reprise: my conviction of the lifelong impact of children's literature and its power "to engage the reader in a dialogue, not only with universals, but with himself, as part of the universe."

Some of those to be publicly thanked connect to earlier "patchwork" quotes from my 1985 book, *Library Literacy Means Lifelong Learning*. Again, for "her gift of able ear and blue pencil" go flower-baskets of thanks to my colleague/editor, Kathryn Shohl Scott. Dale W. Brown of the Arlington County Schools, Arlington, Virginia, has been an almost career-long mentor as has Dr. Elizabeth W. Stone, Dean Emerita of the Catholic University School of Library and Information Science. An illustrations credit to my artist husband, Dr. William M. Michaels, for the sketches that help create the book's illustrative quality. My daughter, Madelyn Leopold, now a lawyer and formerly an editor at Little, Brown, used her broad skill base to gentle me toward reconciling disk and hard copy. Joan Kuhn Thomas, a beloved Holton-Arms colleague, once more put my chapter quotations into calligraphy. Editorial considerations kept this labor of loving expertise from seeing print, and her sudden tragic death on October 8, 1992 will keep Joan from seeing the finished book.

Arthur Plotnik, former editor of *American Libraries*, gave me the chance to hear from collectors and collection managers nationwide through that magazine. Among those experts who contributed priceless peer review are Carolyn W. Field who read chapter 1; Nancy Larrick, who with Lee Bennett Hopkins and Myra Cohn Livingston served as poetry consultants; and Maria Salvadore, who read an early draft.

Peggy Coughlan was an invaluable answerer of questions and a properly severe sounding board. Mae Durham Rogers, Linda K. Murphy, Anita Silvey, and Ginny Moore Kruse generously gave unique, hand-tailored help. From the faculty of the College of Charleston, Dr. Charles E. Matthews provided online searches and Dr. Mary Blake insisted that holistic reading instruction be included. For their gifts of personal communications thanks are due to Jane K. Adelson, Allen Ahearn, Betty and Douglas Duffy, Dr. Donald Farren, Doris Frohnsdorf, Scott Husby, Gil O'Gara, Blanche Ebling-Koenig, Jo Ann Reisler, Martha Smith, Dr. Dale A. Sorenson, and Peter Stockham, and to the many others for their generous comments. By including me in Library of Congress seminars, Sybille Jagusch, Chief of the Children's Literature Center, provided opportunities for dazzling anecdotal research. Jim Presgraves of Bookworm and Silverfish, Wytheville, Virginia, and Amelia Wolf of Charleston's Atlantic Books contributed their dealer ears and advice. Finally, for TLC hands-on education in the mysteries of word processing I'm indebted to a superb teacher, Carolyn Scott Miranda, and a fine technician, Larry Olson.

CAROLYN DENNETTE CLUGSTON LEOPOLD MICHAELS
Washington, D.C.
Charleston, S.C.
December, 1992

1

Children's Literature: A Brief Historical Overview

We children's book collectors search for pieces of publishing history and cozy our homes with these tangible reminders of our own childhood. The collector's interest in children's books goes many dimensions beyond that of the first readers—the children themselves. We search to repossess experience, either of the physical book itself or of the text's window to memories of powerful early pain or joy. Those who re-read and thus re-internalize can relive some of the strongest emotions underlying adult personality.

Wordsmiths create literature, but without visual artists it could not become that singular literary collectible, a children's book. As an art form, its development and continuing existence rest upon the creative efforts of centuries of literary and graphic artists—authors, editors, illustrators, designers, paper makers, printers, and binders. Content and format—message and medium—combine to create this artistic power. Some content and illustration prove timeless, new talents appear, and changing technology affects format and offers challenging illustrative opportunities.

Children's literature encompasses everything children have chosen or has been chosen for children. In a narrow sense, it includes only that writing intended for their instruction or entertainment. In a broad sense, it embraces all literature marked by simplicity, healthy humor, vividness of expression, and imagination. That explains why folktales, ballads, legends, poetry, myths, stories of magic, adventure, exploration, and worlds and characters made intelligible by the great novelists have always belonged to children. To go back to the beginnings—the rhymes and stories that form the most enduring elements of children's literature—returns us to listening beside the fires of our earliest ancestors. Characters from this long history of "story" belong to all categories of earth's animate and inanimate denizens—the "Family of Man," the "Kingdom of the Animals," the plant world, and a whole catalog of objects.

This overview proposes to give collectors a foundation from which to extend their knowledge. It must be selective and therefore not inclusive, can only be organized in one logic, and primarily addresses the concerns of the English-speaking world. In spite of the intertwining of text and illustrative material in the book, for convenience sake text is discussed first here, with illustration following. In addition to an ever-growing knowledge of the tools and topics of children's literature, we who seek it out as adults need to be familiar with the publishers that give it life and substance within a book, the libraries that maintain and provide access to it, and its societal roles.

Imaginative literature is composed of several separate storytelling forms. These are familiar to us, but in everyday use the distinctions between things both familiar and related blur easily. Being knowledgeable about children's literature requires sensitivity to these differences.

Myths are explanations of the how and why of the world; in a sense they are the antecedents of scientific truth.

Folklore is a synonym for the oral tradition, a mirror for the social history of a people, and the primary instrument for cultural continuity. Its use formalizes tradition within the noninstitutional culture and creates the special rites that identify and unify family groups—our "only ways" to trim the Christmas tree, and stuff the Thanksgiving turkey.

Fairy stories or *Tales* employ magic in "once upon a time"—the indefinite past, the deliberate "not now." They are usually short pieces with a human protagonist.

Fables have animals or inanimate objects as protagonists and are told to point a moral.

Legends concern heroic achievements—real or imaginary—with more history and less of the supernatural than a myth. In an urban setting, they may be rumors; in the life of a country they are Switzerland's William Tell or America's Paul Bunyan. Legends serve to reinforce the edges of what is otherwise hard to express concretely.

Fantasy employs superstition in a modern form, belonging to the time of the novel. It requires a suspension of physical reality such as the creation of a new world or a time shift.

Science fiction moves into the future from a basis of known scientific facts, given the advances promised by fact or theory. It allows travel to new worlds to discover their landscapes and inhabitants and depends heavily on technology.

A basic definition separating poetry from prose describes poetry as having poetic qualities of spirit, feelings, and rhythms characterized by basically regular recurrences of elements such as beat or accent. Poetry can be considered as oral literature, and its ability to communicate depends upon the precise correctness of each word, which, in turn, depends upon hearing each word with our minds as well as with our ears.

According to the British critic, John Rowe Townsend, in his celebrated book, *Written for Children*:

> Poetry wanders unconcerned across the vague and shifting border between children's books and just plain books. A great deal of lyric poetry lies open to young readers, and children's poetry anthologies normally include a high proportion of verse that was written without any special thought of a child readership. This is not surprising, since in one respect at least poet's and child's eye work in the same way. The gift of seeing and feeling things afresh, as if they had never been seen or felt before, is traditionally a quality of the lyric poet; it is also a childlike quality. . . . Children can grasp imaginatively a great deal that in literal terms they cannot understand. (p. 131)

Elizabeth Nesbitt, writing in *A Critical History of Children's Literature*, adds:

> It is desirable that writers of prose for children should retain, in their maturity, vivid memories of childhood impressions. It is essential that writers of poetry for children should do so. Poetry is inherently a thing of mood and emotion, of response to impression. Except for the straightforward, objective narrative and purely nonsensical types, it is a form of literature innately tended toward the subjective. The subjective either in its retrospective or introspective mood, has no interest for children, who have not lived long enough to know the wistful longing for things possessed and lost, and who feel intensely, but never analyze their feeling. (p. 407)

Prose and poetry—all of children's literature has its deepest roots in the stories told around family hearths or in the halls of the high kings. All gathered to listen, to be entertained and informed, just as all did the same work, wore the same clothes, and ate the same food. They heard explanations of the beginnings of the world, the coming of their own family or tribe, heroic deeds, and the natural phenomena that delighted or terrified them. Mothers sang to their babes, old people recounted tales, both homely and adventurous, and professional storytellers polished their favorites into ballads and hero tales. The symbolic wisdom of folk literature and the growing reservoir of practical knowledge were precise and limited enough to be of value for the whole community.

When parents first share tales with their children, they set the pattern for productive and imaginative lives. Oral communication—whether heard around a campfire in prehistory or in Yellowstone Park, or shared from a book in a family room—has proved the most effective medium for imprinting language. In his book *Wordstruck*, Robert MacNeil says:

> Laid down . . . is the term used in sound and videotape editing. . . . It must be with words as it is with music. . . . Words and word patterns accumulate in layers, and as the layers thicken they govern all use and appreciation of language thenceforth. Like music, the patterns of melody, rhythm, and quality of voice become templates against which we judge the sweetness and justness of new patterns and rhythms; and the patterns laid down in our memories create expectations and hungers for fulfillment again. (p. 23–24)

Historians describe four fairly distinct time periods covering the development of children's literature. The first would begin in prehistory, could we know it, and continues as the earliest known precepts, tales, songs, and poems were recorded. Next comes the period of compilation during the Middle Ages (4th to 15th centuries) when literary continuity depended upon energetic and dedicated monks. The third period begins with the 15th century establishment of the printing press. This technology made possible a widespread dissemination of literature which, in turn, revealed a popular fondness for recreational literature, which, in turn, revealed its base in an international, multicultural interrelationship of lore and tales. This domino effect culminated in the clergy's determined efforts to counter it with new religious publications. The fourth period, termed "modern," dates from the 18th century, when children's own interests began to be considered and authors and others worked to please them, the ultimate consumers. This time period now forms the available practical collecting universe for most of us.

‖ BEGINNINGS: THE AGE OF PRECEPT AND LORE

Ancient Egyptian records provide two very early examples of "for all ages" literature. The oldest manuscript yet discovered that addresses children directly, *The Precepts of Ptah-Hetep* (c. 2600 B.C.) directs that "a good son is a gift of the gods"; and a story, "The Shipwrecked Sailor" (c. 2500 B.C.) prefigures Daniel Defoe's 1719 *Robinson Crusoe*. From Greece in 850 B.C. came Homer's two epic poems, the *Iliad* and the *Odyssey*, which are the text for all versions of the Homeric legends. The Greek slave, Aesop (c. 620–560 B.C.) gave his name and dramatic liveliness to fables, that class of early didactic animal tales told to point a moral. To childhood's store of instruction,

Greece added the first great histories—the words of Herodotus (c. 484–424 B.C.) and Thucydides (454–399 B.C.). Caesar's *Commentaries on the Gallic Wars* (c. 50 B.C.) represents a textbook for the Roman child who read it as modern history.

‖ THE MIDDLE AGES

What ensured the safe passage of story during the Middle Ages—those ten centuries from about 476 A.D. to 1450 A.D.? We owe this debt to the monastic scribes who labored to preserve and increase society's accumulated literary store. Few children survived to adulthood, and far fewer of these could read. Oral literature still dominated. Those English children that did learn to read were usually taught by such outstanding scholar-teachers as Bede, Alcuin, and Aelfric. Current theology did color the lesson books they authored, but most had additional secular content. A form of writing termed *dialogues*, based on an ancient Greek form, was introduced as was teaching with riddles. The forerunner of encyclopedias appeared in the 12th century developed by Anselm, Archbishop of Canterbury. The indigenous store of literature remained internationally interconnected with Egyptian tales, Indian fables, Persian romances. Some scholars view *The Arabian Nights Entertainment* or *The Book of A Thousand and One Nights* as drawing from virtually all existing literatures. One textual version from 8th-century India includes "Ali Baba and the Forty Thieves," "Aladdin or the Wonderful Lamp," and the "Merchant and the Genie."

Growing from the folklore and romance cycles of the unlettered medieval populace outside monastic walls, there came into existence five great pieces of enduring folk literature that children took for their own. Romantic France contributed the *The Song of Roland*, (mid-11th century Brittany), whose hero, a mythical knight, accompanied Charlemagne's army to Spain. *Jack, the Giant Killer* derives from one exploit of the Anglo-Saxon hero Beowulf (existing medieval manuscript dated c. 1000 A.D.) when he battles the monster Grendel in the hall of a king. This ancient, oral saga was probably first set down following the 5th century German invasion of Britain. Scandinavia contributed a cycle of heroic legends, called the *Eddas*, comparable to those of Homer, that survive from a manuscript of the 13th century. One of the most popular collections of tales from England's Middle Ages that, in modified form, provided juvenile adventure story reading was *Gesta Romanorum*, or *Deeds of the Romans*, compiled in Latin around the end of the 13th century. The English legend that has produced the greatest number of literary descendents is the cycle built around the figure of King Arthur. Most celebrated of these works inspired by the *Historia Regum Britanniae* of Geoffrey of Monmouth (c. 1100–1154 A.D.) is *Morte D'Arthur*, published by

Sir Thomas Malory in the first half of the 15th century. It is remembered today chiefly for those parts that Chaucer, Shakespeare and Howard Pyle appear to have borrowed. *The Canterbury Tales* of Geoffrey Chaucer (1340–1400) warrants mention for its record of emotions, activities, and physical settings which has both supplied authors with a continuing font of material and supported the development of realism.

‖ THE EFFECTS OF THE PRINTING PRESS: 1500 TO 1800

After hundreds of years of refining that began with the Chinese, the process of printing from moveable type was established in England by William Caxton (1422–1491). Children's literature owes him a great debt for printing the old tales, crudely translated or adapted, and making use of the English dependence on sea trade to speed his English language versions to the European market. Some noteworthy Caxton editions are Malory's *King Arthur, Fables of Aesop, Reynard the Fox,* and *The Golden Legend.*

During all these years material that later became literature for children was not created for them. Instructional books represented the only concession to children as special consumers of books. In the early days of printing Europe favored more fanciful writings than did the English.

In Italy, Giovanni Francesco Strapola had published in Venice *Le Piacevoli Notti* or *The Entertaining Nights* (1553), a collection of retellings that included renditions of "Puss in Boots" and "Beauty and the Beast" and had wide influence for fairy tales; and Giovanni Battista Basile (1575–1632), a poetic soul, survived soldiering by collecting versions of "Snow White," "Hansel and Gretel," and "Sleeping Beauty" in *Pentamerone* (1634–36) the Spanish novelist, Miguel de Cervantes (1547–1616), a contemporary of Shakespeare, gave children that great romantic hero, *Don Quixote* (1605).

France was the first to imbue traditional fairy tales with enough charm and dramatic style for them to be considered great literature. Members of the court of Louis XIV receive credit for this new way of amusing their worldly circle. In 1697, an elderly architect, Charles Perrault (1628–1703), published a collection of eight historic fairy tales, including "Little Red Riding Hood," "Sleeping Beauty," "Bluebeard," "Cinderella," "Puss in Boots," and "Tom Thumb." The book became known by the words appearing on the frontispiece of the first edition, *Contes de Ma Mere l'Oye,* or *Mother Goose Tales,* meaning old wives' tales. The 18th century English translation was titled *Histoires, or Tales of Past Times* (1729).

About 1500, clerics and lay church leaders alike began to view an increasingly literate populace with apprehension. The rapid spread of chapbooks helped the power of the press become a tangible social force. Their content of fancies and controversy created and nurtured a freedom of thought and the printing process permitted enlarged dissemination of such knowledge and ideas. The clergy responded by a move to make religion the dominant theme of children's books which reached its English zenith around the year 1649. England had experienced a tremendous religious revival and the Puritans became an overriding social influence. Their broadmindedness about freedom of conscience did not extend to religious observances. To defend their rigid moral code and morbid fear of death, they mounted an aggressive attack on secularism which took the form of a flood of moral tracts for the young. *Pilgrim's Progress* (1678) by John Bunyan is the only page-turner among these religious tracts. Reading it, children can enjoy the allegory without having to understand the theology.

Bunyan's *Book for Boys and Girls* (1686) is perhaps the first example of the Puritans' use of poetry for religious instruction. The English clergyman, Isaac Watts (1674–1748) in his preface to *Divine Songs* (1715) wrote: "What is learnt in verse is longer retained in Memory, and sooner recollected." The didactic purpose of the *Divine Songs* was balanced by the memorable simplicity of the verses. That "How doth the little busy bee," and "Birds in their little nest agree," remain familiar lines, and two of our best loved hymns are "O God, Our Help in Ages Past," and "When I Survey the Wondrous Cross," show the extent of our debt to Watts.

Colonial culture was both borrowed and indigenous—English and American. Sterner aspects of religious precepts and attitudes did not soften as they took root in New England. The Puritans considered children miniature adults and dedicated juvenile instructional literature to the salvation of their souls, but they forbade its illustration. The preacher Cotton Mather (1663–1728), wrote voluminously to terrify and exhort the children of the colonies to stifle their inherent depravity. That he hoped to inculcate Puritan theological strictures and codes becomes evident in his titles: *A Family Well-Ordered: or An Essay to Render Parents and Children Happy in One Another* and the 1700 supplement to the English cleric James Janeway's conversion treatise, entitled *A Token for Children of New England, or Some Examples of Children, in Whome the Fear of God was Remarkably Building Before They Dyed in Several Parts of New-England.* Apart from *Pilgrim's Progress*, this is considered to have had the most lasting success of any Puritan book for children.

The New England Primer, compiled by the English bookseller Benjamin Harris in a first edition of c. 1686–90, was the first important textbook of our fledgling land. It used elements taken from Harris' English originals, the alphabet and a catechism. Each printer of the *Primer* felt free to adapt it to timely events such as changing rhymed alphabets from a line praising kings by name to one lumping them all under "Kings should be good."

The history of American children's books is in part a record of changing expectations about language. From early alphabet books and didactic religious tracts on to 19th century instructional and narrative literature, texts focused on instruction in language systems. This inclined child readers to an awareness of the written word as it develops narrative context and codes of thought. John Cotton (1584–1652) onetime don of the English Cambridge, afterwards a Boston minister, authored *Spiritual Milk*, the first children's book written and published in America (1648). It contains such exchanges as:

> Q. What hath God done for you?
> A. God hath made me. He keepeth me, an he can save me.

Children were expected to memorize this dialogue form, the catechism. When viewed as a social work, it teaches proper roles—dominance and authority for the adult and innocence and obedience for the child. Seen as a religious tract, it teaches the fundamentals of Puritan doctrine.

‖ THE MODERN PERIOD

Until at least 1769, almost all books produced for children continued to be designed solely to instill virtue, morals, religion, timely correct manners, and academic subjects. Their text was catechism, advice, sermon, and juvenile elegy, genres that allowed narrative only when it served their instructional purposes.

In England, fresh visions were changing the momentum of publishing. John Newbery (1713–67) generally receives the credit for being the first to see the potential market for books whose content would interest and entertain children and whose format would make them desirable childhood possessions. The research of Iona and Peter Opie and others indicates that two other London publishers, Thomas Boreman and Mary Cooper, probably were the trailblazers. They demonstrated two things that had not been done before: that there was a place for playfulness in children's books, and that this idea could be used to produce a list of books consistently edited for such a market. Their work apparently served as an inspiration for John Newbery who successfully put children's books on the commercial map. In 1744, he published the first of his new type of children's book, A *Little Pretty Pocket-Book Intended for the Instruction and Amusement of Little Master Tommy and Pretty Miss Polly with Two Letters from Jack the Giant Killer*. Being a publisher as well as a writer, Newbery was able to put his intentions into covers, hard or soft. He published about 200 stories, including, in 1768, an English version of Perrault's "Cinderella." An understanding of and an affection for children happily colored his output.

Poetry turned cheerful now too. The great poet, artist and visionary, William Blake (1757–1827) gave children *Songs of Innocence*, a collection full of the youthful radiance that precedes the first stirrings of adult knowledge. For us, as book people, much of the sum of this remarkable man can be compressed into the statement that *Songs* was written, illustrated, lettered, engraved on copper and printed by Blake's own hand.

The precise genealogy of Mother Goose is likely to remain unknown, but around her name can be grouped the oldest surviving nursery-rhyme book, *Tommy Thumb's Song Book* published by Mrs. Mary Cooper in 1744, which included "Sing a Song of Sixpence," "Hickory Dickory Dock," and "Baa, Baa Black Sheep." Better remembered today is the difficult to date *Mother Goose's Melody* which contains both nursery rhymes and songs from Shakespeare.

A pair of English poets, popular both in America and England were the sisters, Ann (1782–1866) and Jane (1783–1824) Taylor. Their first book, *Original Poems for Infant Minds* (1804), set out to teach lessons, (a prerequisite to publication), but the meter and the children it portrays have that vitality necessary for survival. Kate Greenaway illustrated some of their work. Other notables from this period are Charles and Mary Lamb and William Roscoe, author of the popular *The Butterfly Ball and the Grasshopper's Feast* (1807).

The close connection between Newbery's publications and John Locke's childrearing philosophies offers a collecting trail of special value to those interested in early childhood education. Locke (1632–1704) replaced a French Protestant cleric of the Reformation, John Calvin (1509–64), as a childrearing guru. Locke's many times reprinted *Some Thoughts Concerning Education* (1693) set forth his beliefs that instruction should be combined with entertainment and that children learn most effectively when enjoying themselves. Newbery publications such as *A Play Book for Children* (1694), apparently the first native English alphabet book designed to amuse as well as instruct, reflected these beliefs.

An educator and writer, Jean-Jacques Rousseau (1712–78) led a group of French educational reformers in a direction that limited the spread of Newbery's influence. His book, *Emile, ou Traite de l'Education*, conceives of childhood as a self-propelling quest for information to be derived from the child's own surroundings. He held that there is no original sin born into the human heart, therefore every entrance of vice can be accounted for. In England, Thomas Day (1748–89) and Maria Edgeworth (1767–1849) were among those carrying these ideas into children's fiction. His *Sandford and Merton* (1783–89) and her *The Parent's Assistant* (1796) show their child protagonists learning by doing in stories which became increasingly moralistic as the ideas passed from France to England to America.

The efforts of the American Sunday School Union represented a broad effort to continue the flow of uplifting literature. The outgrowth of several religious publication societies, it had an important influence on contemporary writers, and through them on the character of juvenile literature, especially the development of periodicals. Expanding in 1824, it formed a committee to "jury" all submitted manuscripts. A board of publication, composed chiefly of clergymen of approved denominations, chose and edited acceptable works. The tales published by the Union were of two sorts. One told of the good child, faithful churchgoer, who died young. The other featured an unregenerate youth who scorned the wisdom of his elders, avoided religious attendance and consequently "went bad."

As we look back across more than 200 years to Daniel Defoe's *The Life and Strange Surprising Adventures of Robinson Crusoe* (1719) and Jonathan Swift's *Travels Into Several Remote Nations of the World by Lemuel Gulliver* (1728) there can be no doubt as to the staying power of amusement and invention versus didacticism. Johann David Wyss (1743–1818), a Swiss pastor whose attitude toward education resembled Rousseau's, wrote another classic, the Crusoe-inspired *The Swiss Family Robinson,* of which the first English version was *The Family Robinson Crusoe* (1814). To charm his four sons, Wyss spun out the tale, episode by episode.

Enlightened 18th century opinion disapproved of fairy and folk tales. Impossible, nonsensical, unduly fanciful tales had not suited the Tudors, the Stuarts or the Puritans. The print diet for their children was either approved didactic or tolerated popular. Many specialists feel that children owe the literary rescue of their innate child to the work of the German brothers Grimm. While studying law, Jacob Ludwig Carl (1785–1863) and Wilhelm Carl (1786–1859) became interested in German folk poetry, which led them to collect local folk songs and tales supplied them by close friends and neighbors. Though the tales were viewed as material for an eventual history of German literature, the Grimms were prevailed upon to publish them. The first volume of *Kinder- und Hausmarchen* appeared in 1812. As collecting continued, their work swiftly became international, resulting in the first English version, *German Popular Stories* (1823), set down by a London lawyer, Edgar Taylor. His notes explain that his editing "gentled" the tales for his desired young audience. Joined by a second volume (1826), the impact of the Grimms' work is considered to have radically reversed the existing English attitude and made fairy tales and fantasy acceptable.

England's forte, imagination, now emerged from its imprisonment and the old fairy tales moved from the humbler print of chapbooks into more formal guise with fresh humor, fantasy and romantic adventure. Victorian morality now found proof that fairy tales produced moral good. Unlike the ancient genres of imaginative literature—myth, fairy tale, folk tale, and legend—fantasy is a modern literary art form. It took wing in the decade of the 1860s with the special talents of Lewis Carroll, pseudonym of the

Rev. C. L. Dodgson (1832–98), and the Rev. Charles Kingsley (1819–75). Carroll, in his *Alice* books, *Alice in Wonderland* (1865), and *Through the Looking Glass* (1871), and Kingsley with *The Water Babies* (1863) were able to build on the Grimms' groundwork and liberate children's books from the restraining hand of the moralists.

The true first edition of *Alice* was actually sold in America. The American publisher, William Worthen Appleton, was the instrument for this. Macmillan of London contracted to publish *Alice* in 1865, illustrated with wood engravings by the Dalziel brothers made from John Tenniel's drawings, which were, in turn, based upon Carroll's own sketches. Author and illustrator, however, were disappointed enough with the printing of the engravings to cancel that press run. Macmillan thereupon went back to press for an edition that appeared with a date of 1866. Meanwhile Appleton happened to be in London and obtained a "lot" of the rejected first printing. He cancelled the title page, substituting one for his firm dated 1866 like the official and definitive English first. Thus the true first edition was really sold in America.

Carroll has emerged the acknowledged master, but 19th-century England saw the publication of many other classics in fantasy for children. George MacDonald (1824–1905), was another minister turned author, but, if my childhood constitutes any proof, his books such as *At the Back of the North Wind* (1871), and *The Princess and the Goblin* (1872), though religious allegories, continue to speak experiential truth. The thus-far eternal "Peter Pan" of J. M. Barrie (1860–1937), began as a play, published in 1911, creating the icons of Tinker Bell and the eternal child. There are several versions of the story, not all by Barrie. The brilliant and enigmatic Rudyard Kipling (1865–1936) touched fantasy in *Puck of Pook's Hill* (1906) and in the same year the fascinating Edith Nesbit (1858–1924) published *The Story of the Amulet*, a fantasy unlike her family stories of the Bastables. James Makepeace Thackery (1811–63) contributed an important light-hearted make-believe, *The Rose and the Ring* (1855). John Ruskin belongs here for *The King of the Golden River* (1851), as does Charles Dickens for his *Magic Fishbone*.

The English poet Christina Georgina Rossetti (1830–94), sister of the artist Dante Gabriel Rossetti, told an original fairy tale in verse in her 1862 *Goblin Market*. "Come buy, come buy" chant the goblins as they lure a pair of sisters with their spells. Her 1872 book of rhymes, *Sing Song*, offers brief, quiet verse with haunting undertones. Another poet of fairyland is Rose Fyleman (1877–1957), best remembered for a single line: "There are fairies at the bottom of the garden." Credit is due to her, however, for inducing A.A. Milne to begin writing verse for children.

In *Children and Books*, May Hill Arbuthnot singles out four poets of nonsense verse—Edward Lear (1812–88), Lewis Carroll, Laura Richards (1850–1943), and L. Leslie Brooke (1862–1940) as logical successors to Mother Goose. Lear's 1846 *Book of Nonsense* contains limericks, a poetic form of rhythmic strength that appeals to childhood's almost instant adoptive mimicry. The rhythmic images in "The Owl and the Pussy Cat" (*Nonsense Songs*, 1870) are so memorable the poem is continuously re-illustrated and reprinted in picture books and anthologies. Carroll's poems like "The Jabberwocky" from the *Alice* books continue to enchant word-lovers. From Germany came *Struwwelpeter*, or *Slovenly Peter* (1845), rhyming stories some consider prankish humor and others plain horror. Only a small amount of good nonsense verse exists—which tells us that those who write it well possess a peculiar genius.

Clement Moore's "A Visit from St. Nicholas" and Sara Josepha Hale's "Mary Had a Little Lamb" made them the first remembered American poets for children. Moore (1779–1863) was a professor of biblical learning at the General Theological Seminary in New York. His world renowned 1822 Christmas poem was written for his own children and slipped into print in the Troy, (New York) *Sentinel*, anonymously and without his permission. It has been illustrated and re-illustrated so often most people believe it began as the picture book, *The Night Before Christmas*, rather than as a poem. Mrs. Sara Josepha Hale (1788–1879) wrote several books of poems and was the first editor to print stories by Frances Hodgson Burnett. The American Poet Laureate of Nonsense for Children, Laura Richards, is best remembered for her 1932 collection, *Tirra Lirra*, which contains some 19th century verse.

Homegrown, American-grown imaginative literature sprang from such sources as the genial warmth of Washington Irving (1783–1859) and the poetic spirit and style of Nathaniel Hawthorne (1804–64). Historically, the contrast between the writings of Cotton Mather and Hawthorne describe in extreme, but nonetheless real terms, the history of American children's books from the early colonial period to the mid-19th century. Society's assessment of the place of reading in our culture had changed as had perceptions of the social, imaginative and moral nature of the child; the place of the child within the natural scheme; and the use of literary language. Sadly, Hawthorne's retellings of Greek myths that blend pastoral themes with the reentry of "fairy" have paled in spite of the charming sensibilities of his *Sketchbook*, and *Tanglewood Tales*.

America's children's books became realistic pictures of domesticity and adventure as some 19th-century writers strove to describe our continuously changing country. Their efforts lessened competition from English markets and helped produce a fresh expression of our national compulsion for self-improvement. Jacob Abbott (1803–79) and Samuel G. Goodrich (1793–1860) were among the authors who based their work on Rousseau's ideas of childhood as a self-directed inquiry classroom. Their names may draw a blank, but not those of Rollo and Peter Parley. Abbott, an educator, wrote twenty-eight volumes of Rollo travel books. Goodrich used the pseudonym of Peter Parley for over 100 informational books which allow children to learn art, history, science and geography through the vicarious experiences of travel writings.

Louisa May Alcott (1832–88) pioneered in the establishment of a new pattern for American children's fiction that broke with both English and continental traditions but grew from the Puritans' emphasis on the family unit with the father as priestly head. Her teacher-father, Bronson Alcott, authored child-rearing texts portraying children as innocents and parents as guardians of their morality. Miss Alcott's books provided fictional experience to match his professional beliefs. Their detailed, factual domestic narrative of Concord, Massachusetts created a believable world inhabited by some seemingly eternal characters.

Kate Douglas Wiggin (1856–1923) expanded upon Miss Alcott's domestic realism. We who collect her and read our purchases can be assured of a vacation from the unease of today. Frances Hodgson Burnett (1849–1924), Lucretia Peabody Hale (1820–1900), Margaret Sidney (Harriet Milford Lothrop) (1844–1924), and Sarah Orne Jewett also wrote of settled domesticity and idealized youth. Currently, some parents have found a new role for books of this period, such as Martha Finley's *Elsie Dinsmore* series (1867). These are deemed authoritarian enough to be used as texts for at-home instruction by fundamentalist parents.

When entertainment became an aim for the authors of children's books to consider, it became evident that reading tastes were a function of gender as well as age. Older girls had the home stories. What about the boys? Boys' adventure stories, one of the important features of Victorian children's literature, derive chiefly from two sources—*Robinson Crusoe* and the historical novel as established by Sir Walter Scott. Scott's romantic adventure stories first came to children through the listening pleasures of family reading. Though he wrote only one children's book, *Tales of a Grandfather* (1827–30), his fictional treatment of history became an important precedent for the popularity of the juvenile historical novel. *Ivanhoe* (1819) sold out in a week.

The importance of real experience characterizes the historical adventure fiction of England's Captain Frederick Marryat (1782–1848). At thirteen, inspired by Nelson's victory at Trafalgar, he joined the navy; in 1818 he was awarded a gold medal by the Royal Humane Society for his many acts of naval heroism. The three volume *Masterman Ready: Or the Wreck of the Pacific* (1841–42) was his first children's book. George Alfred Henty (1832–1902) was perhaps the most notable of those who continued stories of Victorian reality. Henty's experiences as a British war correspondent gave rise to a string of boys' books with accurate history but cardboard characters which were much read in the United States as well as Britain. Mayne Reid (1818–83), an Irishman, came to America and fought in the Mexican War, where he gathered material for western adventure stories. Another adventure spinner is his contemporary, the Scotsman Robert Michael Ballantyne (1823–94), who also journeyed far to gather material for his eighty adventure books. Novels with a strong ethical purpose and graphic particulars of a world being set to rights appealed then, as now, to youthful idealism.

During the years after 1840, these books sent boys sailing, exploring, being trapped and escaping in the company of heroes who were more stereotyped adventurers than differentiated characters. This changed in the 1880s with the appearance of another children's literature milestone—the recognizable genius of that spinner of unforgettable yarns and children's poet sublime, Robert Louis Stevenson (1850–94). To the accepted novelistic attributes of excitement and color, he added realized, memorable characters. *Treasure Island*, which appeared in the magazine *Young Folks* in 1882 and in book form in 1883, survives as reading because of the power of the heroic villainy of Long John Silver. When Andrew Lang wrote "Except for *Tom Sawyer* and the *Odyssey*, I never liked a romance so much" (Meigs, p. 238), he gave conclusive evidence that it had passed the toughest test—adult appropriation.

The continuing enthusiastic joy with which collectors pursue the myriad illustrated editions of Stevenson's *A Child's Garden of Verses* (1885) testifies to the staying power of a great collection. These poems demonstrate poetry's power to recreate the inner feelings and outward experiences of childhood. Stevenson wrote as a child might do were he articulate enough to express his feelings about wind and rain, shadows and dreams. Readers in both their first and second childhoods feel and treasure the "I" of childhood that is constant throughout these poems.

One strong thread of America's literature of the 1880s and 1890s celebrated the "common man" who brought shrewdness and homely wisdom to western settlements. Some of these pioneers lingered in America's heartland to build the stability that still identifies the Midwest as the "backbone of America." James Whitcomb Riley (1849–1916) is not considered a great poet, but because he characterizes his time and place, his work has significance. The fame of America's Eugene Field (1850–95), a Chicago literary columnist, also barely survives to the present. Anthologists and picture book illustrators guarantee continuing exposure for Riley with "Little Orphant Annie" when Halloween is their subject and for Field through their pleasure in his most remembered poems, "Wynken, Blynken and Nod" and "The Duel," the story of a warring gingham dog and calico cat. Carl Sandburg (1878–1967) built enduring fame in two areas, Lincoln scholarship and nonsense tales. His 1922 *Rootabaga Stories* describe Rootabaga country which is reached by riding the railroad to where the track zigzags.

"Make way for the children's magazine . . . with a face as fresh and handsome as a school boy's, and with contents more varied and precious than he carries in his pockets." Thus began an announcement for *St. Nicholas*, Scribner's illustrated children's magazine. The number and variety of stories in 19th- and 20th-century magazines, of which *St. Nicholas* was the most famous, greatly increased opportunities for children's authors and illustrators. Its first and landmark editor in 1873 was Mary Mapes Dodge (1831–1905), a poet and juvenile writer whose most important novel is *Hans Brinker or The Silver Skates*. A later editor, May Lamberton Becker, describes the magazine as "owing its distinctive character to the constant cooperation between youth and maturity" (Commager, p. xvi). In 1899 the St. Nicholas League for Young Writers was established with such writers as Edna St. Vincent Millay on its honor roll. Adult contributors included Louisa May Alcott, Frances Hodgson Burnett, Emily Dickinson, Lucretia Hale, Joel Chandler Harris, Rudyard Kipling, Jack London, Howard Pyle and Mark Twain. Another magazine, *The Brownies' Book* (1920–21), edited by W. B. DuBois, was the first major publication for African-American children. American children also enjoyed *Youth's Companion* (1827–1929), *Riverside Magazine* (1867–70), *Our Young Folks* (1865–73), and *Harper's Young People* (1879–99). *Boy's Life* and *American Boy* are two later juvenile magazines with a targeted audience of older readers, which printed, for the most part, only quality writing. Many serials, novels, and short stories which originally appeared in those publications later appeared in hardcover editions. Frederick Warne published an edition of *St. Nicholas* for the English market, and many copies of their *Chatterbox* reached American children.

America was producing its own novels of adventure and bravery. The novels of James Fenimore Cooper (1789–1851) earn him a first in literary realism for opening authentically portrayed, vicarious windows onto America's forests and prairies. Yet he had no first-hand knowledge of the frontier life. His *Leather-Stocking Tales, The Pioneers* (1823), *Last of the Mohicans* (1826), *Pathfinder* (1840) and *Deerslayer* (1841) are among the books that earned him the accolade of "America's Sir Walter Scott." Today, the art of N. C. Wyeth seems to be what keeps Cooper in print as a children's author. The illustrated editions begun by Scribners' in the 1920s live on as collectibles, enshrining now somewhat unreadable stories.

Harry Castelmon's (Charles Austin Fosdick, 1842–1914) *Frank on the Lower Mississippi* (1867) so charmed the great Indiana collector E. K. Lilly that he bought everything Castelmon had written, and commissioned Jacob Blanck to write *Harry Castelmon, Boys' Own Author; Appreciation and Bibliography* (1941). "Oliver Optic" is one of the pen names of William

Taylor Adams (1822–97), another writer of prodigious output whose books included *Outward Bound* (1867), the Boat Club series, and juvenile magazines such as *Oliver Optic's Magazine*. Perhaps what might now be justly and kindly said is that, for him, output exceeded talent.

Samuel Langhorne Clemens (1835–1910), Mark Twain, showed that adventure could be found at home in two beloved and famous children's books, *The Adventures of Tom Sawyer* (1871) and *The Adventures of Huckleberry Finn* (1884). His characters were not "little prigs" but real live boys enduring small town life and enjoying its river, the Mississippi. Amazingly, the accurately portrayed, deservedly immortal, world and characters of Tom Sawyer and Huck Finn attract the ire of current censors who seem not to comprehend the importance of preserving America's past. Howard Pyle (1853–1911), our first celebrated artist-author, re-worked Arthurian legends in books that form individual, visually satisfying wholes. Horatio Alger (1833–99) authored 130 scenarios, creating the genre of "Street Arab" or rags-to-riches fiction. He made his name a symbol for America's belief in bootstrap success by creating books that boys could read for ideas of how to become successful men of their own time.

One southern author who gave children a memorable window onto the Civil War was Thomas Nelson Page (1853–1922) with his novel *Two Little Confederates* (1888). By 1876, the Georgian, Joel Chandler Harris (1848–1908) had made a reputation as a newspaper humorist. In his work for a plantation newspaper-owner he absorbed a good deal of black folklore. The much re-illustrated and revised Uncle Remus tales, which strongly reflect his African-American scholarship, began running in the *Atlanta Constitution* in 1879 and first appeared in book form in 1890 as *Uncle Remus: His Songs and Sayings*.

Most of the varieties of children's literature began beyond our shores. One of these literary debts to English-born genres is for the "school" story which took hold in Britain with the publication of Thomas Hughes' *Tom Brown's School Days* (1858) and another title, not a recognized piece of American cultural literacy, F. W. Farrar's *Eric, or Little by Little* (1857). As the genre moved to America, young Tom Bailey, the hero of Thomas Bailey Aldrich's autobiographical *Story of a Bad Boy* (1870) becomes our closest equivalent. Edward Eggleston's *Hoosier School Boy* (1883) is as American as it sounds, as is the later private academy series of Ralph Henry Barbour (1870–1944) which was first published in *The Youth's Companion*. "School" appears throughout all realistic children's literature as a part of daily life, but as a separate genre it really did not outlast the Victorian era. As such, it is valued because school is a self-contained country, where pupils separate from their families for a prescribed time to live as citizens responsible to the laws of the school. This setting effectively showcases the conflict between authority and the individual, a storyline with considerable dramatic potential. Related to this theme is the story of "children on their own." Under the pseudonym of Margaret Sidney, Harriet Mulford Lothrop (1844–1924), created the series beginning with the *Five Little Peppers and How They Grew* (1881) that signaled the appearance of the poor—as distinct from the merely hard-up— family.

Much poetry survived the Victorian age to be happily inherited by a new young audience, and once begun, American children's poetry flourished. Rachel Field's first book of children's poetry, *The Pointed People* (1924), came out at the same time as Milne's *When We Were Very Young*, but it was not overshadowed by the fanfare for it. Many consider the city poems in *Taxis and Toadstools* (1926) to be Field's unique poetic gift to children. Though Robert Frost did not write for children, time, anthologists, and illustrators are demonstrating that his poetry is accessible to them. Another great American, Carl Sandburg, did give children two collections, *Early Moon* (1930) and *Wind Song* (1960). Elizabeth Maddox Roberts (1886–1941) is remembered for the unpretentious, un-cute verses about children's everyday experience in *Under the Tree* (1922). The Benéts, Stephen Vincent (1898–1933) and his wife, Rosemary (1898–1962) created *A Book of Americans* (1933) which describes notables—mostly historical. The adult poet many consider the most influential of his day, T. S. Eliot (1888–1965), whose fame England and America share, gave children *Old Possum's Book of Practical Cats* (1939). Public libraries still hold and circulate copies of Sara Teasdale's *Stars Tonight* (1930), a collection of lyric poems transformed by the illustrations of Dorothy Lathrop into a book of rare and enduring beauty. Elizabeth Coatsworth (1893–1986) a 1930 Newbery winner for the fanciful tale, *The Cat Who Went to Heaven*, produced some lovely nature poetry that was originally part of her historical tales: *Away Goes Sally* (1934), *Five Bushel Farm* (1939) and *Fair American* (1940).

American series books embody the idea that a child can accomplish any goal while still retaining a childlike innocence. Gil O'Gara, publisher of the periodical *Yellowback Library* described them to me:

> A phenomenon of the 20th century, they were in many respects an outgrowth of the dime novel publishing world. One of the most famous entrepreneurs in the marketing of children's literature was Edward Stratemeyer, a former editor of dime novel material and a writer of nickel weeklies, boys' fiction serials, and hardbound juveniles. Though he didn't invent the genre, his literary syndicate established in 1904 became the catalyst for the distribution of inexpensive hardcover adventures. He paid his pseudonymous writers a flat fee for fleshing out the plots he dreamed up and then convinced his publishers to issue the books at a price affordable for the majority of American families. The Stratemeyer Syndicate eventually created more than 100 series with an estimated sale of over two million copies before being acquired by Simon and Schuster in 1984. This

number is but a fraction of the overall sales of independently created series. Several publishing houses had their own series, and writers such as Percy Keese Fitzhugh, Leo Edwards (Edward Edson Lee), Margaret Sutton, and John Blaine (Harold Goodwin) continued the series tradition from its Golden Age in the teens, twenties, and thirties through to the genre's decline in the fifties and sixties. Even Frank Baum wrote some—the *Aunt Jane* series, *Boy Fortune Hunters*, and some series for small children, all under different pseudonyms. Joseph Altsheler (1862–1919) authored a wealth of historically set books including the *Guns of Bull Run* (1914).

Lucy Fitch Perkins' *Twin* series, which began in 1911 with *The Dutch Twins*, had current literary approval and is still readable historical fiction. Today, older series titles are returning as paperbacks featuring revamped versions of the Hardy Boys and Nancy Drew. Current ones appear, including the popular reader-controlled "choose your own adventure" game books and novels for preteen girls such as the *Babysitters' Club* books by Ann M. Martin and the *Sweet Valley High* series created by Francine Pascal.

Until mid-century, 20th century children's literature, like everything else, was shaped by the two World Wars. John Rowe Townsend writes:

> We all inhabit the twentieth century, but the twentieth century is not the same for everybody. Events which loom large in one part of the world may have only minor significance in another. For the British, the two great shocks and shakings-up have been those caused by the two World Wars. . . . but for Americans the depression, the Korean and Vietnam conflicts, the racial turmoil and political scandals of recent years have had additional impacts. . . . On its smaller scale, the twentieth-century history of children's literature reflects the differences of pattern. In Britain it could be said, as a crude generalization, that the Victorian-Edwardian heyday ended in 1914, and that children's literature picked itself up uncertainly in the twenties and thirties, only to be knocked down again in 1939. . . . In the United States, where solid institutional foundations had been laid much sooner than in England, progress was steadier, and not so seriously interrupted by the World Wars. Part of the price of institutional support in America has been a general assumption that children's books should be a visible good influence on the educational and social development of the nation. . . . The belief that books could be an important influence on children's attitudes reinforced, and was reinforced by, the tendency of American children's books to relate to the here-and-now (whereas the British imagination strayed perpetually towards fantasy, and few people in Britain were serious about children's literature anyway). (Townsend, p. 209–10)

For American children's literature, 1919 was quite a year. It saw the establishment of Children's Book Week, designed to promote the best books for children, and the hiring by Macmillan of Louise Seaman (later) Bechtel as the first American children's book editor. Anne Carroll Moore had been Director of Work with Children at the New York Public Library since 1906. Her Room #105 could be termed the traffic control center for this decisive period in the publication of American children's books. Each member of the artistic team needed to produce a book streamed through her office—authors, editors, illustrators, reviewers and educators. Librarians, typified by Miss Moore, provided a powerful force that helped to drive the publishing industry's crucial 20th-century development in the field of books for children. Oliver Garceau, in *The Public Library in the Political Process* delivers high praise:

> Another outstanding success . . was the development of reading for children. . . . This was much more than the simple opening of a room for them. . . . To the children's librarians, perhaps more than to any other group, is due the modern revolution in literature for children. (p. 48).

Factors that promoted the growth of the public library were the training of children's librarians; the appearance of school libraries, finally recognized as basic educational resources providing valid educational tools; and the close interaction between children's librarians and the growing group of children's book editors, many of whom came from the library profession. According to Margaret McElderry, herself one of the greatest of the librarians become editors, "Editors and librarians naturally formed strong relationships of great mutual benefit. Such a relationship has never existed to any degree between adult editors and librarians. It continues to be a particular strength of the children's publishing and library world" (*Horn Book*, October 1974, p. 86). These children's librarians demanded high standards in story, art and format and rewarded the efforts of the best publishers with handsome purchase orders.

Between the two World Wars, the Depression greatly increased American public library use. Library books were one of the few free sources of entertainment and amusement. Two outstanding people exemplify the many talented, far-sighted librarians and publishers whose efforts shaped children's literature. Virginia Haviland (1911–88) contributed a very special force to these years.

> Virginia Haviland served nearly one half-century as librarian, writer, anthologist, folklorist, historian, lecturer, reviewer, and promoter of international understanding. . . . Her dream of establishing a national reference library of children's books was realized as the first Chief of the Children's Book Center at the Library of Congress. (American Library Association, ALSC Item 46)

Another influential giant was Frederic Melcher (1879–1963), the editor of *Publishers Weekly*. In 1921, when the Children's Section of the American Library Association, at his suggestion, had voted to award a medal annually to "the most distinguished children's book written by an American author in the preceding year," Melcher provided the endowment for the Newbery Medal. In 1938, he established the Caldecott Medal, a picture book award, in honor of the English artist Randolph Caldecott. He also offered to give a third award for poetry which was not accepted by ALA.

In *A Critical History of Children's Literature*, Ruth Hill Viguers pays tribute to Melcher:

> There is no doubt that the fortunate relationship between children's librarians and children's book editors, between the readers of children's books and the publishers of them, and the strides made in the publication of children's books in America in the past thirty years were accomplished largely because of the existence of such a unifying factor as the warm personality of Mr. Melcher, a great publisher who never lost the viewpoint of the reader—of any age. (Meigs, p. 430)

With few exceptions, the authors who achieved prominence in the United States between the wars were American, but many had been born in Europe and its perspectives and traditions enriched their work. The books from 1920 to 1940 glow with a special, fresh brilliance which was honored by large numbers of Newbery awards. To a Dutch-American, Hendrik Van Loon, went the first Newbery in 1922 for the informational *The Story of Mankind*. The wartime letters of Hugh Lofting, who emigrated from England in 1912, grew into a self-illustrated series that began with *The Story of Doctor Dolittle* (1920) and won the 1923 Newbery for *The Voyages of Doctor Dolittle*. The 1928 Medal went to a transplanted East Indian, Dhan Mukerji, for *Gay Neck: The Story of a Pigeon*.

American institutional support helped English children's authors recover from the horrors of the First World War. Townsend tells us, "The best work of the post-war decade was mainly in poetry, or fantasy, or poetic fantasy" (p. 164). Two leading writers, Walter de la Mare (1873–1956) and Eleanor Farjeon (1882–1965) wrote both poetry and prose. De la Mare's ways of invoking the supernatural—weird, grotesque, mysterious—are one quality that set him apart. His first children's collection, *Songs for Children* (1902), was published under the pseudonym of Walter Ramal by Andrew Lang. It was followed by *Peacock Pie* (1913), *Poems for Children* (1930), *Bells and Grass* (1942) with its early, never-before-published poems, and the 1944 *Collected Rhymes and Verses*. What some consider the best of his tales were brought together in the 1947 *Collected Stories for Children*. As a novelist, Farjeon, who like Stevenson remembered how it felt to be a child, wrote of the Sussex spring in *Martin Pippin and the Daisy Field* (1937), and made English history delightful in the 1932 *Kings and Queens*, written with her husband, Herbert. *Over the Garden Wall* (1933) and *Sing for Your Supper* (1938) hold poems full of dance, games, and play. The works of humorist and playwright A. A. Milne also belong here. His lasting fame rests on four books for children written between 1924 and 1928—two *Winnie-the-Pooh* books and two books of verse. He did as much to popularize poetry for children as Stevenson had earlier, and quotations from his poems have become household lore. Christopher Robin's omnipotence gave children a welcome role model, and Milne's facility with words made him a favorite choice for reading aloud.

In the twenties progressive education and the development of nursery schools influenced realistic writing for young children. Lucy Sprague Mitchell of New York's Bank Street School wrote to fulfill the young child's absorption with self and interest in a daily, immediate world. *Here and Now Story Book*, published in 1921, created a story type adopted by others. Margaret Wise Brown was among Mitchell's pupils, and her early books, such as *The Fish with the Deep Sea Smile*, *The Noisy Book*, and others followed Mitchell's lead. Brown's *The Little Island* (1946), illustrated by Leonard Weisgard, won the Caldecott and *Goodnight Moon* (1947) is the quintessential bedtime story, with a continuous sale for forty-five years.

Collectors of Little Golden Books know that this chronology must mention Simon and Schuster's successful mass-marketing venture. Their project of publishing these inexpensive books for children, in cooperation with the Artists' and Writers' Guild, a subsidiary of the Western Printing and Lithography Co., began in 1942. The first twelve titles appeared just before wartime paper and press shortages—critical factors in publishing—became determinants. Picture books in full color, a majority of them new stories, at a price of 25¢ each, gave full credence to America's faith in mass marketing. They were followed by a more expensive series, the *Giant Golden Books*. Aficionados, whether parents from the post World War II generation who did the reading, or those children who listened and then read, were a satisfied audience.

Those of us who are *Oz* fans share the opinion of many including *The Oxford Companion to Children's Literature* that L. Frank Baum (1856–1919) was "the first writer to create an unforgettable, full-length American fantasy" (p. 51). Scholar Mark I. West in *Before Oz* supplements this with "Baum's book had many predecessors, some of which were written by the leading authors of the nineteenth century." This, he adds, "raises some interesting questions about the historiography of children's literature" (p. 1). However, the key to reconciling these two comments is the word "unforgettable." Ozites have no doubt about this as they go on buying whatever they can afford, like my recent purchase of Charles Santore's definitely different illustrations for a condensed edition of *The Wizard of Oz*. This unforgettability is also continuously reaffirmed by current writers and commentators each time they employ the Emerald City or the Wicked Witch of the East as a figure of speech.

More recent English embodiments of fantasy demonstrate both its deep humanness and its hospitality to imaginative elements. J.R. Tolkien (1892–1973), Professor of Anglo-Saxon at Oxford, published *The Hobbit* in 1937. When, after its success, his publisher pressed him for more, he received valuable writing support from an Oxford colleague, C. S. Lewis, in completing its sequel, *The Lord of the Rings*. This trilogy (1954–55) created cult status and disciples with buttons announcing "Tolkien is Hobbit-forming."

Other most special post-war English authors include C. S. Lewis (1898–1963) whose allegorical *Narnia* series began with *The Lion, the Witch and the Wardrobe* in 1950 and ended with *Last Battle* in 1956; Mary Norton whose small protagonists from *The Borrowers* series (1952 to 1961) have made "Borrowers" the equal of earlier fey folk; and Lucy Boston, whose "real" fantasy began with *The Children of Green Knowe* (1954). As Alan Garner's name is emblematic of England's decade of the sixties for *Owl Service*, so is Lloyd Alexander's in America. The fact that Alexander's creation of Prydain does draw freely from the whole reservoir of story burnishes his gifts while reminding us of the ancient history of children's literature. His images, such as the Cauldron Born, burn deeply and, seemingly, forever. For quiet writing grace and deeply felt humanism, E. B. White's three children's books, *Stuart Little* (1945), *Charlotte's Web* (1952) and *The Trumpet of the Swan* (1970) excel. Each are beloved by children and contain those qualities necessary for eternal book-life.

There are more than several meritorious American poets writing during this period. Dr. Seuss (Theodor Seuss Giesel, 1904–91), published his first children's book *To Think That I Saw it on Mulberry Street* in 1937. He has earned three Caldecott Honor awards: *McElligot's Pool* (1947), *Bartholomew and the Oobleck* (1949), and *If I Ran the Zoo* (1950). In 1955, his alma mater, Dartmouth College, made real his self-conferred "doctorate" by noting that he had long possessed a "D.D.C."—Doctor of Delighted Children. With a *New York Times* bestseller in 1990, *Oh, The Places You'll Go*, Giesel, at over eighty, must have thoroughly enjoyed having more than the last word.

David McCord's first book of children's poetry, *Far and Few* (1952) was really his fifteenth book of verse, followed by *Away and Ago* (1968) and *Stars in the Pail* (1975). The verse of Ogden Nash (1902–71) goes off in search of a rhyme and wanders back with something as ingenious as the "elderly poems for youngerly readers" in *Parents Keep Out* (1951). According to John Ciardi (1916–86), author of such books as *The Peddling Man* (1968), "Children are born with a love of poetry, but school takes it out of most of them." *Catch a Little Rhyme* and *There is No Rhyme for Silver* are two of Eve Merriam's collections of poetry that cloak memorable fun in a modern vein. X. J. Kennedy excels at molding ideas into verse that uses precise rhymes without sounding forced or contrived. As lighthearted nonsense verse for the youngest to authentic lyric poetry for the oldest, Harry Behn's poetry, from the 1949 *Little Hill* to the 1971 *More Cricket Songs* can be compared to that of Milne and Rossetti. Myra Cohn Livingston both interprets poetry as a teacher, anthologist and writer of textbooks, and speaks it as a poet. Her prolific voice takes us from *Whispers and Other Poems* (1958) to her most recent book, a 1990 collection of essays, *Climb the Bell Tower.*

Two important African-American poets of the middle to later part of this century are Langston Hughes (1902–67) and Eloise Greenfield. The jacket from Lee Bennett Hopkins' anthology, *Don't You Turn Back* (1969) says of Hughes, "Here is poetry that speaks of love and hate, hope and despair— treats the basic elements and emotions of humanity in language keyed to our time." Eloise Greenfield's poetic gift is to speak in the voice of a young black child and it can be heard in such books as *Honey I Love You* (1978), illustrated by Leo and Diane Dillon. Greenfield, Hopkins tells us in a letter to the editor of the July/August 1990 *Horn Book Magazine,* "is the only black writer of children's poetry currently being published in the United States. . . . It seems quite incredible that, with over four thousand books for children being published annually, America is not seeing work produced by black poets. . . . Langston Hughes is represented, in print, only by *The Dream Keeper and Other Poems*, a volume published in 1932, with illustrations so stereotyped I cannot, will not, bring them to the attention of children I work with, black or white."

What happened to American realism in these postwar years? Slowly accelerating forces began to alter dramatically both the Newbery Medal and the popular market. The list of Newbery winners from 1945 to 1949 shows us a realism in *Johnny Tremain* by Esther Forbes and Robert Lawson's *Rabbit Hill*; *Strawberry Girl* by Lois Lenski; *Miss Hickory* by Carolyn Sherwin Bailey; William Pène du Bois' *Twenty-one Balloons*; and *King of the Wind* by Marguerite Henry that pales startlingly beside that for the sixties, seventies and eighties—*It's Like This, Cat* (1964) by Emily Cheney Neville; *Sounder* (1970) by William H. Armstrong; and Katherine Paterson's *Jacob I Have Loved* (1980). Family stories like those by Eleanor Estes and Elizabeth Enright turned pastel when Louise Fitzhugh made spying and much else acceptable in 1964 with *Harriet the Spy*. Social unrest, ignited by the Vietnam War and the human rights movement, overtook America. The dominant, visible "we" accepted the topical urgency of divorce and new sexual codes along with loss of innocence and language tolerance. Taboos dropped like leaves. The poetic voice of Shel Silverstein seems appropriate to these musings. Amidst the quick laugh and the hilarious imagery that delight today's children, his highly imaginative verses address larger concerns.

An overview of the history of pictures in children's books needs to distinguish between their use as art for decoration, as illustration, and as a major component of a picture book. The first implies only the inclusion of visual images within the text; the second puts some part of the story, a character or an incident, into visual language; and the third, picture book illustration, dances along with the words to tell the story. Story-hungry children of long ago curled up with woodcut-brightened popular chapbooks. William Caxton's 1484 edition of *Aesop's Fables* exemplifies early illustrated adult books children found and devoured, as does John Foxe's *Actes and Monuments, or Book of Martyrs* (1563) which depicted Christians tortured in crackling infernos.

Juvenile illustration is considered to have begun with Thomas Bewick (1753–1828) and Newbery's *Little Goody Two-Shoes* in 1765. In general, artists did not sign their work and individual cuts were re-worked and recycled. The English collector and author, Eric Quayle, believes that

> It is only recently that the first picture book for children was recognized . . . in a . . . case in the backroom of a small bookseller's shop within a mile of the British Museum . . . *Kunst und Lehrbuchlein* was first published in Germany in 1578 . . . composed of a hotch-potch of illustrations. . . . [As] *Books of Art and Instruction for Young People* . . . [it] was re-issued in 1580. (Quayle, p. 11)

In the English edition the German publisher Sigmund Feyerabend (1528–90) used full-page woodcut illustrations by Jost Amman (1539–91) picturing almost every aspect of everyday European life with rare views of children using hornbooks.

Another landmark "first" picture book also demonstrates a conscious effort to associate words with pictures for instructional purposes. The Moravian pastor, Jan Komensky (John Amos Comenius, 1592–1690), argued that a pupil must observe something sensually before being able to grasp its meaning in words. This belief in the efficacy of pictorial methods of teaching induced him to produce the *Orbis Sensualium*, printed in Nuremberg in 1658. Shortly afterwards it was translated into English as *Visible World—For the Use of Young Latin Scholars*, and remained in print for more than a century.

These early informational books were bent on saving the soul from hell or informing the mind about reading, spelling, and manners. Illustrated alphabets and cuts to illustrate such famous verses as "In Adam's fall, we sinned all" provided what entertainment children could find in the books of James Janeway, Cotton Mather and in Benjamin Harris' *Primer*, which became America's *New England Primer* (c. 1686–90).

Though John Newbery's books were literary landmarks, scholars agree that he did little to further the art of illustration. His only book in which the art was truly illustrative was the aforementioned *Little Goody Two-Shoes* (1765) with work attributed to Thomas Bewick, the finest contemporary English wood engraver. Bewick's first known book meant for children was *A Pretty Book of Pictures for Little Masters and Misses* (1779), published by Saint of Newcastle, apparently from the earlier Newbery edition of the same title. After Bewick, we find known artists signing their work in children's books. Leonard de Vries, compiler of *Little Wide-Awake: An Anthology from Victorian Children's Books and Periodicals*, feels that "the influence of [Newbery's] precursor, Thomas Boreman [flourished 1730–1742] must be recognized" (de Vries, p. 15). Beginning in 1741, Boreman published ten "Gigantick Histories," measuring 2½ by 1¾ inches, with appropriate illustrations.

The poet and artist William Blake brought the added delicate beauty of water colors to illustrate his *Songs of Innocence* (1789). John Harris produced an acknowledged illustrative milestone with the bestselling *The Comic Adventures of Mother Hubbard and Her Dog* (1805), one of the first children's fiction books done with color. Wood and copperplate engraving were the artistic media for these books and their coloring, either freehand or by a stencil process termed *pochoir*, was done by children as a cottage industry. These illustrated books were small, averaging 4 by 6 inches, and what they depicted was so accurate that, as the distinguished children's literature specialist Paul Hazard noted, "England could be reconstructed entirely from its children's books" (Hazard, p. 128).

Pictures were still a curiosity and with color added they became popular attractions indeed. The first American professional book artist was Alexander Anderson (1775–1870), a New York physician turned engraver who became fascinated with the new style of engraving perfected by Bewick and used it in imitation of the master's style, copying and reinterpreting many of Bewick's blocks. Although most of his work was for adults, he did illustrate a *Mother Goose* and an edition of *The Children's Friend*.

The prolific F.O.C. Darley (1822–88) was the leading American mid-19th-century illustrator of the books of Washington Irving, Dickens, Poe, Longfellow, Harriet Beecher Stowe, James Fenimore Cooper, and Mary Mapes Dodge—many in large gift editions. He was a friend of Irving's and illustrated his *Rip Van Winkle* and *Legend of Sleepy Hollow*. His children's audience grew from this artwork as well as that in *Hans Brinker* (1866), and *Aladdin: or The Wonderful Lamp* (1888).

The distinguished British printer and engraver, Edmund Evans (1826–1905), made color printing a fine art as a showcase for the three great picture book artists of Victorian times, Walter Crane (1845–1915), Randolph Caldecott (1846–86) and Kate Greenaway (1846–1901). The attraction of color for young readers interacted with the development of technical processes able to replace handcoloring at this time. Crane designed some fifty picture books, usually with fairy story texts, printed on paper or linen. Later, also with Evans, he produced books such as *The Baby's Opera* (1877) that lavishly combined color and music. For each Christmas over a period of eight years, Caldecott and Evans produced two of the "toy books" that displayed the artist's virtuosity in illustrating texts of nursery rhymes or nonsense verses.

The first two of these were *John Gilpin* and *The House That Jack Built* (1878). Maurice Sendak, one of the great illustrators of the mid-20th century, wrote, "Caldecott's work heralds the beginning of the modern picture book. He devised an ingenious juxtaposition of picture and word, a counterpoint that never happened before. Words are left out—but the picture says it" (Sendak, p. 21). Greenaway's verses are innocuous, but her drawings of children became determinant pictorial icons. Their clothing, still worn by many fashionable children (and their mothers), was solely her invention. Sir John Tenniel (1820–1914) first came to fame for his illustrations for an 1848 edition of *Aesop* and remains immortal for visualizing the first *Alice* in 1865.

Arthur Hughes (1832–1915), who illustrated George MacDonald's *At the Back of the North Wind* and *The Princess and the Goblin*, also created important visual support for the texts of other writers including Rossetti. Two other important early 19th century artists are William Mulready (1786–1863), who is remembered for his black-and-white drawings that were hand-colored for Roscoe's *The Butterfly Ball* and *Tales from Shakespeare*, and George Cruikshank, like Tenniel a satirist for *Punch*, who illustrated the first English translation of the Grimms' *Collection of German Popular Stories* (1823).

Because the icons of Victorian illustrators have proved so strong and enduring, their familarity makes them valid references for considering the social effects of art in children's books. The story MacDonald tells in *At the Back of the North Wind* does contrast the warm comfort of Diamond's nighttime rides on the North Wind's back tucked into her flowing hair and his own chill bed, but Arthur Hughes' pictures give the reader only comfort and security. Until the 1960s American children's books gave the same sort of glossy, limited image of the African-American world, Lucy Fitch Perkins' *The Pickaninny Twins* being a dramatic case in point. The openness that came with textual realism is only now being matched by the wave of worldwide multicultural publishing.

The later 19th and early 20th century saw new English and European artists. Richard Dalby, author, bibliographer, and antiquarian bookseller, writes, "The Golden Age of the children's book reached its undoubted peak in the decade from 1905 to 1914" (Dalby, p. 7). Original editions ranged from quarto gift, deluxe or limited editions, to trade editions and all manner of continuing reprints with fewer plates and variant picture quality. Dalby lists forty artists, from which I'll pick my notables. Arthur Rackham (1867–1939) and Beatrix Potter (1866–1943) were opposites in everything but genius and appeal. One showed a mysterious and sometimes menacing view of fantasy and fairy; the other, a comfortable natural and settled domestic world. Publicity attending the 1988 Pierpont Morgan Library's exhibit of Potter's original art and early books in New York helped to make her tiny books picture book stars, duly honored for their new brillance of color, faithful to the originals. Her last published story was the posthumous *The Faithful Dove* (1955). Rackham's sinister creatures and gnarled, groping anthropomorphized trees give a fantasy presence to the more than ninety books which he illustrated with great versatility. His final book was the Limited Editions Club *Wind in the Willows* (1950), the last illustration for which was finished shortly before his death.

A Frenchman come to London, Edmund Dulac (1882–1953) created stylized, decorative art for a version of the *Arabian Nights* (1907), which was the first of ten ornate gift books he illustrated over the next ten years. The brilliant colorist, Danish Kay Nielson (1886–1957) produced celebrated book illustration as well as stage designs; *East of the Sun and West of the Moon* (1914) is the most spectacular. Books illustrated by another stage designer, the Hungarian-born Willy Pogány (1882–1955) include several by the Irishman Padriac Colum (1861–1972)—a lovely *My Poetry Book* (1934), and his now most sought after title, *Mother Goose*. The English Robinsons, Charles (1870–1937) and W. Heath (1872–1944), Cecil Aldin (1870–1935), Harry Clarke (1889–1931), Edward J. Detmold (1883–1957), and Ernest Howard Shepard (1879–1976) who created images of Toad and Winnie-the-Pooh, all transformed great stories to high book magic.

It is interesting to follow the history of major texts as authors and editors searched for definitive illustration. The original depictions of John Tenniel for *Alice* seem inextricably interwoven with the text, though the Rackham illustrations offer a superb alternative. Yet, in the opinion of many, the stories of Hans Christian Andersen had to wait until 1900 for the "proper" art of Hans Tegner (1853–1932).

There were many American artists whose work bridges the 19th and 20th centuries. The genius of Howard Pyle (1853–1911) and his Brandywine School met a watershed moment, when in the last quarter of the 19th century, the invention of photoengraving replaced wood engraving. This technological advance provided great creative opportunities for book illustrators. Pyle gathered and trained a company of young talent who went on to make famous his pictorial beliefs—Maxfield Parrish, (1870–1966), Jessie Wilcox Smith, (1863–1935), N.C. Wyeth (1848–1929), Frank E. Schoonover, and Pyle's sister, Katherine, among others. In style, Pyle is likened to Walter Crane for his unitary view of book design and his decorative floral borders. Two humorous artist-illustrators, Palmer Cox (1840–1924) and Peter Newell (1862–1924) produced books of guileless fun, the Brownie and Hole books. Charles Falls (1874–1960) was among those who used woodcuts for children's book illustration in the 1920s. The first picture book to look forward unmistakably to the 20th century in its graphic style was the *Alphabet* of the Englishman William Nicholson, which appeared in 1898, twenty-five years before Falls's famous *A.B.C.*.

Between the wars the starred American artists, like the writers, were either Europeans or had strong, Old World ethnic roots. The Hungarian-trained Miska Petersham with his American-born wife, Maud, produced *Poppy Seed Cakes* (1924), and won the 1946 Caldecott for *The Rooster Crows*. They also did a series of "Story" books between 1933 and 1939 that remain valuable informational reading and were the predecessors of Holling C. Hollings' *Paddle to the Sea* (1941). Two Swiss-born artists, Edgar and Ingri d'Aulaire, won in 1940 for *Abraham Lincoln* and another Swiss, Roger Duvoisin (1904–80), won for *White Snow, Bright Snow* in 1948. Wanda Gág (1893–1946) grew up amid Old World customs which helped her art transmit the settled reassurance of her *Millions of Cats*, a 1929 Honor Book. The success of Ludwig Bemelmans (1898–1962), an Austrian who came to America in 1914 and saw war service, was established with *Madeline* (1938). Another great artist of the period was the Russian emigre, Feodor Rojankovsky. Near the end of World War II, Caldecott Medals had come to Virginia Lee Burton for *Mike Mulligan and His Steam Shovel* (1939), Robert Lawson for *They Were Strong and Good* (1941), Robert McCloskey for *Make Way for Ducklings* (1942), and James Thurber for *Many Moons* (1944). Children rate H.A. Rey's *Curious George* an unforgettable monkey and Jean Charlot's Miguel in Krumgold's *And Now Miguel* a lasting role model.

Theodor Seuss Giesel must also be mentioned as illustrator as well as poet. In *American Picturebooks* Barbara Bader terms him "Piper, prophet, magician, priest—these are the words for Dr. Seuss . . . entertainer-in-chief" (p. 302). Some consider Edward Ardizzone (1900–79), another storytelling father, to have been the most eminent English illustrator working between 1945 and 1970 with a fame undimmed in America. He blessed his "Tim" books with watercolor backgrounds of seascapes and port towns, and also illustrated splendid books for other writers.

A roster of the important American artists from World War II to today is very long. These are some favorites, with birthdates added (when readily available) to provide some order. James Daugherty (1889–1974), Gustaf Tenggren (1896), Lynd Ward (1905), Munro Leaf (1905), William Pène du Bois (1916), Ezra Jack Keats (1916), Barbara Cooney (1917), Alice and Martin Provensen, Ed Young (1931), Nonny Hogrogian, Nancy Ekholm Burkert, Anita and Arnold Lobel (1934) and (1933), Tomie de Paola (1934), Trina Schart Hyman (1939), Susan Jeffers, Barry Moser, David Macaulay, Chris Van Allsburg, Molly Bang, Michael Hague, Maurice Sendak (1928), and Leonard Weisgard. An Englishman, Brian Wildsmith (1930), and a Japanese, Mitsumasa Anno (1920) have also captured our hearts.

The turmoil over definitions of childhood still rages, which worries many children's literature specialists. More than ever before, kids are street-wise, TV-wise and R-rated-movies-wise. But what does the future hold for an information-processing society that neglects to pass on the "old" wisdom that has so successfully transmitted our civility from one generation to the next? The book is a safe testing ground of vicarious experience—of what others think and do. Fiction, especially the adventure genre, allows the young reader to make decisions while keeping him or her from having to participate personally in the consequences of such choices. In *Summoned by Books*, Frances Clarke Sayers recalls C. S. Lewis praising Potter's *Squirrel Nutkin* for showing him loveliness. She goes on:

> [It] is a complex and beautifully wrought story in which riddles are asked and answered, the hero an impudent fellow, taunting and teasing. But the moral strength is there. The hero got what he well deserved, which no present day squirrel is allowed to do. In the latest squirrel literature I have read, the hero takes all the nuts which have been saved for Thanksgiving dinner and goes out to play with them. A wily old squirrel tricks him out of them. When he tells his mother what has happened, she replies, "Don't worry, we won't tell father." She then persuades father to take them all out for Thanksgiving dinner. (p. 18)

"It is grown people who make the nursery stories," wrote Robert Louis Stevenson; "all the children do is jealously preserve the text." The truism that nostalgia ignites our collecting fire implies that few of us begin our collections with books that were not part of our personal childhood. Except for children fortunate enough to reside in generational households where the books of parents and grandparents can be at hand, applying this truism puts the date at which today's youngest collecting rememberers connect to the history of children's literature at about 1975—a history as short as their young lives. However, once collecting takes a scholarly shape, knowledge of the history of children's literature and its illustrators provides one sure road map for achieving both context and organic unity in our collection design.

2

Underneath the surface of Today, lies Yesterday, and what we call the Past, the only thing which never can decay.

—Eugene Lee Hamilton, *Roman Baths*

A Foundation for the Collecting Process

Collecting success depends heavily on knowing what one is about. In order to follow a better mentor than impulse we must be knowledgeable about today—current desirability, availability, and price—and yesterday, which brought us to today. Collecting is an item-by-item process by which we strive to complete some predetermined finite unit. It is the art of balancing instinct, intellect, and passion. True collecting evolves as experience translates the accumulator's urge and transforms enthusiasm into physical entities. Each new purchase, each successful quest, fills a niche within the overall plan and increases the visibility of the mental design.

My metaphor for this process replays the children's card game of "Go Fish," a form of rummy, in which a player asks, "Do you have any Queens?" For a moment, don the cloak of invisibility and imagine yourself at a book fair. Entering a dealer's booth, you eavesdrop as a customer makes the request that always begins, "Do you have . . . ?"

Linking an adult hobby to a children's game can reinforce its genesis in the *rememory* of childhood. The author Virginia Hamilton gave us this term. "Rememory is a 'reword' out of my past. It is not poetic license, but a volunteer, like a self-sown seed come forth unbidden . . . At fourteen, a dashing fellow told me he wasn't much on names, but he had a perfect rememory of my smile." She continues: "If one recalls or remembers something remarkable, such as a high compliment from a jiving dude, then one must need to use one's rememory in order to do so. Therefore . . . Rememory: an exquisitely textured recollection, real or imagined, which is otherwise indescribable" (Hamilton, p. 6). The "Fish" dialogue broadens to reflect the specifics of each person's quest, but "Do you have?" remains constant.

Knowing what one is about demands an adequate foundation of information about children's books, which are multifaceted artifacts with almost limitless collecting possibilities. There are roughly sixty-nine generally accepted genres within children's literature. An annotated list appears here in chapter 3. To these can be added all the hybrid fields conceivable for individualized cross-collecting. A collector's success at "Do you have?" depends upon knowledge of books in general and children's books in particular. We need to master this broad foundation upon which to build the database of specifics that describe and support personal goals.

‖ BOOK COLLECTING COMPONENTS

As children's book readers, we know the power of the number three in tales of three brothers, three riddles, or three tasks. Collecting also has its three: 1) an emotional response to a material object; 2) the desire to possess it; and 3) money spent with some hope of successful investment. Narrowing these to book collecting, the first two become specific thus: emotional response relates to book content or internal attributes, and the desire to possess a book relates to edition or bibliographic description, its external components. Cost will be discussed after we've developed an understanding of the elements upon which pricing is based.

"Why am I attracted to this particular item?" you ask yourself. "This is a rare Alcott title," you respond. Content, an internal attribute, is a primary criterion. This promotes simplified, speedy, and satisfactory decision making about a title. When you tell yourself, "I've never seen *Little Women* in this binding before," you are thinking of its edition, an external factor. If your immediate reaction to a book is, "This is a must. Can I afford it?" price is what you are reacting to. Successful collecting depends upon having a well-honed reason for making each choice at the expense of alternative possibilities. It will therefore be easier to resist irrelevant charms and successfully resolve the final outcome—to succumb or to resist.

‖ WHAT ARE INTERNAL COMPONENTS?

Internal encompasses most of the collectible categories: author, illustrator, title, subject, and designer. For anthologies, compilers are authors and, for all books, editors share the creative acknowledgment, though this is rarely expressed. Dealers say that most of their "Fish" queries are for either the artists or writers whose creativity establishes each book's primary identity.

‖ OUR INTERNALS BEGIN OUR COLLECTIONS

The book elements labeled as internal created the feelings that began our hobby. We collect authors and illustrators because, in the main, they are "our people." If the combination of our past and present emotions pulls us into series books and the historical periods they represent, or to family stories, or Christmas, or Disney, or fairy stories, or teddy bear or travel tales, we understand where we are and how we got there. Most collections are built upon a "first love"—a book fiercely remembered from childhood. To repossess it, a collector must add adult thought processes to emotional impetus. Authors who continue to exert such magic wrote from personal connective rememory of their own childhood. It is their vivid and "true" recollection of those qualities with which life is endowed in childhood—the auras and aromas of life's morning—that speaks to children with unforgettable conviction and clear images. The visions of childhood are small—objects and happenings. Those who draw on the intensity of their own rememory to describe them in detail reach the spirit of the children we once were so exactly that we eagerly seek the chance to "go home again."

Once we've chosen our internals, serious collecting strongly suggests that we add the excitement of scholarship. An obvious way to do this is to explore a title's context. For example, we could extend our pleasure in *Little Women* to related titles like *Little Men*, then to other Alcott books beyond the family tales, and then go on to a biography of the author and bibliographic sources that list the body of her work, such as Gloria T. Delmar's *Louisa May Alcott and "Little Women."* That is one way to become an Alcott scholar. Or we may become fascinated with her father, Bronson Alcott, and seek out some of his writings. The town of Concord, Massachusetts itself may draw us into the part that it played in her life and then lead to the books in *The Five Little Peppers* series, the world created by another Concord dweller, Margaret Sidney (Harriet M. Lothrop).

‖ GENRE AS AN INTERNAL COMPONENT

If our collection centers on an internal, we need to be familiar with its history, authors, component parts, and current status. To view the history of children's literature through a subject genre such as animal tales puts the fables of Aesop first. They, however, were not written for children. A search for animal stories written for children turns us to John Newbery with his first 1760 title, *A Pretty Book of Pictures for Little Masters and Misses; or Tommy*

Trip's History of Birds and Beasts. The genre includes stories about animals both as humans and as their natural selves, and both encourages kindness to all living creatures and illustrates the code of morality for an era. Several examples of this genre follow.

The survival of Anna Sewell's only book, *Black Beauty*, is due to its power to arouse the compassion of children and to the conviction of Sewell's dedication to the cause of the working horse. The Canadian Marshall Saunders' *Beautiful Joe* (1893) allows the dog, Joe, to recount his own tale of fellow-creature kindness. Ernest Thompson Seton (1860–1946) wrote naturalistic tales derived from personal experience as founder of the Woodcraft Movement and a Chief Scout of America. His pen-and-ink sketches, both illustrative and decorative, combine with the authority of his writing to create impressive examples of that magical package—the illustrated book. Kipling's *Jungle Book* and *Just So Stories* show us one facet of this exceedingly complex Englishman. Kenneth Grahame's power lies in creating universal animal-humans—"ourselves in fur," as May Hill Arbuthnot called them. Beatrix Potter accomplished that with miraculous economy, and illustrated her books as well. For Peter Rabbit alone we are forever in her debt. These are but a few possibilities. I finish the animal kingdom with a favorite, Munro Leaf and Robert Lawson's *The Story of Ferdinand* (1936), about a bull whose preference for flower-smelling over fighting mirrors my own inclinations and that of the right thinking of any age.

‖ WHAT CREATES EXTERNAL COMPONENTS?

"External" describes the physical attributes of a book. The evolution of these components has a long history. As written language developed, literature was recorded on tablets of stone, clay, or wax. The tablets were replaced in time by spindle-turned papyrus scrolls. Because papyrus was fragile writing material, it was replaced by tougher parchment or vellum made from animal skins, and, in the 13th century, by the introduction of paper. The rectangular book form derives from the shape of an animal skin: folding it in half furnishes two leaves; another fold, four; and another, eight. Eight leaves became a gathering, which, when stitched together, formed the medieval manuscript. Multiples of the eight-page "signature," when bound together within a cover, comprise the traditional book form.

To turn an illustrated manuscript into a book requires decisions about format, illustrative process, page layout, type design, paper, binding, dust jacket (or not), and number of copies. Making these decisions is a process that involves author, editor, publisher and book designer. A designer's responsibilities include the selection of typeface, paper, page layout, cover and dust jacket design—each of which strongly affects the character of a book. Paper choice is chiefly determined by type of illustration and price. Photographic illustration can require heavy coated stock. Woodcut art needs paper with a textured surface. Endpapers are normally one folded sheet, either white, colored or printed, that covers the juncture between the covered binding board and the sewn or glued sheets of the text. For hardcover books, our binding choices begin with the material we see (paper, cloth, leather, or a combination of these) which covers the binding board—once thin pieces of real wood, and now cardboard. All cases thus made require cover and spine design—color, typeface, and illustration. Some titles appear only in paper, though most modern collectible books are hardcover editions.

‖ EDITION DESCRIBED

Edition points, or bibliographic description, define any given specific edition. Once you've learned what comprises edition, you'll be able to write these descriptions yourself. Each external feature plays its part. These include:

1. Precise form of all names—author, illustrator, editor, etc.
2. Exactitude of text with any errors or particularities spotlighted
3. Publisher
4. Place and date of publication
5. Descriptions of binding, including color
6. End papers, decorated or not
7. Dust jacket or not
8. Number of pages
9. Book size
10. Kind of paper
11. Artist's original format
12. Printing process
13. Number and kind of illustrations.

The full and *half* (partial) *title* pages are information sources of primary value to the bibliographer as is the *verso* or back of the title page, which is the major place that may contain each book's publishing history to date. The verso's listing includes the notation of successive printings of the same work and of enlargements or abridgments of content that create a different edition. This will not usually describe the changes that constitute a new edition. Do remember that having the publication date appear on the title page establishes it as the actual date, whereas its presence on the verso does not do so. Where art is an important book feature, the title page or verso may carry a notation such as this: "The original pictures for *I Have A Friend* are watercolor paintings." Sadly, many publishers are eliminating this bibliographic information as cost-cutting dilutes the industry's traditional integrity and sense of mission. To be a true first, second, or any specific edition, all known edition features must be present. For some, such as the *Oz* books, identification is very tricky and, for *Oz*, only a bibliography like Justin Schiller's can identify with certainty an edition such as a first of the *Wizard* that sold in late 1991 at Sotheby's for $24,000. Therefore, keep abreast of new bibliographies in your collecting field that list edition points and all of the author's known works. Publication of such a scholarly compilation, just by itself, increases interest and thus raises prices.

‖ BOOK TERMS BRIEFLY DESCRIBED

Though the glossary in the back of this book provides full definitions, I'll tuck in some brief ones here. Bibliographers and catalogers (librarians) define *author* as the person having major intellectual responsibility for the text and *illustrator* as the same for original artwork. A *compiler* decides what work of others to include in a particular volume of poetry, speeches, stories, and the like. The *editor* shapes the work of each of these in varying degrees. *Publisher* indicates a business institution that contracts to put the work of an author and illustrator into book form, and promotes and sells it. Informed collecting means being knowledgable about the history and practices of "your" publishers. The trade designation for book size is based on measures that derive from the folding of a sheet of paper measuring roughly 19 by 25 inches. When folded once to make two leaves it is termed a *folio*; twice, to make four leaves, a *quarto*; and so forth. Usual library practice for modern trade books measures in centimeters and refers to the height of the binding, not the size of the book's leaf or page.

‖ ILLUSTRATIVE PROCESS

Because many collectors value illustration above text, an understanding about how illustrations are made is essential knowledge. Book illustration combines several processes: the hand work of the artist and the pre-press and press work that transfers an image of the artist's original onto the page by printing. Important information about the book artist's technique is sometimes included in one of three places: the title page, its verso, or a colophon or note at the end of the text. As graphic techniques developed over time, woodcut, wood engraving, etching, engraving, lithography, serigraph, silhouette, collage, and photography have been and are among the media of book artists. Book illustrators also create their original work as paintings done in watercolor, oil, pastel, and acrylic, or—as showcased by Eric Carle—paper collage. When an artist considers his or her original art finished, its journey toward the printed page begins.

For early books the artists alone could do everything needed to create art.

The techniques they used were termed *direct*, because they employed immediate hand-controlled methods of printing, as opposed to *indirect*, which infers the need for other specialists and technology. These are *relief printing*, which begins with a woodcut or wood engraving, and *intaglio*, which begins with an etching, or copper or steel engraving. Our introduction to these techniques comes in definitions prepared for their patrons by Betty and Douglas Duffy, owners of the Bethesda Art Gallery:

> For a *woodcut* the artist draws his design on the surface of wood . . . a soft wood which has been cut with the grain. Areas not meant to print are then gouged out, creating the design in relief. The raised surface of the wood is inked and the paper to be printed is pressed against it, thereby transferring the relief image to the paper. For a *wood engraving*, the artist cuts his design into the surface of a hard wood which has been cut across the grain, thereby providing the smooth, hard surface required for the fine lines which characterize the wood engraving. Sharp, fine-pointed tools are used. The block is then inked and printed, as with the woodcut.

Because woodcut and wood engraving are relief techniques, the blocks can be set up to be printed along with and at the same time as the text. The presswork that transfers the artist's image to the page of book paper involves setting the block, and any text for that page, into a hand press and pressing down on the paper by hand or with the help of simple technology such as a turn screw. Color in early books printed on hand presses was hand-applied, usually with watercolor by a process termed *pochoir*.

The Duffys continue:

> With *etching*, an intaglio form, the artist draws his design on a metal plate which has been covered with a wax-like acid-resistant material called a "ground." A sharp tool or "etcher's needle" is used to cut through the ground, exposing the metal beneath. The plate is placed in an acid bath where the exposed metal is eaten away (or etched) by the acid. After the design has been etched into the metal the ground is removed and the plate is inked. The ink settles into the etched grooves. The surface is wiped clean. Paper is placed over the plate and run through a high-pressure press. The ink from the grooves in the metal is transferred to the paper, creating the finished etching.

Engraving differs from etching in that the artist cuts his lines directly into the metal plate with an engraving tool. It is printed in the same way as an etching. During the 18th and 19th centuries this process was much used in juvenile books. With the coming of photography, designs were transferred onto a woodblock by photomechanics rather than by hand. This change meant less work for artists and more for printers. We can see examples of this artwork in magazines such as *St. Nicholas*.

The term *reproduce* has broader meaning than does print. It means "to duplicate," and can be said of a photocopying machine, while printing implies the impression of inked type or plates on a flat surface by means of a printing press, to make what is termed an *impression*, not a copy. To an artist, a "copy" occurs when one copies work of another artist. It is equatable with plagiarism in the print medium.

There are two other directly printable artistic techniques that we need to understand: *lithography* and *serigraph* (or silkscreen). The Duffys describe a lithograph (or stone drawing) as follows:

> The artist draws his design directly onto a carefully ground stone (usually limestone). He draws with a greasy crayon or with greasy ink (tusche). The drawing is then fixed on the stone by a chemical process. The stone is then dampened with water. The water is absorbed by the open surfaces of the stone and repelled by the greasy crayon areas. The stone is inked, the ink clinging to the greasy areas (the design) but not the dampened stone. The paper to be printed is pressed against the surface of the stone and the ink from the crayoned areas is transferred to the paper.

A great variety of effects can be achieved and virtually any graphic form imitated because all drawing instruments can be used as long as the medium or vehicle is greasy. Plates of prepared zinc are sometimes used in place of stone.

A strolling player and playwright by the name of Alois Senefelder discovered lithography in Germany in 1798. He was neither an inventor nor an artist. His motive was to find a cheap means of engraving or etching upon stone in order to get his plays printed and circulated. His was the first entirely new printing process since the invention of intaglio in the 15th century. What financial success he gained came from using his process to print music. By 1845, Europe was producing lithographic illustrated books in great quantity and shipping them to the English market.

Chromolithography, the process of color lithography, was patented in Paris in 1837 by Godefroy Englemann, and had its first major use in England with Owen Jones's *The Alhambra* (1836–42, 1846). It was not initially successful as an illustrative medium for good-quality children's books there. Most English artists disliked the brilliant, almost tactile, colored surface. The volume of these books published by the New York firm of McLoughlin Brothers (still available to collectors at a reasonable cost), testifies to the American popularity of this illustrative process. When the technology developed to the point where chromolithography could be used in the offset printing process, the French-produced *Babar* stories (1931–) of Jean de Brunhoff and his son Laurent helped the technique gain favor in England as well as America.

Serigraph is an original art form also popular with those illustrating children's books today. According to the Duffys,

> It was the American artists of the 1930s who first popularized the use of the silkscreen method for the making of creative images. The method is relatively

simple and inexpensive and has since achieved great popularity around the world. The silkscreen, by nature, is a color medium. The artist uses a fine-mesh fabric stretched on a frame to screen each color, one at a time, onto the paper. He controls the areas of placement of each color by blocking out, with glue or a similar substance, those portions of the screen where he wishes the color to be denied. With the screen mounted just over the paper, he forces the pigment through the unblocked areas of the screen and onto the paper with a squeegee. This stencil-like process provides the artist with a highly flexibly and accurate method for applying color to paper.

‖ MECHANICAL PRINTING

Printing is the process of transferring an image from an inked surface (the printing plate) to another surface (such as paper) by means of pressure. *Letterpress* and *offset lithography* are the processes most used for book making. Letterpress is direct—a relief printing process. The image, usually type, photoengraving, woodblock, or rubber stamp is raised and the raised areas take ink and print. Offset lithography is indirect. The image is first transferred from the printing plate to an intermediate surface (rubber blanket) and from there to paper. The printing plate is made photographically and then treated chemically. Because film preparation and platemaking use photo-sensitive films and plates, the process is known as *photo offset*.

Color printing can be done in any number of colors up to at least ten, but the most popular process used today is four-color. This comes close to replicating the full color range of complex art, such as a painting or photograph. It requires four printing plates, one each for blue (cyan), red (magenta), yellow, and black. The plates are made from film, in which the colors have been separated out electronically into the four process colors, which will recombine on press to come close to the original art in value. Before the use of four-color process printing, color pre-separation had to be done by the illustrator with successive overlays of color on the artwork. Printed together, the colors from the overlays combine to form an image in as many colors and combinations of colors as the artist intended.

Although the printer's desire is to employ technology to come as close as possible to the artist's original work, reproduction can never exactly match the original, and some kinds of original art do reproduce better than others. Book artists and production staffers strive to make the book faithful to their original art, and collectors will profit by comparing a book to an original when possible. Book art must stand as such in the printed medium.

For children's book people, it is satisfying to recommend David Macaulay's *The Way Things Work* for a diagrammatic, illustrated explanation of printing. Checking the card or online catalog at your public library can lead you on to any additional details you seek.

‖ DETAILS THAT INDICATE PROCESS

When an intaglio plate is forced into the paper and run through the press, a "plate mark" is created by its edges. Lithography as original art is not easily mistaken for intaglio because it does not have the plate mark. There are also other ways in which the trained eye can differentiate between these processes in original prints or hand-printed books. For example: an engraved line can usually be distinguished from an etching by the ends of the lines. Engraved lines, being cut, taper to a point and are sharp and clean, whereas the ends of the etched lines, being drawn and bitten unevenly by the acid, end with slight irregularities. Chromolithography looks thick with color that can be truly tactile while lithography has no such surface texture; and woodcut illustration is usually coarser, lacking the fine details possible in wood or metal engraving. Art that began as watercolor does carry its appearance of "thin" color onto the printed page, as does the thick color of much of chromolithography. Eyes thus trained are better prepared to evaluate original art when used in a printed book, even though most fine distinctions do require a hand lens to find. Such knowledge adds greatly to one's collecting skill and allows us to understand what artist Christopher Wormell means in the colophon to *An Animal Alphabet*:

> The art for this book was created from handcut linoleum block prints. Several blocks (generally five) were cut for each picture. Each block was inked with a roller and printed separately by hand, producing the black images and the color areas. In certain instances, to achieve a shading or blending of colors, more than one color ink was applied to the same block. All of the art was color-separated by scanner and reproduced in full color.

Most artists worthy of being collected contract to see progressive color proofs until what comes from the press matches as closely as possible the colors in their original art. It pays to remember that whereas many artists closely monitor publisher's proofs for the first one or two printings of a first edition, they don't always do this for further print runs of the same edition. If you're an art-gallery-goer, you can experience this color difference by comparing an original you've seen to its reproduction in the show catalog, gallery print, or postcard. Another visible difference is paper quality, which can be changed between print runs. These are details to be overlooked at your pocketbook's peril.

‖ HOW ART IS USED

There are two main uses of art within children's books: for illustration and for the picture book. *Illustration* is subordinate to the text. It serves to illuminate, explain, or re-create ideas, scenes, and characters from the text. How it accomplishes this function is easily demonstrated by the simultaneous examination of variant editions of the same text, both illustrated and not. An "elderly" public library with a large collection of older children's books is the most appropriate and usually most available place to master this component of bibliographic understanding. The term *picture book* applies when both words and pictures are equal storytelling partners. The pictorial art *can* be the sum of the book; there may be no text at all. However, one cannot say with impunity that a book's text cannot have a life of its own. This is especially true right now when there is much use of short, classic poems and stories as picture book texts. Robert Louis Stevenson's poem "My Shadow" appeared thus in 1989, and *Lon Po Po*, a picture book retelling of "Little Red Riding Hood," captured that year's Caldecott Medal. This practice allows the illustrator (and probably the publisher) greater income, because these folktales and poems are not under copyright and so there is no author royalty to be paid. Its use also reflects a dearth of original texts acceptable to publishers. In general, though, it is axiomatic that neither part of a picture book stands alone.

A child's first exposure to vicarious worlds comes with the spoken word of stories told or poems recited—often sung or chanted. Picture books provide another medium for widening personal experience that children can often gain on their own, without the need for the mediation of a reader. As Frances Clarke Sayers, Professor of Children's Literature at the UCLA Library School, writes in *Summoned by Books*:

> Color, line and design—these are the forces that break down the gates of infancy and lay bare the world for the youngest eyes to see. It is an illuminating experience to watch the response of children to picture books; to see, time and again, certain books lay hold upon their minds and imaginations with the strength and certainty of all art which is capable of transmitting emotion to the eye of the beholder. (p. 145)

‖ TEXT AS AN ART FORM

The often dramatic use of text in picture books makes it easy to visualize type as an art form. To recognize the artistry of planned visual impact that designers have created on a page of "ordinary" print comes harder. But book collectors—especially children's book collectors—need well-trained artistic senses. This should encourage us to consider the differences between visual symbols and word symbols or printed words. Visual symbols are addressed to the eye and word symbols to the ear. So much for the obvious. But how obvious? Reading translates a line of print into sounds addressed to the ear and accessible to the mind's comprehension. Printed words can be pronounced in an almost infinite variety of ways—and clothed in an almost infinite variety of typefaces each possessing a visual image. Words have dictionary meanings and typefaces have historic and artistic connotations that the collector needs to be sensitive to. A last page colophon to Anne Tyler's novel, *Breathing Lessons*, tells us how seriously some book designers take the role of a typeface:

> The text of this book was set in a digitized version of Electra, a Linotype face designed by W. A. Dwiggins (1880–1956). This face cannot be classified as either modern or old style. It is not based on any historical model, nor does it echo any particular period or style. It avoids the extreme contrasts between thick and thin elements that mark most modern faces and attempts to give a feeling of fluidity, power, and speed.

‖ PAGE DESIGN

When illustrated books employ pictures as full-page art, text pages are affected, but not seriously. Where art shares the page with text in headpieces and tailpieces, or other pictorial elements, its size and shape exert major control over page design. Type then must be designed with that art in mind. No creator or serious appreciator of the wonder of a great picture book would fail to understand its special use of the double-page spread. The same appreciation is also due the designer responsible for all the choices that contribute to the creation of a handsome page of text. In children's books it is especially important to comprehend the potential of "handsome" to encompass the humorous, the old-fashioned, the ghostly, the cute, and the like as attributes of style.

‖ CONDITION, EDITION, AND PRICE

Physical condition, the giant book-collecting external, determines value and use. Top dollar demands pristine physicality—this is the book that actually does glow. Did any child really ever open this? You gaze and wonder. A reputable dealer will note any repairs that might otherwise remain hidden. The purest distillation of the collecting essence requires an item to be in the exact state in which it was first issued. This produces a special use of the term connoisseurship to mean establishing as direct a connection as possible with the original creators of a book as time allows. Another way to describe coming as close as possible to the genesis of a book is to say that the author saw this edition through to its completion on press.

Experiencing an exact, brilliant first edition from our memory bank allows us another way of tampering with time. Fred Woodworth, the editor of *The Mystery and Adventure Series Review*, provides a "for instance" of this in a vignette about a lawyer's obsession with Genghis Khan. What the collector said about his area of expertise gave Woodworth

> an odd sense of *dèja vu* . . . and after selecting a copy of a certain book . . . I knew why . . . Of all the volumes on Mongol history that the man has

> accumulated, the one that fueled his imagination enough to quote it as his own was a 1949 boys' series book. (Woodworth, pp. 2–3)

Children's books from our past, met again today, double their power because we come face-to-face with the child we were. In a sense, we encounter our own autobiographies.

The direct relationship between edition and price puts all buyers on their mettle. Edition points, the specifics that create a specific edition—author, title, date of publication, number of pages, illustrated or not, details of binding, etc.—determine rarity and thus price. Though to err is human, it is not the policy of dealers to forgive with a refund what they view as ill-informed purchasing. Therefore, always examine a prospective purchase to ensure its completeness. Take the time to page through to the end, checking each page for possible tears or stains. The newer the book, the less likely dealers are to inspect it for a missing page.

If a book has plates, find the page that lists them and check to see that they, as well as tissue guards (when used), are all there. In series books, the presence of cover art determines those editions that are currently prized and thus pricey. Without colored plates, an *Oz* book is probably not a first. A first edition issued with a dust jacket is still a first even when the jacket is missing from a particular copy. It just isn't a complete first. The presence of the dust jacket is a prime collecting point. It should always be either removed to a safe roost or covered in plastic. Other than just making the edition complete, it carries valuable information and historic context: biographies of author and artist; story synopsis; excerpts from favorable reviews; and ads for other titles. Historic context can be derived from the jacket's calligraphy and typography, author or illustrator photographs, the style of its art, and the slant of its story synopsis. Consider, for a moment, the bibliographic excitement in a dream collection of the jackets from all editions of A *Child's Garden of Verses* or *Robinson Crusoe*. It is ironic that our hobby dictates that what was made to protect the stainable cloth or paper cover now, itself preserved, merits special housekeeping care because it can increase a book's value at least twofold.

All serious collecting must operate within sight of the value of the finest available copy of any title; otherwise, there is no price guide. As dean of London's booksellers, H. M. Fletcher of Cecil Court advised me in late 1989: "For a fine book, price is never too high, if you have the money. Once spent, the pain and money are gone and you have the book." Corollary counsel was: "Try not to buy someone else's experience. You have to learn to depend on your own."

"If you have the money." What better phrase with which to continue to analyze the bottom line of children's book collecting—price? It isn't the dream, but it is the reality that permits the dream. Another British expert, Eric Quayle, counsels, "There is no half-way house; the seller either knows what treasure he is offering on his shelves, on his stall or in his hands, or he remains blissfully ignorant that the book he is about to part with for a few pounds could, and should, command a ransom" (Quayle, p. 8). Folk of the book remain a genteel lot, and all but the fringiest fringe deal honorably with their customers.

Pricing is a function of the interaction of supply and demand, and book dealing, though special, is no exception. Dealers price with the market, but if demand seems too slow, especially for high ticket items, they will lower prices. Today, perhaps the most important relevant generalization for juveniles is that the combination of age, rarity, quality, edition, condition, and demand concentrates top prices on the illustrated classics. Have them you still can, but paying for such prizes implies that your shopping luck runs to finding winning lottery tickets. Building a complete set of first editions of the likes of *Oz*, Kate Greenaway, Kay Nielson, Arthur Rackham, Jessie Wilcox Smith, or Maurice Sendak realistically dictates both a dealer's help and the willingness to live with incompleteness. But if you can think small at first, then early plates, distinctive bindings, and other external amenities are affordable. In a large shop in Rutland, Vermont in 1989 I paid $2 for a library discard copy of a first edition of De Angeli's *Bright April* (1946) with dust jacket. Now I can read, study, and savor its special qualities and trade way up if I choose to be more serious about De Angeli.

For series buffs, an important price note concerns the cost (and concomitant difficulty) of getting the last items in any series. One rule of thumb cautions that the last title, and often the last few titles, of any long-running series will prove elusive. Gil O'Gara, editor of the series magazine *The Yellowback Library*, described this phenomenon to me:

> This is a matter of simple arithmetic. A series with new titles issued every year for twenty or thirty years is certainly going to end up with more copies in print of the earlier volumes than the last ones. In fact, sometimes the last title may have had only one print run before the series was canceled. Thus, while thousands of copies of the first volume may have survived the generations, often no more than a hundred or two of the last titles are still to be found.

A successful collector must speak "condition language" while keeping in mind its subjectivity. The place to begin is with mint or fine firsts. So much of a first's power concerns its connection to the author or artist's own supervision that a collector's insistence on newness is really very logical. If it looks other than brand-new and untouched, how can one sustain the illusion that it comes directly from its creator? One reading of anything but a highly illustrated book can remove it from being "mint."

Here is one set of definitions adapted from those in AB *Bookman's Weekly* and Allen Ahearn's *Book Collecting*:

Mint or *as new* is what first edition collectors want—unreal, a "glower."

Fine approaches *mint* without being "crisp" and also without defects.

Very good, the next notch down, has more wear and still no defects.

Good describes the average used and worn book, still complete and with no major defects.

Fair is a worn book with complete text pages but major defects that must be noted.

Reading copy describes a poor copy whose only virtue is a complete text.

"Antiquarian," "collectible," and "out of print" are terms in common use, but with no commonality of definition. The Smoot-Hawley Tariff Act of 1931 defined "antique" as something that was made before 1831 (a date for machine manufacture), which defined antique as something made at least 100 years ago. Some experts feel that an *antiquarian* book should be one printed on a hand-set press. This sets a date of 1885, when machine composition arrived with the invention of the Linotype by the Baltimorean Ottmar Mergenthaler. *Out of print* (*o.p.*) technically means no longer available from the publisher. In reality, a book can be o.p. from the publisher but still available from a bookseller. *Collectible* seems to mean anything for which a market demand has been created. Some specialists choose to define antiquarian as any *significant* book, and if one then adds, "such as a Medal book," all other caveats vanish.

Rarity and historical time period do often intertwine, of course, but not always in terms of dollar value, therein misleading the beginner. Collecting fashions and just plain literary and bookmaking quality of any book deny high value to many, many ancient tomes. When the appraiser comments, albeit gently, "A publication date of 1600 does not automatically provide great intrinsic value," we empathize with the disbelief of the book's owner. For children's books, it stands to reason that time and the enthusiastic pleasure of the original child reader makes availability the second time around a direct function of publication date. Fine copies of currently sought-after 19th-century children's books, and, of course, earlier treasures when they can be bought, now command high prices and indicate collectors with deep pockets.

|| A PRACTICAL TIME SPAN FOR CURRENT COLLECTORS TO CONSIDER

Two facts encourage me to feature materials published after 1840: price and the seemingly universal practice of building collections around works we knew first as children. In 1992, there will be precious few active collectors much over eighty years of age. Think through a timetable for someone born in 1912. One's detailed aural memory for literature begins about age four—1916; personal reading ability about age six—1918. If this eighty-year-old heard some earlier literature—perhaps parental books read by a thirty-year-old—we are back to 1885. If a grandmother read or lent her own childhood treasures, we could be back another forty years to 1845. Thus for our hypothetical collector, the collecting world—the childhood regained—could fall as far back as 1840.

You can use this formula to find your own collecting span. If you are thirty in 1992, born in 1962, when you were four in 1966 your thirty-year-old mother born in 1936 could be reading you something stretching back in time to *her* mother's four-year-old memory! Certainly this is no hard-and-fast rule, but it does serve to demonstrate the long echo of children's literature from the past.

‖ REFERENCE SOURCES AS LEARNING GUIDES

To further enlarge your knowledge, discover the reference books that support your chosen collecting area. Buy them when issued, and get a first. Somewhat later, you might find one on a remainder table or at a secondhand bookstore such as the Strand in New York. Otherwise, much later, you will find yourself paying high prices for key reference sources, such as $85 for a dust-jacketed copy of William Targ's *Bibliophile in the Nursery* (1957) that originally sold for $12.50. Your pocketbook and shelf space will greatly profit if you let libraries come into your collecting life. Most public library children's rooms have relevant reference shelves and many of the collectibles that you need to be able to see. Their interlibrary loan capability can bring you titles not in the local collections. Children's librarians will put their professional competence at your disposal, giving you both knowledge and the companionship of another adult who believes in and reads children's books. Senior professionals in the field carry much of the collection within them. Newcomers can offer the fresh perspectives of their library-school learning, which now includes the insights of popular culture, a new academic discipline that relates closely to children's book collecting.

Courses in popular culture can now be found near you in the offerings of municipal departments of recreation, community colleges, museums, or art schools. This exploration of the connections between mass and high culture mirrors and extends our hobby, as was demonstrated in an exhibition at the Library of Congress from March 1986 through July 1987 that was held over by popular demand. The brochure for "Childhood Choices: American Pastimes and Everyday Fantasies, 1900–1950" noted, "This glimpse of yesterday's childhood . . . is set in three broad locations where children have made choices . . . 'At Home,' 'Backyard, Street, and Beyond' . . . and 'Main Street' . . . suggest the progressive independence of childhood, and the display of personal possessions underscores the impact childhood choices may have on later life." The exhibit visually and verbally explored and exploited the connections among everyday books, toys, games, and radio, and the economic realities of child labor in the years between 1900–1950.

‖ CLASSES IN BOOK ART

Extending your learning by more structured methods can give you quantum leaps in expertise. Classes in any field of book art will train your eye as well as your hand, and a trained eye is a necessary collecting tool. Studying bookbinding can help make you a connoisseur. Practicing what you've learned gives you a highly demanding craft useful for working on your own books or those of others in a skills market crying for practitioners. Creating slipcases (covered boxes) for your most valued books is an acme skill. Creating Pliofilm jackets for everything is a kindergarten example. Some hands-on training in bookbinding is available if we can momentarily suspend our reverence for books and meticulously dismember a to-be-trashed hardcover volume. Becoming equally knowledgeable about book art has no known comparable immersion for learning "how to."

‖ COLLECTING CHOICES MAKE OUR MAPS

Once the adult discovers how easy it is to relive the games, shared secrets, and memories of the "then" child-self, another antiquarian chidren's book buyer may exist. He or she is then launched into collecting, away from the dock under the power of reminiscence but still charted for only random dockings. Adult interests connected to early book loves often determine direction. Two vignettes from my interviewing exemplify this. A young woman enthusiastically explained how she had used her childhood delight in Laura Ingalls Wilder as the spark to design a collection of related early titles that allowed her to experience American pioneer life. When I asked one man, "How did you develop your focus?" he told of spontaneously entering a children's bookstore to find Michael Hague autographing his illustrated edition of *The Wizard of Oz*. "*Oz*. How I loved that," he told me, and was moved by this chance encounter with the impulsive power of rememory to take home an affordable first edition of a favorite from his window-seat years. Now he collects both Hague and variant modern editions of the *Oz* books. He has become a collector. He has a map.

One strength of personal, not institutional, collecting lies in having just one captain to satisfy. Committees can, and do, require formal constraints such as consistency, line-item budgets, justification by more than faith, and such. You alone, until you run out of money and space, know your direction. Simply rearranging familiar books according to some constructive plan gives them new significance. Unfamiliar or neglected titles, juxtaposed, acquire fresh interest. Every book—being a multifaceted art object—holds many directions within its covers to give us entry into the process of creation in special ways. If we re-trace the historical path of a chosen book to its beginnings, what we find is an already existing integrity. Within our collection, each book makes and takes its own place through an affinity of form, and intellectual and emotional content. For us that place enlarges a passionate personal vision as we seek and find things that belong together. Indeed, collecting seems to be a kind of love story.

3

Books are perhaps the last vestiges of everyone's childhood to be given up. I write these words in a room with piles of books from my most recent move above me . . . Each time I pack and unpack them, I think some must go, but I remember the birthday or achievement that brought them to me as gifts and they stay with me, long after books I bought as an adult have been given away or mislaid.

—Peggy Sullivan in
Carolyn Field's *Special Collections*

The Collector's Universe

Somewhere between our first purchase, subsequent accumulation, and established collecting, we become self-conscious and, seeking reassurance, ask, "What else is out there?" "What to collect?" or "What can be collected?" addresses the totality of publishing for children and its related print, paper, cloth, glass, ceramic and metal ephemera. Chapter 2 of this book treats that world holistically. But we don't collect holistically any more than we live that way. Our collecting represents innumerable, individual but needfully related decisions.

In order to tame the world of children's books into comprehensible manageability, you must divide and conquer. A division into the broad categories of internal and external serves well again. Here, internal focuses upon literary genres, or kinds or types of literature, and external examines the features or *points* that establish edition identity. External features require only the straightforward bibliographic description that establishes edition. Not so for exploring the limits of a universe as imprecise as that of genre, from which one can build a collection of children's literature.

This inventory does not attempt the impossible—a complete catalog. I began with the helpful dictionary arrangement of *The Oxford Companion to Children's Literature*, our only encyclopedia. Because currency and an expansion of American coverage were needed to balance the 1987 English *Companion*, I also depended upon two very important children's literature textbooks: *Children and Books*, begun by May Hill Arbuthnot and continued with Zena Sutherland, and Charlotte S. Huck, Susan Hepler, and Janet Hickman's *Children's Literature in the Elementary School*. The booths of specialized dealers at antiquarian book fairs also offer a valuable additional reference source. I scanned them, using their wares as libraries and examining their arrangements for collectible fields. The amount of annotation for each genre to follow is designed to define, provide historical context, and encourage cross-collecting. Any information duplicated in earlier or later chapters is given to provide a concentrated, alphabetically arranged database that can be supplemented with the index. The references in chapter 10, "Printed Helpers," can lead to answers for your continuing queries.

‖ GENRE CLASSES

ABC BOOKS. These are also termed Abcee, Abcie, or Absey books. From the Middle Ages until the 18th century, alphabet learning was tied to religious and moral instruction. Primers and hornbooks contained alphabets and prayers. John Locke made the case for teaching by entertainment in *Some Thoughts Concerning Education* (1693); his influence lightened this genre with such as "A Was an Archer" in the 1694 *Playbook for Children* by "J.G." *The Child's New Play-Thing* (1742) by Mary Cooper used a version of this. With pleasure approved, artists went on to explore the ability of these books to organize graphic experience by helping children identify objects with the use of key words. History appeared in *The Alphabet of Peace* (1856), which celebrated the end of the Crimean War; nonsense charmed in *An Edward Lear Alphabet Book*; beauty triumphed in Crane's *Baby's Own Alphabet* (1874) and Kate Greenaway's *A Apple Pie* (1886); and Ruth M. Baldwin's *100 Rhyming Alphabets in English* (1972) produced scholarly help. The genre continues to produce splendid examples to charm parents, collectors, and children.

ADVENTURES OF INANIMATE OBJECTS. See Personified Toys and Other Inanimate Objects.

ADVENTURE STORIES. Cornelia Meigs writes, "The adventure story, after the folk tale, was probably the first form of literature that children took for their own" (Meigs, p. 482). The first format available to them for medieval romances was the chapbook. Modern versions developed from *Robinson Crusoe* (1719) and its imitators, which have been continued by English authors: Marryat, Ballantyne, Darton, and Henty, with Stevenson starred; and Americans Cooper, Fosdick (Harry Castlemon), Elijah Kellogg, J. T. Trowbridge, Noah Brooks, Charles C. Coffin, and Charles Boardman Hawes.

Beyond Ernest Thompson Seton, the American special contribution to adventure writing of the 20th century may be the breed of superheroes that began in the 1930s with Superman and Batman.

ANIMAL STORIES. These are divisible into stories about animals as such and those about humanized animals. Wild animal biography demands writers with storytelling skills plus detailed authentic knowledge needed to present the animal as nearly as possible in its animal nature. Important masters of this genre are the Canadian Charles G. D. Roberts, Ernest Thompson Seton, and Jean Craighead George (1919–). Other important stories are Russell Freedman's *Buffalo Hunt*, Holling Clancy Holling's *Paddle-to-the Sea*, Marjorie Kinnan Rawlings's *The Yearling*, and Sterling North's *Rascal: A Memoir of a Better Era*. Beatrix Potter's *Peter Rabbit* is probably the best incarnation of a humanized animal character, followed by *The Velveteen Rabbit*, the Cowardly Lion, and legions of stuffed favorites. *See also* Cat, Dog, and Horse Stories.

ANNUALS. These are yearly publications beginning with independent forms such as Mrs. S. C. Hall's *The Juvenile Forget-Me-Not*, and usually associated with a magazine from the mid-19th century on. Boys' Victorian annuals are more factual than those for girls.

AUTHOR. Collecting a single author requires seeking, finding, buying, and storing works—perhaps the rarest ones—that you may not like at all. This creates a negative implicit in pursuing this genre in a pure form. Obvious inclusion possibilities are editions illustrated by differing artists and introduced by various relevant literary figures.

BATTLEDORES. After about 150 years of satisfactory instructional use, the hornbook began to be replaced by another form of primer, the battledore. This invention was claimed by the Salisbury, England bookseller, Benjamin Collins, who manufactured a *Royal Battledore* in association with John Newbery in 1746. Some were tablets of wood, rounded like rackets, which could be, and often were, used for playing shuttlecock. Others, like the *Royal*, were made from heavy paper folded into book form. The printing was sometimes protected by a coat of varnish. Now, when found, they are usually in mint condition—often hidden within a larger book.

BESTIARY. Popular in medieval Europe, this is a form in which real and imaginary animals are used to illustrate Christian morals and dogma. Newbery's *Pretty Book of Pictures for Little Masters and Misses* relates to these, and T. H. White translated one from Latin under the title *The Book of Beasts* (1954).

BOOKS OF COURTESY. These are handbooks of instruction in the manners and customs of polite society for children and youth, written from the 15th to the 19th century with a straight face. Judith Martin, "Miss Manners," offers a current example of this genre.

BOOKS OF INSTRUCTION. Bede (c. 700) and Aelfric (1006) wrote early versions for teaching Latin, and the *New England Primer* is America's most famous example. This genre comes down to us in textbooks, nonfiction or informational trade books, and children's encyclopedias.

BROADSIDES. Format description for single, large sheets of paper, with printing on one side only, often illustrated and generally containing the text of a ballad. Current events—often crimes or scandals—and the romances of chivalry comprised their usual subject matter.

CAREER NOVELS. These appeared for both boys and girls in British and American versions in 1936. Britain's was *Ballet Shoes* by Noel Streatfield and America's was *Sue Barton, Student Nurse* by Helen Dore Boylston. The best featured being "something" professional or work-related, but mass-marketed formula titles and series were just thinly disguised romances.

CAT STORIES. Perrault gave us *The Master Cat* or *Puss in Boots* (in English in a 1729 chapbook). Dr. Seuss's *The Cat in the Hat* (1957) now amuses a third generation of beginning readers. For lyrical feline beauty, I suggest the work of author/illustrator Clare Turlay Newberry (1903–70) for her output that includes *April's Kittens* (1940) and *Smudge* (1948).

CAUTIONARY TALES. Poetic or prose warnings against foolish behavior. *Vice in Its Proper Shape* by Elizabeth Newbery (c. 1774) is one of the earliest and Heinrich Hoffmann's *Struwwelpeter* (*Slovenly Peter*, 1845) one of the most fearsome. Gelett Burgess (1866–1951) wrote humorous advice in books such as *The Goops and How to Be Them* and Munro Leaf created the Watchbirds in his picture books of the 1940s (some of which are now back in print).

CHAPBOOKS. Once the masses were encouraged to read so that they might know their Bible, they sought to find in print the lurid improbabilities of oral gossip and superstition. Thus, from the 16th to the 18th century, the English chapbook or cheapbook became an important bookish format for popular literature. These generally consisted of from four to twenty-four folded but unstitched pages, with some texts illustrated with crude woodcuts. They were sold at door and fair by "Flying Stationers," itinerant peddlers or chapmen. By 1800, chapbooks for children were being produced in some quantity and children could devour in travestied form nursery rhymes and adventure stories.

CHILD AUTHORS. *The Young Visiters* (1919) by Daisy Ashford is the best known of these.

CHRISTMAS BOOKS. Strictly defined, this term describes a series by Charles Dickens. The first was *A Christmas Carol*, which was written during 1843 when sales of his current serial, *Martin Chuzzlewit*, were slow. It saw print that Christmas and its wild success resulted in the publication the next Christmas of *The Chimes*, a tale of a dream of New Year's bells. *The Cricket on the Hearth* appeared in 1845, followed by the last two books in the series: *The Battle of Life* (1846) and *The Haunted Man* (1848). Broadly defined, this genre includes any book with Christmas as its subject; under this definition, I've been building a collection for thirty-five years.

CINDERELLA. Folklorists claim to trace this fairy tale's variants from sources as diverse as China and Peru. As English-speakers, we prefer the French version as set down by Perrault. Each index entry for Cinderella carries an author and illustrator note (Marcia Brown, Rackham, Cruikshank, etc.) that tells us how each slightly altered tale will be remembered—from Disney until forever.

COLLECTING AIMS. The North Pomfret, Vermont dealer Jane K. Adelson contributed this concept and under it lists: "one's special hobbies, such as pigs or bees; interests such as airplanes, trains, cities; books to republish; likeness books—age, geography, sex, sports in common with the collector; a shelf of the right color bindings to match your library walls; and, of course, investment."

COMICS. Defined as sequential drawings telling a satirical story or chain of events, this art/story form is found in prehistory on cave walls and later on Greek vases. In Britain the format was a weekly tabloid and in the U.S. a daily comic strip. "Little Orphan Annie" (1924), "Dick Tracy" (1931), "Flash Gordon (1934), "Oaky Doaks" (1935), "Superman" (1938), and "Batman" (1939) are some important examples. The original drawings for these are now collectible art. The comic book format descends from penny dreadfuls and can be defined as an anthology of comic strips.

CORRESPONDENCE. Letters received or written are tangential fields for a book collector. Price makes retrospective acquisition impractical, but for those collecting the works of living authors and artists, obtaining letters offers personalized connections and potentially lucrative holdings.

DEATH BED SCENES. The teary demises in *Elsie Dinsmore* come easily to mind. More universally affecting is Beth's death in *Little Women*. Cotton Mather, other American Puritans, and the authors writing for the American Sunday School Union (c. 1824) excelled at portraying these, as did their English predecessors and counterparts.

DETECTIVE STORIES. Tentative appearances of criminal activities and Gothic horrors in late 19th-century chapbooks led to Poe's *Murders in the Rue Morgue* (1841), considered to be the first true example of a detective story—a literary coup for America. Dime novels found this genre and by 1879 it went West in the Deadwood Dick series. Another hero is Sexton Blake, whose detectings first appeared in *Marvel* (1893), and who connects in energy, if not brains and class, with Sherlock Holmes. Detection is an important plot in series collecting with England's C.D. Lewis' *The Otterbury*

Incident (1948), Enid Blyton's Famous Five series, and America's Tom Swift, Hardy Boys, Nancy Drew, Linda Craig, etc.

DIME NOVELS. Sensational subjects such as Gothic novels, sea stories, sports, and Westerns were published in this cheap paper format that sold for a dime. These were largely the work of hacks. See also Penny Dreadfuls.

DISNEY ITEMS. Walt Disney (1901–66) founded the studio that produced the animated films that form the basis for these books and related artifacts. Currently this is a very hot and pricey collecting area, with the fiftieth anniversary of *Snow White* just observed.

DOG STORIES. *Lassie, One Hundred and One Dalmatians, The Incredible Journey, White Fang*, and the stories of Albert Payson Terhune, Jack O'Brien, Jack London, Farley Mowat, Wilson Rawls, and others are examples.

DOLL HOUSE STORIES. Frances Hodgson Burnett's *Racketty Packetty House* imprinted this genre on me. Flora Gill Jacobs of Washington, D.C., describes their world thus: "Dollhouses cast the spell of the small as they embody the history of architecture, the decorative arts, and domestic culture. They represent historic preservation in miniature." She has written two doll house stories: *The Doll House Mystery* (1958) and *The Toy Shop Mystery* (1960), as well as *A World of Doll Houses* (1967), a children's version of her adult reference source, *A History of Dolls' Houses* (1953).

DOLL STORIES. Two of these won the Newbery: Rachel Field's *Hitty* (1930) and *Miss Hickory* (1947) by Carolyn Sherwin Bailey. Rumer Godden's dolls are often boys, and all strongly portray human conflict. My sources did not put Johnny Gruelle's Raggedy Anne and Andy here, and I wonder why.

DOMESTIC DRAMA. See Family Stories.

EPHEMERA. Short-lived or transitory items that can add value and interest to a book collection. Advertising posters, programs, publishers' catalogs, newspaper clippings of reviews, and fliers from programs all make worthwhile supplements, especially if one is alert and brash enough to snatch opportunities to get them autographed—free. (Paid-for poster signings are no·challenge). Printed textiles are one variant form. Possibilities for these range from the well-preserved handkerchiefs printed with useful knowledge and moral precepts for juvenile instruction that are part of the Betsy Beinecke Shirley Collection at Yale University's Beinecke Library to the more obtainable ones printed with Disney characters that sold in the 1940s for 35¢.

ETHNIC AND REGIONAL STORIES. The "all-white world of children's books" Nancy Larrick described in her September 11, 1965, *Saturday Review* article is still all too accurate, with America's present influx of Hispanic and Asian-American children joining African-Americans and Native Americans as underrepresented faces in mainstream publishing. Though publication of books with African-Americans as characters has increased, *Shadow and*

Substance by Radine Sims, published by the National Council of English Teachers in 1982, observed that most were written by white authors. Virginia Hamilton's Newbery award for *M. C. Higgins the Great* (1975) honored the first black. Many writers in the 1940s broke through publishing taboos against African-American and non-middle-class characters: Marguerite De Angeli with *Bright April* (1945), about a middle class black family; Doris Gates with *Blue Willow* (1940), about California migrant workers; and Lois Lenski's Newbery *Strawberry Girl* (1945) about Florida "crackers." Native American books are a sub-genre including Grace Moon's *Chi-Wee* (1925), Louise Adams Armer's Newbery winner, *Waterless Mountain* (1931), and Eileen Nusbaum's *Seven Cities of Cibola*, and books by more recent notables such as Paul Goble and John Bierhorst.

FABLES. A fable is a fictive narrative with a hidden meaning. They are often animal tales that illuminate a human foible; some famous examples are by Aesop, La Fontaine, and Joel Chandler Harris.

FACSIMILES. Exact replicas of early books gain in popularity as the originals increase in price and decline in availability. There are fine ones published in sets by the Osborne Collection, the Library of Congress, the Huntington Library, and Green Tiger Press and Scolar Press. Scribner's exact reprints of the Wyeth-illustrated books are related collectible editions.

FAIRY TALES. These are among the oldest children's fare, coming from oral literature and appearing in some form throughout literary history. They are usually short narratives with either popular or identifiable authorship set in times past with mortals as heroes or heroines interacting with fairies, giants, talking beasts, and trees. According to Bruno Bettelheim, "The fairy tale's deepest meaning will be different for each person . . . and the child will extract different meaning from the same fairy tale, depending on his interests and needs of the moment" (Bettelheim, p. 12). My canon chooses Andrew Lang (1844–1912), who gave us a series of "color" books, largely a by-product of his scholarship in mythology and folklore, which began with *The Blue Fairy Book* in 1889 and ended with *The Lilac Fairy Book* in 1910. Virginia Haviland also deserves mention for her compilation of a splendid series of books of traditional fairy tales, each with a different national origin.

FAMILY STORIES, OR DOMESTIC DRAMA. These began by using the events of ordinary home life to point a moral. The 19th-century English-women Catherine Sinclair and Charlotte M. Yonge added entertainment to balance instructional content. These books are thought to be models for Alcott, whose *Little Women* (1868) began the American genre, which continues with Sidney's *The Five Little Peppers*, and books by Martha Finley, Elizabeth Enright, Eleanor Estes, Beverly Cleary, Madeleine L'Engle, E.L. Konigsburg, and others. Home reflects society's continuum, and in the early 90s junior novels now reflect our growing Asian population.

FANTASY. This is briefly defined as a work of fiction by an identifiable author involving the supernatural. And what special human beings are among its creators—Ruskin, Kingsley, Carroll, Stockton, Lofting, Travers, Tolkien, C. S. Lewis, Alan Garner, Lloyd Alexander, L'Engle, Ursula Le Guin and Lindgren. What a company!

FOLKTALES. Stories from folklore, with universal themes and motifs, found among almost all peoples. Folktales were begun orally, then set down in the earliest writings. They are collected by scholars who analyze them from historical, literary, religious, and psychological points of view. The Celtic inhabitants of the British Isles were telling theirs before the Romans came. The two hundred tales and legends that Jacob (1785–1863) and Wilhelm (1786–1859) Grimm collected earn them a starred mention as the virtual founders of the scientific study of folktales. These continue to be used by illustrators as picture book texts.

GAMES. The rhyming games that children play spontaneously were brought into the area of modern scholarship by the Opies, who collected and publicized *Children's Games in Street and Playground* (1969). This describes the long, continuing history of games of seeking, fighting, daring, racing, guessing, pretending, etc.

GEOGRAPHIC LOCATION. Pick your locale and start researching. General or centrally done juvenile cataloging does not use subject headings, so you won't find geographic headings there, and I did not find a bibliography so arranged. This means that your best sources will be local special collections in museums that do use location as a bibliographic access point.

GHOST STORIES. These have both a long history as oral literature and a marked overlap with adult literature. Three editions to note are Mrs. Molesworth's *Four Ghost Stories* (1888), Oscar Wilde's *The Canterville Ghost* (1906), and *Doctor to the Dead: Grotesque Legends and Folktales* by John Bennett (1943). Virginia Haviland's collections also hold some. The National Book League (London) did a 14-page bibliography, "Ghostly Encounters," in 1978. Authors to look for are Leon Garfield and Ruth Manning-Sanders, plus recent collections by Alfred Hitchcock, Susan Hill and many folklorists.

HISTORICAL NOVELS. Sir Walter Scott's first novel *Waverley* (1814) set a precedent for this genre for children. His success encouraged British writers of moral tales to set theirs in time past, and adventure story writers used history as a source to replace much-used geography after the mid-19th century. Robert M. Ballantyne (1825–94) is thought to have paved the way for George A. Henty. Some of the most lasting late 19th century fame goes to Robert Louis Stevenson, Mark Twain and Howard Pyle. By 1900 the genre had become established and continues to be an important resource for making history real to children.

HISTORICAL TIME PERIOD. These collections include both fiction and nonfiction. Quality in both requires authors to be accurate in the details they select to clothe the bare historical facts, to bring them to life. A collector must decide whether to include books written after, as well as during, the chosen era.

HORNBOOKS. Scarcity of paper inspired the development of a unique instructional format, the hornbook, which became common in England from the 16th to the 18th century and came to America with the Puritans. These sturdy primers were built by applying thin sheets of horn to wooden paddles and then binding the whole with brass.

HORSE STORIES. Anna Sewell wrote *Black Beauty* (1877), which starts our list. Some followers could be Walter Farley's *The Black Stallion*, Lynd Ward's *Silver Pony*, C. W. Anderson's *Blaze* books, Marguerite Henry, and Enid Bagnold's *National Velvet*.

ILLUSTRATOR. To collect one illustrator successfully, and somewhat independently, one must be bibliographic-entry-wise. Author entry is always given in standard bibliographic form, but not illustrator. For now, and probably into the future, this is the most pricey modern collecting area. Dorothy Lathrop has recently become "collectible." The original art for many books has become a hot collectible, available from a few children's book dealers, and general and specialized art galleries. Prices for it vary in relation to sources and the importance of the book from which it comes.

INFORMATIONAL BOOKS. These discuss science, health, music, art, medicine, law, sports, government service, military service, history, etc. Although collectible, they generally show a poor track record. The planned speed of our technologically-driven society that causes these topical accounts to date very quickly, plus their lack of illustrations, help account for little collecting interest. One hopes, though, that some institution has gathered and retained this valuable informational literary record. Since about 1960, however, illustrators—led by David Macaulay, Leonard Everett Fisher, and Brent Ashabranner, among others—have discovered this field, with noteworthy present and future collecting prospects.

INSCRIBED COPIES. This describes books with special, handwritten comments, dedications, memorializations, and/or unique illustrations such as cartoons or an illustrator's "chop." Attendees at annual American Library Association (ALA) meetings who are willing to exercise their minds and their feet, standing in line sometimes for hours, carry away vast numbers of such books. Publishers' booths feature Caldecott and Newbery winners and as many other authors and illustrators as can be cajoled into participating. A subgenre of inscribed copies could be award books inscribed just at ALA. Establishing guidelines, such as defining when the autographing practice began, would lend research spice to this collecting.

JEST BOOKS. Now called joke books, this genre of short comic anecdotes and sayings has been traced from 16th-century chapbooks and is considered an ancestor of modern comic books. The 1739 *Joe Miller's Jests* is the origin of our term "Joe Miller," meaning a stale joke. The title relates to Joseph Miller (1684–1738), a Drury Lane comic actor who was a reputed wit.

JUVENILE INCUNABULA. In bibliographical terms, incunabula ("cradle books") denotes books printed before the convenient date of 1501. The Victorians were familiar with these "fifteeners," which we find listed in their antiquarian booksellers' catalogs, but juveniles were still extremely rare and the majority of these cradle (of printing) books now can be seen only in museums and national libraries.

MAGAZINES. These collections of stories, verse, and instructive articles, usually illustrated, are distinguished by their periodic publishing schedule from those issued as single copies. The earliest American juvenile was *Children's Magazine* with three issues in 1789. Those with an interest in the view of childhood's history that they afford may find these magazines rewarding collecting material.

MORAL TALES. Nonfanciful, often religious didactic juvenile fiction, developed to counter the allure of chapbook fiction, appeared first in the mid-18th century and became the predominant genre by 1800. These books featured childhood sins, requisite punishment, and repentance. Adults were pictured as omnipresent, guiding figures. Newbery's *Goody Two-Shoes* (1765) is one of the earliest. Around 1825, America saw what Cornelia Meigs terms the "Sunday School Tracts" flourish—printed books whose object was "to do what they can to counteract the prevailing thirst in the rising generation for the mere entertainment of high-wrought fiction" (Meigs, p. 134). Moral tales survived in differing forms through to the evangelical and temperance stories of the 19th century. Within the literary mainstream, gradual lightening triumphed, aided materially by the first English translation of Grimms' fairy tales, called *German Popular Stories* (1823). Fiction seems to require morality, and moral education appears as an intrinsic thread of children's literature.

MOVABLE PICTURE BOOKS. Lothar Meggendorfer (*Comic Actors*, 1891) is the current buzz-word for these fragile fascinators that accomplish scene changes with flaps and tabs (before they get broken). As early as 1766, harlequinades, or turn-ups, appeared. The mid-1890s saw Ernest Nister's English series that began with *The Great Panorama Picture Book*. In the mid-1960s, with the help of "paper engineering," Bennett Cerf of Random House revitalized this collectible, now so "hot" that dealers seek and salt away current publications. Look for a bibliography in the near future.

NOBEL PRIZE WINNERS. Among those who also wrote for children are Pearl S. Buck, Rudyard Kipling, Selma Lagerlof, Maurice Maeterlinck, Anatole France, Sinclair Lewis, and Sigrid Undset.

NONSENSE. *Webster's* defines nonsense as "words that convey an absurd meaning or no meaning at all . . . foolish, unintelligible." Parents almost unconsciously create this when they play with language to amuse small children. Edward Lear used the alphabet as material for such playfulness, and Lewis Carroll's tale of the Walrus and the Carpenter shows us some unpleasant results of such a subversion of sense. Carl Sandburg's *Rootabaga Stories* (1929) offers a highly literate example. Later practitioners include Ogden Nash, Dr. Seuss, and Shel Silverstein. Modern poetry abounds with nonsense.

NURSERY RHYMES. This term for verses spoken or sung to small children is apparently of mid-18th-century English origin. "Mother Goose" continues as the American name for these folk verses that originated "long ago" as adult chants, rituals, numerations, and riddles. About 500 of the English versions remain "traditional," that is, remembered and handed down through the generations. Some ditties appeared in medieval texts; some were in use by 1650, with about half of those we use today known by the mid-18th century. America's fondness for Mother Goose—rhymes and name—invented a historic connection with a Boston lady named Goose or Vergoose who died in 1690 and is buried in Boston Common.

PARALLEL COLLECTIONS. Since duplicates of most books are available, you might choose to make a personal selection from the catalogs of famous collections. One example would be the two-volume 1931 catalog by K. A. Gumuchian & Cie. of Paris, reprinted by London's Holland Press in 1967. With 336 plates, many hand-colored, illustrating 186 of the 6,000 items described in its more than 400 pages of text, it is a handsome representative of collection catalogs such as Rosenbach, Osborne, d'Alte Welch, or, on a smaller scale, *Peter Parley to Penrod*.

PENNY DREADFULS. This is the British term for our "dime novels." A penny bought one of these serial story-parts, magazines, or novelettes containing cheap, sentimental, and sensational mass-market fiction published from 1830 onward. *The Oxford Companion to Children's Literature* offers this quote from Robert Louis Stevenson on the subject of reading them: "Eloquence, character, thought and conversation were but obstacles to brush aside as we dug blithely for a certain kind of incident, like a pig for truffles" (p. 399).

PERIODICALS. See Magazines.

PERSONIFIED TOYS AND OTHER INANIMATE OBJECTS. Two English sisters-in-law, Dorothy (1755–1836) and Mary Ann (1753–1831) Kilner, are credited with first giving the narrator's voice to animals and inanimate objects. Mary Ann wrote *The Adventures of a Pincushion* (c. 1780), and Dorothy wrote *Life and Perambulations of a Mouse* (1783). Andersen receives credit for inventing the fanciful story about the secret life of these objects which 20th century authors have broadened and used to fashion classics. This genre contains subgenres such as dolls, exemplified in *Pinocchio* by the Italian Carlo Lorenzini (Collodi) and boats, such as *Little Toot* by Hardie Gramatky.

PICTURE BOOKS. "A picturebook is text, illustrations, total design; an item of manufacture and a commercial product; a social, cultural, historical document; and foremost, an experience for a child," comments Barbara Bader in *American Picturebooks: From Noah's Ark to the Beast Within* (1976). "As an art form, it hinges on the interdependence of pictures and words, on the simultaneous display of two facing pages, and on the drama of the turning of the page. On its own terms its possibilities are endless" (p. 1). Because these books embody a most distinctive artistic unity of words and pictures, their history relates directly to that of printing. Two suggestions for learning about picture books are: Read some of Bader's "Starting Point" comments, and follow the history of the Caldecott Award books as one readily visible delineation of genre excellence.

PIRATE LITERATURE. Adventure fiction seems to have discovered pirates as heroes and drawn them from both history and the imagination. Robert Louis Stevenson, J. M. Barrie, and Howard Pyle stand out for their creations in *Treasure Island* (1883), *Peter and Wendy* (1911), a retelling of "Peter Pan" in book form, and *Howard Pyle's Book of Pirates* (1921).

POETRY FOR CHILDREN. This is both a genre and a division of a major literary form. Probably forever, and surely since *Beowulf*, poetry in some guise has been used to teach and entertain children. For joyous parent/young child communication nothing ever has or ever will surpass nursery rhymes, ballads and doggerel. Books of poetry are divided between "collections," the poems of a single poet, and "anthologies," the works of many poets grouped around a subject (Christmas), purpose (family reading), chronology, or age level. An anthologist's creative voice draws collectors to specific books. In a telephone conversation, the distinguished anthologist, author, and educator Nancy Larrick described the spiritual integrity of anthologies:

> Sitting on the terrace one night we heard, with surprise, the unmistakable voice of a whippoorwill. Suddenly, for me, that combination of bird and moment crystallized a subject, sounds of the night. Fall 1992 should bring the publication of *The Night of the Whippoorwill* which will contain the poems that, grouped together, tell my story of the meaning of those night sounds.

"How do you do it?" I asked Lee Bennett Hopkins, another notable writer, teacher, and anthologist. His response:

> To be good, an anthologist must: know the field—the poetry; must have the resources available from which to select and keep abreast; and must have the skill to make a fresh artistic whole from selected parts which, in themselves, are artistic wholes. For an anthology of sixteen poems, I'll read and consider about two thousand. Each new anthology must show a balance, including that between the old and the new. For over twenty years, I've been collecting books of poetry,

and now what I can turn to compares well to the collection of the Library of Congress. Contemporary poets writing for children (as well as for adults) voice the tone of the times, and each generation of children is identifiable by the poetry they have taken unto themselves. Being a wise collector means buying volumes as they are published because many go out of print very soon. For example, numerous books written in the late 1950s and 1960s have already disappeared from the scene. Early books by Myra Cohn Livingston, Eve Merriam, Dorothy Aldis, Harry Behn, and Aileen Fisher are almost impossible to come across. If these works are not collected and preserved, we are losing a large part of this genre forever.

POP-UP BOOKS. A variant of movable books, in which picture parts spring out when pages are opened or tabs pulled. Dating from the mid-20th century, they became a fad in the 1970s. Their distinctive features make them unusually destructible and thus rare, and dear when in mint condition.

PRIMER. Originally describing a prayer book, this term was later applied to elementary textbooks. For Americans, *The New England Primer* is the dream collectible. Early readers are an attainable field, especially prized for their period illustrations.

PRIZE BOOKS. An easy genre to collect, this is an established, historical, finite, and constantly growing universe, the specifics of which are well documented. Beyond the Caldecott and Newbery, a short list of prizes includes: the Laura Ingalls Wilder Award, ALA Notable Books, the Regina Medal, the Coretta Scott King Award, the Carnegie Medal, *Boston Globe–Horn Book* Awards, the Hans Christian Andersen Award; the Scott O'Dell Award for Historical Fiction, National Jewish Book Awards, and many regional and state prizes such as Vermont's Dorothy Canfield Fisher Children's Book Award. More and more groups are adding kudos for juveniles. Even the Edgar Allan Poe Society now gives one.

PROBLEM FICTION. Modern examples began in the 1970s with somewhat didactic books and novels about death, divorce, race issues, the handicapped, and—sex. The latter became a special problem for nonconsenting parents in what we may be tempted to call the Judy Blume era. There are signs that this genre may be waning. Current literary criticism vibrates between the opinion that children were helped by finding that their problems were not unique and the opinion that they were hurt by the apparent sanctioning in print of "far out" actions.

PUBLISHER'S IMPRINT. Except in rare instances, seeking to acquire a publisher's entire output mandates a large budget and potentially infinite shelf space. I started to collect P. F. Volland books with enthusiastic nostalgia—an effort that speedily reinforced the value of learning by doing. To determine the size of an imprint universe offers a challenge in itself because the citation of publisher is not used as an access point in library catalogs or in most bibliographies. The Baldwin Library at the University of Florida has created an imprint catalog for its holdings up to the year 1900, but *Publishers' Trade List Annual,* a compilation of publishers' catalogs for each year, is an excellent reference obtainable in larger libraries and is really the only organized way to search by imprint. Only some juvenile catalogs are included, however. Almost all juvenile publishers put out catalogs, often lavishly illustrated, which can be picked up at appropriate meetings like ALA or obtained directly from the publisher. As these age, they become useful and valuable refrence sources.

RIDDLES. These offer an unusual collecting field with a history of great age—going back to Oedipus and to the Bible. Jumping over many centuries brings us to that successful marketer, Newbery, with his *Food for the Mind, or a New Riddle Book* (1757). In addition to being available in anthologies, some modern examples exist in Potter's *The Tale of Squirrel Nutkin* and Tolkien's *The Hobbit.*

ROMANCES. Around the 14th century in England lengthy narratives, said to recount doings of a "distant past," appeared full of dragons, giants, knights, and chivalrous doings that children found to their liking. Originally verse, part of the oral tradition, they moved into print and became popular chapbooks with abbreviated texts and woodcut illustrations of dragon-killings and other knightly adventures.

SCHOOL STORIES. *Tom Brown's Schooldays* (1856–57) by Englishman Thomas Hughes gets credit for establishing this genre, which came to America with Thomas Bailey Aldrich's *Story of a Bad Boy* (1870), and continued on to Edward Eggleston's the *Hoosier Schoolboy* (1883), the private academy stories of Ralph Henry Barbour (1870–1944), and now Francine Pascal's Sweet Valley High series.

SCIENCE FICTION. "The line between fantasy and science fiction has always been difficult to draw, particularly for children's literature," writes Charlotte Huck (Huck, p. 378). Drawing it raises such definition snags as whether science fiction must use the tools and technology of science and whether its projections about the future must aim at being realistic. Jules Verne established sci-fi in futuristic stories that have turned out to possess amazing actuality. Influenced by such books as H. G. Wells's *The Time Machine* (1895), sci-fi became a popular part of boys' magazines. Robert Heinlein, H. M. Hoover, Peter Dickinson, John Christopher, and Andre Norton carry on most ably in personal versions of Verne. Ursula Le Guin in her Earthsea trilogy and Madeleine L'Engle in her trilogy that began with *A Wrinkle in Time* (1962 Newbery) lean to fantasy. For younger children, I pick Eleanor Cameron's *Wonderful Flight to the Mushroom Planet.*

SERIES BOOKS. A set of books issued sequentially and dealing with the adventures or experiences of a hero, heroine, siblings, or chums. Good examples are the Hardy Boys, Nancy Drew, and the Bobbsey Twins. For fine copies, this field is steadily heating up, with *Tarzan* swinging from a very high-priced tree.

SPORTS STORIES. These divide between books that describe and record children's games and those that tell stories about players, fictional or real.

STREET URCHIN OR STREET ARAB STORIES. A genre of moralist stories that appeared in the 19th century. Most firmly American are the "poor boy makes good" stories of Horatio Alger (1832–99).

TEMPERANCE STORIES. Beginning in late 18th-century Britain, there appeared periodicals and stories aimed at teaching children about the evils of drink. Two well-known late examples are George MacDonald's *At the Back of the North Wind* (1871) and Anna Sewell's *Black Beauty* (1877).

TOY BOOKS. A term used by the English and American publishing trade throughout the 19th century to describe a type of colorfully illustrated book of six to eight pages, with text in large type, printed on paper-covered board or linen cloth, and probably intended for the nonreading child. Their content was traditional tales and rhymes, illustrated first with woodcuts, later with early examples of chromolithography. In England the pioneers were Dean & Son; later, others such as Warne and Routledge became competitors. Crane and Caldecott designed some high-quality toy books printed from Edmund Evans's wood engravings. In America, the genre is represented by McLoughlin Brothers. Special books are a *A Visit from Santa Claus* and *Rip Van Winkle* (illustrated by Thomas Nast); *Camptown Races, Fairy Moonbeam,* and *Baseball ABC.*

TRAVELOGUE STORYBOOK. A fictional form used to impart history, folklore, and native customs (old-fashioned geography). The best of these were written by those who had firsthand knowledge of the countries they described, or who were scholars. This helps explain why Thomas Knox's Boy Traveler series (begun in 1879) and Horace E. Scudder's Bodley books (begun in 1875) remain collectible.

‖ BIBLIOGRAPHIES SUPPORT EDITION KNOWLEDGE

An understanding of the function of bibliographies is a necessary skill for book collectors. *Webster's* defines them as "books having information on editions, dates, authorship, etc., about books and other writings." A librarian defines them as having complete citations, which means they provide author, title, publisher, place and date of publication, number of pages and illustrations, and book size for each book being described. A library catalog is a bibliography of the holdings of that one institution, whether it is published, like the Osborne Catalog, or on cards or online. In her excellent analysis *Children's Book Research* (1989), the custodian of the Renier Collection of the Victoria and Albert Museum, Tessa Rose Chester, comments, "Don't expect the arrangement of catalogues to be convenient," and nudges memory with this poignant reference to World War II England: "An entry in a catalogue does not necessarily mean the book is there: books lost during the Blitz are still listed in the *British Library General Catalogue*" (p. 43).

The bibliography of primary value to us is the definitive author list, or what artists call a "catalog raisonné." It serves three chief purposes: to establish the canon of an author's works; to identify first and later editions of an author's works; and, for at least each major work and edition, to establish full edition description (or points), including precise publication date and number of copies printed (when known), but not prices. Many exhibitions generate published catalogs with full bibliographic information, which, do remember, will not include current value. As you record your own collection, you are compiling a personal catalog or bibliography. "Guidelines for Cataloging Children's Books" in the appendix here tells you how to do this, following the sequence librarians use for a cataloging record.

‖ EDITION OPTIONS

Once you've decided on your subject—author, illustrator, genre, or the like—the decision moves from the consideration of internals to that of externals. What edition shall I collect? A minimum-priced decision would indicate a collection of paperback editions with interesting cover art. Many of these are firsts—especially for science fiction. This decision to publish science fiction in softcover infuriates buffs, who cannot find early titles in libraries, which tend not to keep paperbacks. Beyond the low-budget paperback choice, there are these main options open to you. The cost varies with the internals:

1. First editions—in whatever format each title dictates.
2. Author-inscribed first editions.
3. All first editions in English, including American, British, Canadian, Australian, etc.
4. Hardback editions with dust jacket.
5. Hardback editions, author-inscribed.
6. All English language editions of an author's work, including American, Canadian, British, etc.
7. Only illustrated editions of an author's work.
8. All editions of one title, including reprints and all variant editions.

‖ SOME CHOICES WITHIN EXTERNAL CONSIDERATIONS

ASSOCIATION COPIES. These are individual books with a special provenance such as ownership or inscription or some connection of import that gives them a high appreciation potential. Of any given copy there cannot be a duplicate. Presentation copies are usually first editions—plus.

AUTHORS' PROOFS AND ADVANCE REVIEW COPIES. Distributed by publishers, and sent out before trade and limited editions, these exist chiefly to allow reviewers, acquisition librarians, and booksellers lead time to make advance purchase or review decisions about new books. Electronic publishing is resulting in the demise of the long galley proof, but paginated proofs do exist, often perfect-bound. Sometimes these can be the original author's proofs, showing author alterations, but likely they are simply the first go-around of type before proofing. Proof copies are especially valuable if you are considering eventual donation to a scholarly institution. Advance trade edition copies usually go out with a review or complimentary notice and some bear the publisher's stamp to that effect, which may raise first edition value.

AUTOGRAPHED COPIES. Traditionally these are signed by one of the people who created the book's content—the author or illustrator.

EDITION BY FORMAT. These vary in binding from the paper-, cloth-, or imitation leather-covered "boards" of modern books, to the shiny, stiff covers familiar to us as paperbacks, to those fragile paperwraps whose covers weigh only slightly more than the text, to other special formats listed here.

FINE BINDINGS. These could be termed "book jewelry" without wildly straining the metaphor, as some actually are jewel-encrusted. For juveniles within this book's emphasized time span, limited editions form the main, generally available category. My childhood edition of *Racketty Packetty House* was put in hand-tooled, purple leather binding by a relative. It is my treasure, not as an edition point, but just as a delight for a fine-binding buff.

FIRST EDITIONS. In collecting, *first edition* generally means the first printing of the first edition. A second printing, however identical it may be, is not the true "first." Sometimes between printings, and always between editions, there are differences that are termed *points*. These are sometimes accidental, the result of human error, such as running short of a binding cloth and having to change the color or material, or having a broken piece of type create a typographical error, or deliberate changes such as textual alterations, new illustrations, or other design features. They include all of the above plus the obvious: pagination; misspelling; change of paper; book size; different publisher; different illustrator; and variant front matter or additions such as publishers' advertisements.

What constitutes a point ranges widely, yet this is crucial to edition and thus to value. The informed collector makes sure that those points he needs to know are available while questing, either in his mind or in a pocket-sized reminder. The few children's books that are included in first edition reference works such as Allen and Patricia Ahearn's *Collected Books; The Guide to*

Values (1991), a successor to Van Allen Bradley's *The Book Collector's Handbook of Values* (1972), are usually those of literary authors: an example would be Steinbeck's *The Red Pony*. Joseph Connolly's *Children's Modern Firsts* (1989) covers chiefly British books and lists publication dates, but gives no edition descriptions. Because dealers' reputations depend upon their descriptions, their catalogs become valuable reference books.

From a Justin Schiller catalog comes this example involving four editions of Baum's *The Songs of Father Goose:* "The Songs of Father Goose." Music by Alberta N. Hall. Chicago: Geo. M. Hill, 1900. Illustrations by W. W. Denslow. 4to, 84pp; cloth-backed colored pictorial boards. First edition."

The next citation changes publisher and date with the entry: "Second edition, essentially identical to the Hill printing with slight changes for imprint and the deletion of 'Instructions' at the end."

Then: "Third printing, with a new cover design based on the Geo. M. Hill *Song Folios*, published in 1900."

Then: "Fourth (and last known) printing, with a change in the composer's last name."

In juvenile books, with their preponderance of color and design, variations are more distinctive and thus easier to see than those in adult books.

INDIVIDUAL ITEMS. This describes books that take on significance by virtue of their own distinctive, unique history. The most famous example from the Opie Collection is the copy of *The Wind in the Willows* inscribed by Kenneth Grahame to Alistair, his son, for whose bedtime storytelling ritual the adventures of Toad were first imagined.

LIMITED EDITIONS. These are usually signed, numbered, and in a slipcase, often with the inclusion of an original piece of art for an illustrated book. The few strictly juvenile titles that appear in this form are usually issued by the same publisher who did the trade edition, but classics such as *Tom Sawyer* are to be found. One publisher that specializes in this is the Limited Editions Club (LEC), begun in 1929 and featuring books on good paper, illustrated and signed by famous artists, numbered and originally limited to 1,500, now 2,000, copies. Heritage Press, an offshoot of the LEC, produces what could be termed LEC trade editions (they have the same illustrations, but the books are not signed or numbered). Franklin Press is a newcomer to the field, as is the Easton Press of Norwalk, Connecticut. I sent for and kept *Moby Dick*, one $4.95 promotional sample from Easton Press's collection of "The 100 Greatest Books Ever Written." With imitation leather binding and moire endpapers, it is a $35 reprint of an edition introduced by Clifton Fadiman, illustrated by Boardman Robinson, and first issued by the LEC in 1971. A 1988 concern, First Edition Library, issues exact replicas in slipcases for $35 each, which opens the door to possible deceit—since exact copies of dust jackets create the temptation to put them on actual first editions.

MINIATURE BOOKS. This is another format variant, in existence since the earliest days of printing. Miniatures filled the need for portable editions of such first reference books as the Bible. An example of an early 18th-century juvenile is Thomas Boreman's set of *Gigantick Histories* (1740–43). Maurice Sendak, at the height of his comic illustration career, created *The Nutshell Library*—four small books for the very young reader, including ABC and counting books.

PRIVATE PRESS EDITIONS. Very few juveniles are reprinted in this format. One exception that came to my hand last summer is a totally hand-set edition of *Aesop's Fables*, by the distinguished Vermont graphic artist, Elfriede Abbe. This was published in 1950 by the artist for $35 and listed in a 1989 catalog of David L. O'Neal of Boston as "First edition. Edited, illustrated, hand set and hand printed by Abbe. The illus. are wood engravings, printed from the blocks. Price $450." This book is a masterpiece, waiting for the right publisher to put out a trade edition.

‖ COLLECTING PATHS

After having taken our hobby apart, genre by genre and edition point by edition point, let's select some of these specifics and reassemble them into possible collecting paths. A computer analogy for topical overlapping is Boolean logic, a concept named for its originator, the English mathematician George Boole (1815–64). It allows a single online search to combine, or overlap, several segments or aspects so that one search can locate all items in the database (articles, books, etc.) that contain references to, say, poetry, teddy bears, children, and toy soldiers. An application of Boolean logic that could focus or specify my current collecting map might look like this: Volland imprint—not Johnny Gruelle—not oversize—before 1933—dolls—flowers. Let's think now about some connections you might want to make.

EXAMPLES OF GENRE CONNECTIONS. These can be understood as topical paths that diverge or converge as they touch related materials. Small subjects (horses, dogs, dolls, sports, etc.) appropriately intersect with larger ones such as history (time) and geography (place). Thus historical period, family stories, and geographic location connect to the topics of prairie or pioneer women in the stories of Laura Ingalls Wilder and the 1986 Newbery, *Sarah, Plain and Tall* by Patricia MacLachlan. Historical fiction must deal with time and place, and also offer a point of view (the Depression, poverty, racism, wars, multiculturalism) that can connect you to another genre. For example, Puritanism, combined with Elizabeth Speare's 1959 Newbery *The Witch of Blackbird Pond*, could connect you to witchcraft or other aspects of colonial life discussed by Speare. Another Newbery book, *Caddie Woodlawn* by Carol Ryrie Brink, is set in the Civil War period, but the war is not part of the plot. Pirate literature involves history and geography, but not domesticity. Realistic animal stories connect to geography, and both real and humanized animals meet domesticity. As a group, the books of James Cross Giblin provide easy connections between nonfiction and fiction. His 1991 title, *The Truth About Unicorns*, connects humanized animals to a unicorn and thence to the example in Tove Jansson's *Moominpappa at Sea*, which makes a format link to comics with a 1968 Moomin strip in the London *Evening News*; and to generalized unicorn characters in Marianna Mayer's and Michael Hague's *Unicorn Alphabet*. *George Washington's World* and *Abraham Lincoln's World* (Genevieve Foster) with their indexes of places, nations, and events lay out a connecting hub. Collecting a single, illustrated author automatically touches all his or her illustrators, which then can touch one artist who tempts you to make him or her another internal collecting focus. Poetry can connect you to almost any subject and innumerable illustrators. Seen this way, the infinity of literary subject matter can interact with the infinite arrangements of human mental furniture to produce limitless connections.

"ONLY CONNECT" PERSONALLY TAILORS WHAT WE SEEK. In addition to collecting connections, you can experience personal connections that appear and appeal only to you. E.M. Forster's phrase, "Only Connect," came into the children's literature vocabulary in 1966 when Pamela Travers, author of *Mary Poppins*, used it as title and theme for a Library of Congress Children's Book Week lecture. For her, it meant "the attempt to link a passionate skepticism with the desire for meaning, to find the human key to the inhuman world around us, to connect the individual with the community, the known with the unknown; the past to the present and both to the future" (Egoff, p. 184).

Christina Hardyment brought "Only Connect" alive for me in her book, *Heidi's Alp: One Family's Search for Storybook Europe*. This story describes the adventures of an English family in their Toadish caravan:

> We could spend this summer . . . in search of the roots of the stories that linked our children with children all over Europe in a common imaginative heritage. We could . . . look for witches and wolves in the German forests . . . rout out Heidi and William Tell . . . track down Pinocchio and Punch and Judy. What sort of man could write a book like *Struwwelpeter*? What was the true significance of Cinderella and Sleeping Beauty? Where did Don Quixote tilt at windmills? Was there a jackdaw at Reims, a hunchback in Notre Dame? (p. 3)

Though a car ferry ride can't get us to Europe, in the same spirit, curiosity and homework can send us to New York State to find traces of Rip Van Winkle in the Catskills, to Salem, Massachusetts, now or in 1775 through the eyes of the characters Jean Fritz drew in *Early Thunder*; or to

Boston to re-create the storybook map of happenings in Leonard Wibberley's Treegate series and Esther Forbes's *Johnny Tremain*. This Johnny, being a silversmith's apprentice, could also connect our collecting to jewelry apprentices in Florence, Italy, or to the idea of silver in Lewis's *The Silver Chair*.

Books appear everywhere, and as questers we need only to watch our radar for bookish blips and collecting connections. Just the other Sunday I toured the colonial post office that now houses the Poolesville, Maryland, Historic Medley District Society and its gift shop. There on the counter I noted *A County School Boy*, a history of the local one-room schoolhouse written by Bess Patterson Shipe, and was offered a just-published dust jacket to embellish my first edition, which was published without a jacket. Now I owned two first editions—book and dust jacket. That evening, equally by chance, with the jacket still in our car, I saw the author at a party, and both pieces are now autographed—a rarity indeed. Local history, schoolhouses, and school stories are not a collectible connection for me, but books by friends are.

THE ARABIAN NIGHTS. A STORY OF COLLECTING CONNECTIONS. In an essay in Avery's and Briggs's *Children and Their Books* the distinguished Britisher, Brian Alderson, names *The Arabian Nights*, a group of popular tales gathered over many centuries, as the enthusiasm which drew him into children's book collecting. This book inescapably raises questions about what is or is not a children's book and about the critical relationships between textual abridgement, translation, and adaptation; and it suggests myriad radii of cross-collecting circles. Considered one of the earliest classics, its influences reached out in ever-widening circles to create fresh, continuous intersections between retellers, illustrators, editors, and publishers. The plot concerns a storyteller, Scheherazade, who conceives a scheme to dispense a different tale each night—leaving the punchline blank until the next bedtime—as a device to keep her murderous royal husband stalemated, one night at a time.

Our radiating trails for internals begin with the Frenchman Antoine Galland, whose text of *Mille et Une Nuits*, crossed the Channel, was translated into English, and appeared in a hack-written chapbook version by about 1706 to become part of children's forbidden, but treasured reading. Almost all European versions were expurgations from early Eastern texts. The first selection made for an English children's book, *The Oriental Moralist* (c. 1791), connects to its publisher Elizabeth Newbery and her working relationship with her husband, and touches the hackwriter Richard Johnson, who wrote the text under a pseudonym as the Reverend Mr. Cooper. He introduced it with the observation that finding Galland's book in the library of an inn while traveling on the Continent prompted him to write a cleansed English version shaped to encourage a child's love of virtue. In 1863–65, the connection touches those great wood engravers of Victorian England, the Dalziel brothers, George (1815–1902), Edward (1817–1905), John (1822–69) and Thomas (1823–1906). They made engraving blocks for *Dalziels' Illustrated Arabian Nights Entertainments* "with upward of two hundred illustrations by eminent artists" (Carpenter, p. 140) that connect us to the art of Tenniel, Millais and others which the Dalziels copied, and to later blocks they made to illustrate Edward Lear's enlarged book of nonsense (1860).

Andrew Lang, folklorist and man of letters, intersects at the 1898 version that was the book in his series of annual fairy books (1889–1910). His scholarly interest in anthropology, folklore, and myth supported his argument that folktales are the foundations of literary mythology, not their debased relics. As a publisher's reader and reviewer, Lang worked on behalf of the writings of such as Kipling, Arthur Conan Doyle, and Walter de la Mare, and his efforts add more connections. In the 20th century, the *Nights* touches Edmund Dulac as he illustrated Laurence Housman's text for *Stories from the Arabian Nights* (1907).

"The Accession Diaries of Peter Opie" summarizes these thoughts on collecting connections within the *Nights*:

> I have seen, at last, how to do my book on 18th c. children's books. I was adding another literary reference to my file on the Arabian Nights, and noticed that I now had quotations on it by Wordsworth, Coleridge, & Southey, and realized what a splendid miniature essay could be written on the Arabian Nights. I realized how one might take as one's subject any one of a hundred 18th c. books, authors or themes . . . & then write about it, as an example of its type, listing later editions. (Avery, p. 43)

4

Those piles of ill-assorted volumes heaped together on the floor of a second-hand bookseller's have so miserable and depressing an effect, that you can almost hear the small sigh of pleasure that a book gives when you lift it out of the sorry mess and restore to it some of its true personality. Books have their own very personal feeling about their place on the shelves. They like to be close to suitable companions.

—Hugh Walpole, *Reading*

Collections Great and Small, and Their Collectors

What constitutes a great or major collection of historical children's literature? Must it aim to be representative of the work of all major writers and illustrators of a chosen period who intended their work specifically for children? Most simply defined, a collection is any unity one chooses to establish. For a Beatrix Potter collector, a unity could be all twenty-three of the first editions. For a Little Golden Book collector, unity could be the first twelve titles issued in blue cloth spines with their dust jackets. From such finite examples, "any unity" can grow to the limits of imagination. An important collection must demonstrate depth and internal balance and contain highlights of text, authors, decoration and illustration. It must not leave a great many questions to be answered. It should also be housed, or at least shelved, as a separate entity. As completed efforts, the Elisabeth Ball, A.S.W. Rosenbach, d'Alte Welch, Frederick Gardner, Ruth E. Adomeit, John Mackay Shaw, Ludwig Ries, and Irving Kerlan collections are among the greatest that describe a single personality. Institutional collections are really collections of collections.

‖ GREAT INDIVIDUAL COLLECTIONS

One author of a very important historical collection was heiress Elisabeth Ball (1897–1992) of Muncie, Indiana. Her collecting began by osmosis when, as the child of a loving, widowed and bookish father, she was able to share his collecting excursions. On these joyous learning expeditions she chose richly colored and wondrous picture books by artists who became her favorites—Arthur Rackham, Edmund Dulac and Kate Greenaway. George Ball's collecting had begun at age eighteen, and as his purse and tastes grew he developed an interest in finding juvenile books that authors had noted as greatly influencing them. Among his purchases were several from the famous Gumachian collection.

After-dinner entertainment for their guests was often a chance to sample their collection, enlivened with stories about the artists and the history of each book search. At the end of one such evening, putting away their "show and tell" her father told Elisabeth, "I think you had better consider these your books." "That," she adds, "is the way he gave them to me" (Coughlan, p. 433).

On September 14, 1975, the *Muncie Star* (Indiana) carried an interview with Charles Ryscamp, Director of the Pierpont Morgan Library of New York about the opening of the Library's exhibition, "Early Children's Books and Their Illustration." Ryscamp noted that a large number of the items were gifts of Elisabeth Ball, and praised her determination and unerring gift for detection in acquiring—in fine condition—rarities from the earliest known alphabet sheets of 1544, through to the 1827 *Whittington and His Cat*, and the early editions of *Robinson Crusoe*. The curator of the Library's children's books, Gerald Gottlieb, was quoted as saying "the breadth and variety of her collection make it quite likely the finest in the world."

Quoted too was Elisabeth Ball, who remarked that while she was "still in her right mind and able to see what should be done, she had decided that the books ought to go where they could be seen and used" (Allison, p. B4). She thought of the Morgan Library, although at first its curators were not interested. However, after two men from the Library went to Muncie and spent a week examining the books, they became *very* interested. Thus, the collection, except for the hornbooks that were given to the Free Library of Philadelphia, came to the Morgan in 1964, along with an endowment for maintenance and further acquisition.

A. S. W. Rosenbach was a scholar, writer, and bibliographer. Affectionately known as "Rosy," he possessed a family passport to the collecting of juveniles. In the 1830s, Moses Polock, Rosenbach's uncle, served as a clerk for the Philadelphia publishing firm, McCarthy and Davis. In the 1820s this firm purchased Johnson and Warner, children's publishers since the 1780s, acquiring a large number of children's books, the processing of which fell to Polock. He became enough interested to begin to buy them, as he eventually did the firm of McCarthy and Davis. In 1900 Polock gave his collection to his nephew with the addition of "some extremely valuable examples of early Americana juvenalia" (Coughlan, p. 432).

Taking up his uncle's quest convinced Rosenbach what a true miracle it is that any child's book survives the natural destructiveness of its owner. He captured such choice items as *The Rule of the New-Creature* (1682) and *Peter Piper's Practical Principles of Plain and Perfect Pronunciation* (1836). His collection's richness can be demonstrated by examining its illustrated catalog, "Early American Children's Books" (1933), which Rosenbach prepared to encourage others to collect these survivors of American childhood. His collection was transferred to the Free Library of Philadelphia.

Another important collector was d'Alte Welch (1907–70). By profession a biological scientist on the faculty of John Carroll University in Cleveland, Welch chanced upon his avocation when he was sixteen years old. At that time his father told him the story of the origin of "Little Jack Horner." Young Welch was so intrigued that he used the New York Public Library to research a paper entitled "Old Mother Goose." It was there that he met Leonore St. John Power, Head of the Children's Room, who captured his imagination with early children's books. That made him a collector. Friends, among them Marcus McCorison of the American Antiquarian Society in Worcester, Massachusetts and Ruth E. Adomeit, attested to Welch's charm and boundless delight in the slender volumes from America's past. Welch keenly felt the lack of a guide to collecting children's books—one that would reveal which books were common and which unique—and for this reason he embarked on what was to become his life's work, the compilation of the invaluable *A Bibliography of American Children's Books Printed Prior to 1821* (1963–67) to identify as completely as possible narrative books written in English, designed for children under fifteen years of age, and printed before 1821. It does not include books written by or about children, treatises on the rearing and education of children (with the exception of some etiquette books), school books, sermons, or books of advice.

Welch's important personal collection was divided between two libraries. The English imprints went to the University of California at Los Angeles, and the American ones, along with all Welch's notes, films and photocopies of American children's books went to the American Antiquarian Society.

Our next collector, Frederick Gardner of Amityville, New York, did not begin life as a book lover. A youth in post-World War I Germany, whose memories include being "absolutely hostile to books and the printed word" (Coughlan, p. 435), he was introduced to English literature by six years of service with the Royal Air Force as an English instructor to non-British enlistees. He came to the United States in 1947, and in 1948 joined three cousins in their book jobbing business in Scranton, Pennsylvania, working there until 1966. This intimate contact with books, albeit as merchandise, continued to alter his outlook. On a 1950 trip to London he visited Samuel Johnson's house and Hall's Bookshop, and, intrigued, he immersed himself in Johnson biographies and writings such as *The History of Rasselas* and *A Dictionary of the English Language*. Unwittingly, he'd become a Johnson collector and fan of 18th-century literature.

Seeking original artwork to decorate the walls of a library exhibit room in Amityville, Gardner sent letters to fifteen Caldecott medalists and other artists. A friendship with Robert Lawson's heirs enabled him, over the years, to acquire the greater part of that illustrator's work and ephemera. His complete collection, including all this art, is now at the Free Library of Philadelphia.

In the 1960s Gardner succumbed to the power of children's book collecting and assembled a collection of every "all-important milestone in children's literature, from the worst to the best." Although he had no children, the subject of childhood intrigued him and he studied books about childhood and child psychology, relating them to how "the various elements in children's literature as they evolved, were twisted and often discarded over time."

An avid reader of the books he collected, Gardner was intrigued with the dedications he found in 18th and 19th-century juveniles reflecting "adult striving and the child's reactions to it." The inscriptions he also noted—invectives heaped upon a book thief written by the book's young owner, and marginal notes in early textbooks which personify and humanize each book. As with all enthusiasts, Gardner endured nostalgia for choices not made. "If I were to start over again, I would probably start a collection of editions of Aesop and other fabulists. I believe that almost every illustrator or woodcutter before 1750 has done at least one Aesop (or La Fontaine)" (Coughlan, p. 436–37).

Ruth E. Adomeit's collecting story includes mention of her letters relating how this former Cleveland schoolteacher, secretary, and researcher at Western Reserve University succumbed to the "incurable disease" during the summer she was ten. In Cape Cod antique shops she found a thin chapbook, four inches tall, *Father Shall Never Whip Me Again*, whose title and size tickled her fancy. Her second find of the summer was a tiny wooden book, little more than an inch tall. The dealer, seeing her delight, gave it to her. She writes: "How often I wished it were a real book that size, but I knew that no one could make a book that small. How wrong I was!" (Coughlan, p. 434).

At age eleven her booktrail led to *The Little Pilgrim's Progress*, printed in

1848. The book was only three inches tall, smaller than any she had ever seen, and the urge to possess overcame her. Asking the cost, she heard the dealer utter the dread "Not for sale," to which her reply was tears. Then he smiled and said, "But I am going to give it to you. It belonged to my grandfather and I have no one to leave it to. I know you will take good care of it" (Coughlan, p. 434). His empathetic generosity sparked her dream of owning a library of miniature books.

During Adomeit's college years, her father, a well-known printer and painter, gave her her first real miniature book, three-quarters of an inch tall. *The Addresses of Lincoln*, printed and bound by Kingsport Press of Tennessee, is part of a three-volume set with *Coolidge's Autobiography*, and *Washington's Farewell Address* which, over time, she was able to complete. A fellow collector, Otto Ege of Cleveland, Ohio, showed her an English catalog offering a collection of fifteen miniature books. It was during the Depression and the price of the collection was more than a month's salary. Still she cabled for the books. From that time she began to read catalogs. As she said, "once you find that catalogs are more interesting than bestsellers, you are lost" (Coughlan, p. 435).

The childhood reflections that poetry can mirror captivated another noted collector, John Mackay Shaw (1907–72). In an article for the November 1967 *Top of the News* he wrote that like many fathers, he composed verses for his children. Discovering that this was a common practice he began seeking "a complete delineation of the poetry for or about children, of the poems that children had read, loved, and been influenced by, and of the books and periodicals in which such poems had been printed. Finding none, I decided to make a beginning of one in my spare time." He haunted old bookshops. "Beginning with the more obvious [poets]—Isaac Watts, Jane and Ann Taylor, Field, Stevenson, Riley, Rossetti, Richards, Milne and other 'poets of childhood,' I extended my search to the poets who had written much about childhood, Vaughn, Wordsworth, Tennyson, Swinburne, even Chaucer, Shakespeare, and Ogden Nash" (Shaw, p. 19–20).

He sought writers of prose whose texts contained poetry, such as George MacDonald, J. R. R. Tolkien, Lewis Carroll, Walter de la Mare, and Kenneth Grahame. Among the by-products of his quest are a number of interesting letters, including one by Arthur Rackham that may well have been Rackham's last. He discovered such a rich field in 19th-century magazines, including *St. Nicholas* and *Our Young Folks*, that he was prompted to index poems, poets, and illustrators found in juvenile periodicals. This was the forerunner to his catalog "Childhood in Poetry," which includes a key word index to 100,000 poems.

In due time, Shaw, naturally, became concerned about disposition. He began collecting in the early 1930s, and by the late 1950s his holdings numbered more than 5,000 books. On retirement he visited several educational institutions and selected Florida State University at Tallahassee "on the condition that they would take the donor with the gift" (Shaw, p. 23). Settling in, he received an honorary doctorate from that institution and began work on additions to the original five volumes of "Childhood in Poetry."

The next collecting story begins with a tale of serendipity. Ludwig Ries's serious collecting of children's books was sparked by a visit to a Toronto secondhand bookshop and a chance meeting with Judith St. John, Curator of the Osborne Collection in the Toronto Public Library. He specialized in early editions and finely printed and illustrated volumes published before 1900. In an article for the January 1967 *Top of the News* Ries described as some of his most unusual finds a French book published in Detroit in 1811 entitled *Perfectionner l'Education de la Jeunesse* by Augustin Alletz, and perhaps the only perfect copy of Elizabeth Turner's *The Daisy* (1808). His collection is rich in McLoughlins, fables, editions of *Robinson Crusoe*, alphabets, and books illustrated by George Cruikshank, Thomas Bewick, Alexander Anderson (Bewick's American imitator), and others. Ries compiled title and author (when known) card files for his more than 2,500 volumes, along with a list of publishers. For him, as for all of our collecting heroines and heroes, children's books proved a many-faceted attraction, revealing a period's fashions, lifestyle, psychology, and pedagogy in works of quality and charm. After his death, his wife Vera has continued to add to the collection.

Dr. Irving Kerlan, our next great collector, concentrated on 20th-century books, expanding his scope to include original illustrations and manuscripts, book dummies, letters, and press proofs as well as first editions. In 1949 he gave his entire collection to the University of Minnesota to insure its permanent safekeeping and availability. At that time the university library assumed the responsibility of cataloging, housing, and continually updating the collection. Kerlan promoted and contributed to the collection until his sudden death in a pedestrian traffic accident in 1963.

His collection was originally based primarily on the Newbery and Caldecott Medal books. Dr. Kerlan searched with great persistence for first editions, realizing the special need to preserve mint copies which would become worn in circulating collections. He compiled *Newbery and Caldecott Awards; A Bibliography of First Editions*, published by the University of Minnesota Press in 1949.

Understanding that original art and publisher's production materials are necessary for a full appreciation of a book, he became acquainted with hundreds of artists, authors, and editors, and solicited gifts from them. They responded with great generosity, often personalizing their work by signing both the books and original materials. Kerlan assembled 25,000 individual pieces of art for some 1,200 book titles, representing production states from rough sketches through the artist's dummy to the finished illustration used by the printer. A researcher can study the technique of an individual artist as well as follow the steps in illustrating a book. For example, Jean George's *My Side of the Mountain* is present in sequence from the corrected typescript and original ink drawings to page layout and corrected galleys.

During Kerlan's years as a physician with the United States Food and Drug Administration in Washington, D.C., he gave generously of his time and expertise to the community of children's book people. As he wrote, "Children's books are good-will ambassadors. Our books represent us in all other countries of the world; even more directly we are made known by the many books which are translated and published in other lands" (Nelson, p. 182).

These stories of great collections naturally move us to inquire about important collections now being built. "Who knows whose, what, and where they are?" Dealers, special collection librarians, and competing collectors know. But they don't go public. The dealers involved need to protect their market; special collections librarians need to protect a relationship that may someday yield them the collection; and the collectors need to protect their privacy and their books.

I stumbled upon an exception in the form of an owner-annotated copy of the 1953 (tenth) edition of Bowker's *Private Book Collectors*. It lists collectors under their specialty and under "Children's" I found Adomeit, Ball, Louise Seaman Bechtel, d'Alte Welch, and Kerlan. Bowker editor Marian Sader was firm that there are no plans to update the book. Paging through my copy I realized that its nearly fifty-year out-of-datedness lay as much in what was then a secure invitation to "come and see" as in address changes. Another exception from the more recent past is *American Book Collector*, edited by Bill Barton, which ceased publication in 1987. What I finally found as current is an annual listing of subscribers (dealers and collectors choosing inclusion plus their specialities) in the January issue of *Book Source Monthly*.

|| ONGOING PRIVATE COLLECTIONS

Then, during the 1990 meeting of IBBY, the International Board of Books for Young People, I found a Randolph Caldecott collector willing to allow publicity. Celebrities of the book, those writers and illustrators who produce its "internals," are available to their public at lectures and book signings, but their publishers protect domestic privacy. Such a one is a distinguished citizen of the children's book world—the poet, anthologist, writer, and educator, Myra Cohn Livingston. Her collection is reputed to be the greatest still in private hands.

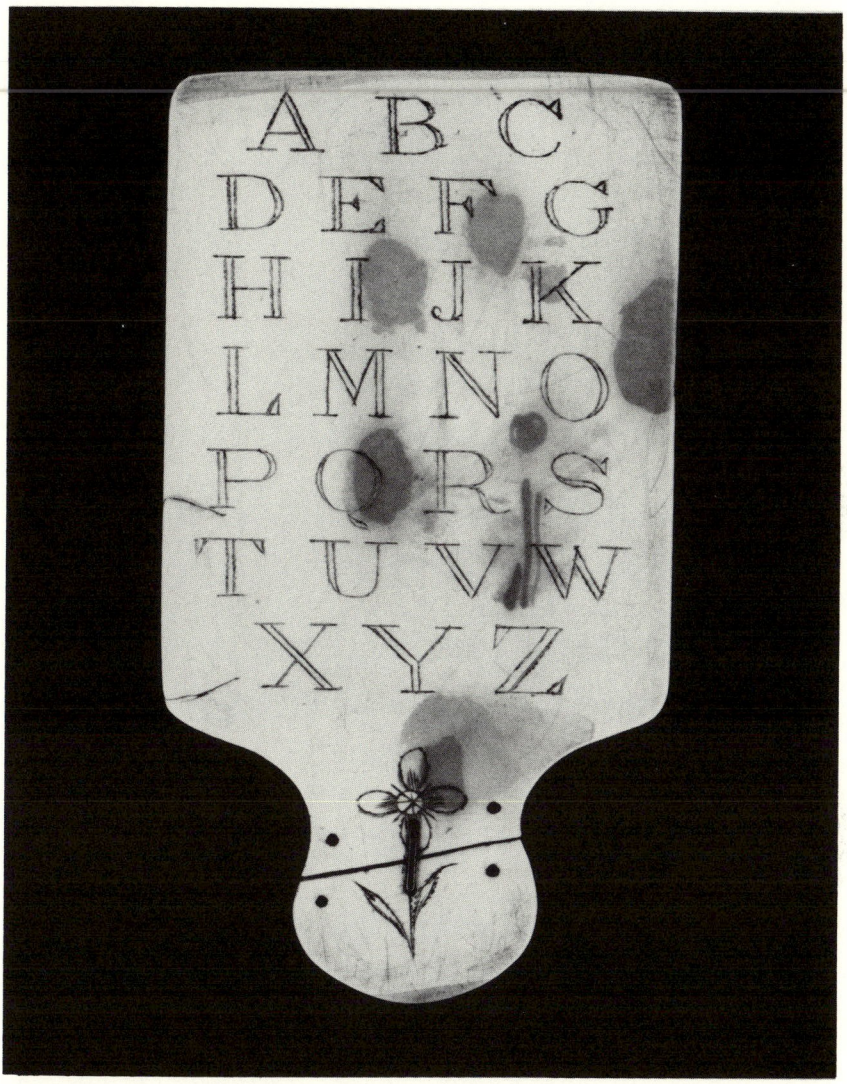

This mid-18th century ivory hornbook (2½″ by 4½″) is an unusual example. The usual format had the text printed on paper, then mounted on wood, and overlaid with horn. Leather backs often held such pictures as Charles I or St. George and the Dragon. *(Courtesy of the Rare Book and Special Collections Division, Library of Congress.)*

Left: Orbis Sensualium Pictus (1658) by Comenius, in a German edition of 1780 is a businesslike, small encyclopedia. He pioneered the concept that, in teaching, pictures must precede words as sensory pathways. *(Courtesy of the School of Library and Information Science, Catholic University of America.) Right: Death and Burial of Cock Robin* (1806 edition). This nursery rhyme commonly appeared in late 18th to mid-19th century chapbooks. Its first four verses can be found in *Tom Thumb's Song Book* (1744), London, attributed to Mary Cooper and generally recognized as the earliest known English nursery rhyme collection. *(Courtesy of the School of Library and Information Science, Catholic University of America.)*

Well, I never faw fo grand a funeral in all my life ; but the money they fquandered away, would have been better laid out in little books for children, or in meat, drink, and clothes for the poor.

This is a fine hearfe indeed, and the nodding plumes on the horfes look

look very grand ; but what end does that anfwer, otherwife than to difplay the pride of the living, or the vanity of the dead. Fie upon fuch folly, fay I, and heaven grant that thofe who want more fenfe may have it.

But all the country round came to fee the burying, and it was late before the corpfe was interred. Af-ter

D

With this image Perrault left scholarship and became, to me, a plump, bewigged, beribboned, satin-clad person. This 1892 book holds a facsimile reprint of both the nursery rhymes we know as "Mother Goose" and Perrault's fairy tale collection, originally titled *Contes de ma mere l'Oye.* *(Courtesy of the Rare Book and Special Collections Division, Library of Congress.)*

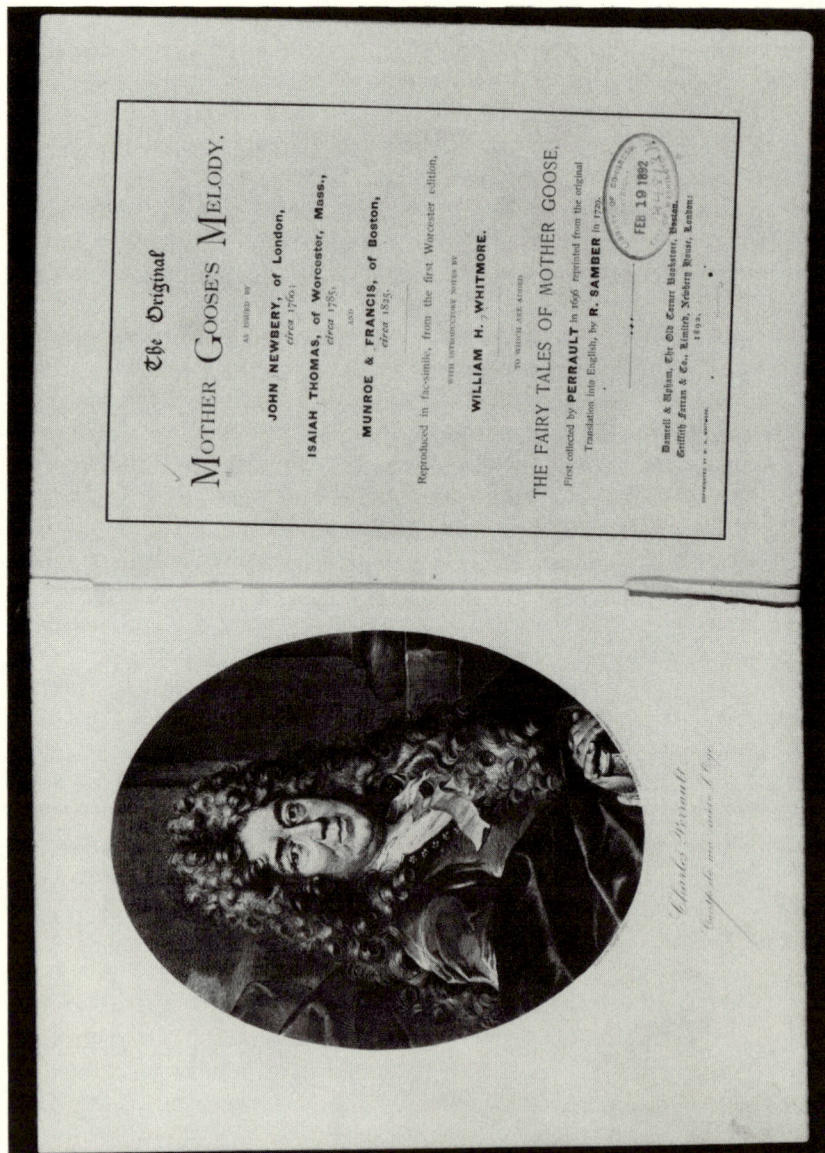

THE OWL AND THE GRASSHOPPER

An Owl was disturbed in her nap by a Grasshopper that refused to stop chirping. Unable to see enough in the daytime to catch him, she thought of a device to lure him near. "Your voice is really beautiful," she said, "I have just received from Athene a gift of nectar, and I would like to give you a taste." Flattered, the Grasshopper approached, and the Owl, sticking her head out of the doorway, snapped him up.

From the countless collectible editions of *Aesop's Fables* are two fine examples of wood engraving. To the left is Thomas Bewick's *Select Fables* (1748), and to the right is Vermont artist Elfriede Abbe's *Aesop's Fables* (1950), completely hand-produced. *(Courtesy of the School of Library and Information Science, Catholic University of America, and of Elfriede Abbe, respectively.)*

THE LION AND THE ASS.

A CONCEITED Ass had once the impertinence to bray forth some contemptuous speeches against the Lion. The suddenness of the insult at first raised some emotions of wrath in his breast; but turning his head and perceiving from whence it came, they immediately subsided; and he very sedately walked on, without deigning to honour the contemptible creature, even so much as with an angry word.

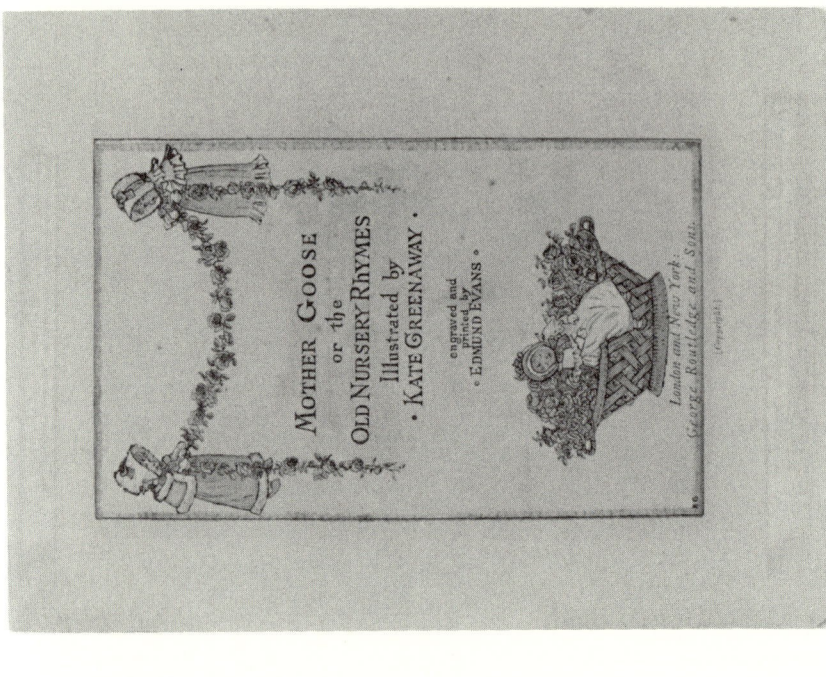

"Mother Goose" came into English translated from Perrault's first edition, which led to the 1765 *Mother Goose's Melody*, combining the rhymes with sixteen Shakespearean sonnets. My McLoughlin Brothers chromolithographic edition and this 1881 Greenaway provide sharp design contrasts. *Fiction, Folklore, Fantasy, and Poetry for Children, 1876–1985* lists some 450 "Mother Goose" titles. (*Author's collection.*)

Her collecting began at fourteen with the works of James Joyce and W.B. Yeats, and crystallized about twenty-five years ago with Randolph Caldecott (1846–86). This collection totals about 800 volumes and includes all of his important children's books as well as many of his adult works plus books about him. It exemplifies a model collection—balance and examples of all of the significant works. There are variant copies of such as titles as *Old Christmas* and *Breton Folk*, first editions of the sixteen picture books published by Routledge, and the Warne reprints of these; early miniature editions from 1950 and subsequent reprints. Books by Henry Blackburn and Edwin Waugh which Caldecott illustrated represent some of his work for adults in her collection.

An important collection of an illustrator doesn't need to have a lot of original art, but a great one does. Livingston has pen-and-ink sketches from *The Graphics*, an English periodical; a book of drawings never published for "Sketches from Buxton"; an original sketch from *Breton Folks*, and a watercolor, the original of the frontispiece from *Jackanapes* (1884) by Juliana Horatia Ewing. One item I star is a silver medal that Caldecott designed for the 1878 Anglo-Afghanistan War.

Mrs. Livingston waited twenty years to get a copy of *The Harz Mountain*, Caldecott's first book, and still has her collecting net thrown out worldwide for her immediate want list. Her goal? "A complete collection of his own work as first published, anything that reproduces a piece of his work such as a contemporary article or book, and anything that bears on his life and work. One of my treasures is a scrapbook of original advertising sketches, ephemera, and finally, sadly, the artist's obituary. Caldecott died at thirty-nine during an American sketching trip, an apparent victim of illness brought on by one of Florida's legendary, exceptionally cold winters."

In November 15, 1991 at a program of the Children's Literature Center of the Library of Congress entitled "A Conversation with Betsy Beinecke Shirley and Lloyd Cotsen," I met Betsy Beinecke Shirley, the daughter of Walter Beinecke, one of the three original donors of the Beinecke Library of Yale University in New Haven, Connecticut. From October to December of 1991 the Beinecke featured selections from Mrs. Shirley's collection in a show entitled, "Read Me a Story; Show Me a Book."

In two decades of collecting, this charming, low-keyed lady has become a recognized authority, anonymously at first as "Yankee Doodle," until 1986 when she published a signed article on the evolution of Santa Claus. Her collection, which the dealer Justin G. Schiller judged to be "virtually unequaled today in private hands," includes books, periodicals, broadsides, games and printed textiles, autograph letters, manuscripts and a large number of original drawings and paintings. Though only a small part of this has been given to Yale, the links that bind the two provide wide-ranging interactive benefits. What follows comes from her speech to the Yale Friends of the Beinecke at a reception that opened the show. She feels this is "more personal" than that in the glorious, full-color illustrated catalog available from the Beinecke.

> Collecting children's books is sheer fun—if only for the friends one makes. . . . It was in a little one-room library on the tip end of Nantucket Island that I was able for the first time in my life to exercise my very own independent judgment! And it may be so for many other children. Freedom of choice—aren't libraries wonderful? I could take out three books at a time, but before making my selection, unused to making any decision, I would spend hours skimming through a story, rejecting, selecting, changing my mind, checking out all the illustrations—then finally, proudly heading home to show my mother and dad the result of my careful consideration. By the middle of vacation I had pretty well cased the books I would want and I learned to double-shelf, in anticipation, those I would take out the following week, always hoping no one would find my secret cache.
>
> *   *   *
>
> Broadly characterized, my collection attempts to make three points. The corpus of children's literature must include the books that youngsters read and enjoyed from cover to cover no matter how critically the writer is judged. Illustration's contribution to the genre should never be undervalued. Art is integral to our genre. My third point is a hope and a wish! None of us really wants a bunch of kids lying on the floor tumbling through today's exhibit at the Beinecke—as I did once in Nantucket. But I cherish the thought that a whole flock of little people will come in to Yale's rare book library, feel warm and welcome and leave with a curiosity that makes them want to come back at a later time to see what else is hidden behind these marbled walls.

That same Library of Congress program brought me publishable access to another significant personal collection, that of the California industrialist, Lloyd E. Cotsen, a member of the new (1990) James Madison National Council of the Library of Congress and a devoted supporter of the work of the Children's Literature Center of the Library. Knowing I would meet him, I'd written and his librarian, Andrea Ummel replied:

> Mr. Cotsen began collecting historical children's books, toys and games in the 1970s. The collection has approximately 15,000 items and includes some incunabula and early modern books for children. It is particularly rich in alphabets, modern American and European picture books, moveables, and John Harris imprints. There is a small group of prints, original drawings for illustrated children's books and some manuscripts, including works written and illustrated by children.

From Cotsen's appearance with Betsy Beinecke Shirley at the Library of Congress in "A Conversation with Children's Book Collectors" comes this quote that allows us to draw something of his collecting persona:

> I'm interested in books as teachers, now with a multicultural focus—how prejudice appears in them; how what we choose tells a story of our roots—our antecedents; where we come from. I only buy illustrated books.

At the reception, I met about as continuous and devoted a children's book person as can be found, Linda Lapides of Baltimore, Maryland. Like Ball, a bookish father was among her collecting riches. Her much-traveled father, Benjamin J. Fishman, never returned without the gift of a book which he always hid somewhere in the house, thus connecting seeking, surprise, and book pleasure. Don't we wish we could say, as Lapides did, "I've saved every book I had as a child"? (Hallstead, p. 2).

A Columbia University-trained librarian, on staff at the Enoch Pratt Library in Baltimore, Lapides's serious interest had been sparked by reading Irving Kerlan's chapter, "Collecting Contemporary Books for Children," in William Targ's *Bibliophile in the Nursery*. She had already built an extensive collection of modern juvenile publications when Ludwig Ries, in Baltimore on a business trip, stopped by the Pratt Library. It was she who was asked to show him the older juvenile collection in the stacks near her office. So contagious was his enthusiasm for early books that she accepted an invitation to come see his collection while in New York for an ALA conference. The first of many visits, Lapides said, "It was like having private lessons in the history of children's books." Now, joined by her politician husband, Julian Lapides, "We suddenly felt that we really didn't have a thing that was any good ourselves" (Hallstead, p. 4). In their quest for the elusive volume they met other knowledgeable collectors, Frederick Gardner and Herbert Hosmer, who also offered inspiration and encouragement.

In November of 1991 Mrs. Lapides wrote to me:

> Let me add that although we stray occasionally, the focus of our collecting is early American children's books, especially those of a nursery nature illustrated with cuts and/or engravings. Being Baltimoreans we do have an interest in such books by local publishers. . . . All aspects of the books appeal to us—the publishers, bindings, illustrations—and, of course, the contents. . . . Within their pages is reflected the history and culture of our country and its attitude toward its youngest citizens.

As one might expect from a service-oriented book professional, Linda Lapides's interest in children's books is not one of horse trading or even long term investment, but of research, writing, and sharing her excitement about them with others and of successfully managing the scary uncertainties omnipresent in the transition from personal to institutional hands.

‖ COLLECTIONS IN TRANSITION

Collection in transition, a moment of truth, gives the next stories their plot twists—uncertainties omnipresent in any transition from personal to institutional hands—but that passage forms an integral part of a story of completed great collections. Charlotte S. Huck is a distinguished educator and coeditor of *Children's Literature in the Elementary School*, a primary text for students of children's literature in schools of education equatable with May Hill Arbuthnot's *Children and Books* for library science students. Miss Huck gave me an interview shortly after her 1988 gift of her collection to the Edgar Dale Media Center of Ohio State University College of Education where she had taught. "I've lived and collected through the time when picture books really started," she told me.

> I credit Wanda Gag's publication of *Millions of Cats* (1928) as the first American picture book and E. Boyd Smith's *Farm Book* (1901) and *Railroad Book* (1913) as the first beautifully illustrated informational books. Maud and Miska Petersham continued this movement with their five fine books, which began in 1933 with *The Story of Things We Use*. I taught in order to share my lifelong love of children's literature with my happily, seemingly countless, students. My books are not firsts. I used them for teaching and research and that is their continuing institutional purpose. They number over 4,000 of which 700 comprise a historical collection going back to 1820. The historical collection will not circulate. Since Myra Cohn Livingston is going to give you permission to publicize her collection of Caldecott's works, I'll mention that two of his original woodblocks for *John Gilpin's Ride* are among my collection's art originals. The appraisal requisite to the deed of gift valued the collection at $21,000 which should be of help to collectors wondering about a price for a less-than-first edition collection.

The next story concerns the May L. Schofield Collection of Children's Literature. Carol C. Jacobs, a collector herself, told it in response to my request for information on collections printed in the journal, *American Libraries*. In 1911, Mary Schofield was a child who played quietly with her dolls in the old Stanford University library while her student mother studied. As an adult, Schofield, unmarried and without children of her own, developed collections of books and ornaments that made her apartment a child's wonderland. Here a china Little Miss Muffet sat demurely near Long John Silver and Old Mother Hubbard. A stained-glass Alice caught sunlight which came in through old-fashioned sash windows. Searching the weighted shelves, a visitor would experience the joy of greeting old friends: *Peter Pan, Cinderella, Sinbad the Sailor, The Wizard of Oz*, and *Winnie-the-Pooh*.

Miss Schofield had been actively collecting for over forty years, assembling one of the very finest private collections, numbering over 14,000 volumes plus related reference works. Her collection is diverse—from early American chapbooks to current picture books. Some are treasured examples of very rare signed limited editions, other books have been lovingly decorated with crayons by previous owners. Her oldest volume is a first edition of Thomas Day's *Sanford and Merton* (1788). She also has a copy of the first edition of the Taylor sisters' *Rhymes for the Nursery* (1806) which contains the first printing of "Twinkle, Twinkle, Little Star." Her copy of *The Emerald City of Oz* contains a letter from Baum, the author, to the original owner of the book. The richness of the Beatrix Potter collection reveals a "favorite:" first editions, signed editions, original drawings, deluxe bindings, and endless memorabilia celebrating Beatrix Potter characters.

Florian Shasky, Stanford University Chief of Special Collections, terms the Mary L. Schofield Collection of Children's Literature one of the most significant of its kind in the western United States. Under terms of the acquisition, Stanford University Library obtained most of the books, selected drawings and prints and biographies of persons important in the field of children's literature. More than forty years of discriminating selection have been shaped into a significant resource for the study of social attitudes toward children. Jacobs reported to me that Schofield told her: "I just hope that people, students especially, will use the books once they're in the library."

Dr. Ruth M. Baldwin is the protagonist of a third transition tale. She created a library, accomplished its move to institutional hands, remained as curator, and retired. Within a year she was dead. She died on a Friday, and the following Monday word was received of a hoped-for grant of a $100,000 book purchase endowment from the Louise Seaman Bechtel Memorial Fund.

"Once upon a time" now moves to fall 1953 to begin a story of love and chance. With her husband, Thomas Baldwin, a professor of English literature at the University of Illinois and an authority on Shakespeare, Elizabeth Baldwin was visiting a London book haunt when a gentleman entered and offered the owner a packet of old chapbooks. When the bookseller refused them as being outside his interests, Mrs. Baldwin bought the lot, and shipped these and hundreds more 19th-century popular children's books home to her daughter. Although Ruth's work as a librarian never involved children's literature, those gifts decided her personal book collecting agenda.

Once begun, book-hunting became Ruth's constant and relentless avocation. In action, she was the incarnation of "practical acquisition methods," buying across the board toward her goal of having a complete popular collection. She scouted thrift stores and could be found first in line at 8 A.M. at the first garage sale she had targeted. On one of her annual buying trips to England she combed no fewer than sixty bookshops, virtually clearing entire segments of their shelves. One "map" of her collection exists in this comment: "I always sought out the kinds of books that children read rather than pristine copies of finely illustrated first editions that would remain on the shelf" (Chernofsky, p. 1906). There is a trail from Louisiana to her summer home in Michigan that can be followed from library bookplates and donor's inscriptions within her purchases.

In 1972, Southern Illinois University Press published *100 Nineteenth-Century Rhyming Alphabets in English from the Library of Ruth M. Baldwin*, and in 1981 G. K. Hall published the *Catalog of the Baldwin Library*. In 1989, the United States Department of Education awarded a grant through which the Library's card catalog will be converted and added to the OCLC and RLIN bibliographic utilities in order to make the holdings more accessible to scholars worldwide.

Reflecting on the value of the Library's content Baldwin commented:

> If the child is the father of the man and if we believe the readings of a child influence him in later life, then this library is where to find those books. Scholars in search of how children were thought of, treated, taught, and affected will find much here. The library provides a look at how death was dealt with, the role religion played and how the sexes were treated through the years. In analyzing children's picture books I found that of the more than 100 pictures of girls on teeter-totters or on horseback, none, not even the smallest one on a rocking horse, was riding astride. Even the old witches rode their brooms side-saddle. (Chernofsky, p. 1908)

In 1975, when Ruth learned that she would be eligible for retirement from Louisiana State in 1977, she began to look for an institutional home for her collection—then numbering more than 35,000 items. The arrangement would have to include her appointment as curator and an agreement that the collection would remain intact always. In 1975, when Professor Joy Anderson of the University of Florida in Gainesville visited Baton Rouge to lecture on historical children's books, she learned about and visited Baldwin's collection. A few weeks later an academic delegation from the University of Florida appeared and the deal was made. In 1977, Ruth opened the Baldwin Library on the Gainesville campus, and until her death in January 1990 it was hers, without benefit of committee. She enlarged her skills to include designing and decorating the space in which the Library was housed. Even without the books, it realized the world of 19th-century childhood. All the furnishings— shelving, catalogs, tables, and chairs—were Victorian oak and walnut originals. Figures of characters from the pages of children's books and old toys peopled the shelves. Such a special space had special rules for researchers, normal for special collections. Within it, one both reveled in and marveled at this accomplishment of an active, dedicated, focused intellect. Her collection merits the only separate entry for a library of children's books in the *Oxford Companion to Children's Literature.*

By the early 1960s, after some ten years of collecting, Ruth had discovered that she could sell duplicates. In November 1984, at the Library of Congress Symposium on Children's Book Collecting, Ruth came armed with a list of 1,500 such duplicates—which I bought. "Transportation for them? I'll bring them up to Charleston in my station wagon." And she did, packed in soft drink flats. While she never considered herself a dealer-collector, her large sales of duplicates placed her in that category. Money from the sale of duplicates was recycled for continuing purchases.

At the Washington Antiquarian Book Fair in March 1990, Jim Presgraves, proprietor of the bookstore, Bookworm and Silverfish, shocked me with word of Ruth's death. She had placed orders until the very last, typical of her intense sense of collecting purpose and pleasure.

Sam Gowan, Associate Librarian for Collections and Services at Florida has continued this story. Monies added to the Bechtel gift from the state and the Baldwin estate will support Louise Seaman Bechtel fellowship(s) for qualified children's librarians wishing to read and study in the Baldwin Library, to be administered by the Association of Library Services to Children of ALA. A draft of this fellowship program reads in part:

> It is the intention . . . to establish an important award which commemorates Louise Seaman Bechtel's work, enhances the recognition of the research resources gathered by Ruth M. Baldwin. . . . the importance of literature to childhood studies, the importance of an historical perspective in library collections for children, the significance of childhood studies as an emerging discipline, and especially the stimulation of children to read for pleasure.

‖ GREAT PUBLIC LIBRARY SPECIAL COLLECTIONS

Many kinds of libraries, including public and academic, hold "special collections" with restrictions on patron use. These contain material which, because of its physical condition (rarity, fragility, value, etc.) requires a method of handling (noncirculating, non-photocopyable, gloves needed, etc.) that differs from the contents of their general collections. The descriptions that follow are for such special collections.

The Free Library of Philadelphia has the Rosenbach trove, which includes books from 1682 through 1836; Elisabeth Ball's collection of over 150 hornbooks; a historical collection of its juvenile publications given by the American Sunday School Union; a Howard Pyle Collection; and books written, illustrated, and published by Pennsylvanians, especially Philadelphians. Much of this was built for the Library under the direction of Carolyn Wicker Field when she was Chief Children's Librarian and Bibliographer.

The Donnell Center of the New York Public Library houses the largest collection of juveniles of interest to those seeking museum-quality children's books and related reference materials in New York City. The Central Children's Room opened in 1911, making real librarian and author Anne Carroll Moore's dream of a visible and accessible collection of rare children's books at the heart of a children's room. Her collection of first editions formed the basis for their Children's Room Research Collection.

Named in honor of the founder of children's services at the Library, the Alice M. Jordan Collection of the Boston Public Library is the largest collection of national and international children's books in New England. In the catalog for their 1989 exhibition, "A Goodly Heritage: Children's Literature in New England, 1850–1950," Linda Murphy, the Jordan curator, wrote: "The Jordan Collection welcomes research and offers this exhibit as a starting point for future study of children's literature in New England."

To top off these public library stories, here is an account of the Toronto Public Library's Osborne Collection by an Osborne librarian, Judith St. John, which appeared in the September/October 1984 issue of *The Horn Book*. It will make collectors who have already appeared in this chapter seem more real.

> During the twenty-seven years that the Osborne Collection was in my care, I witnessed a succession of singular coincidences . . . The fact that the librarian of Derbyshire County in England chose the Toronto Public Library as the home of his collection of bygone children's books can, in itself, be considered miraculous.
>
> Fifty years ago, in the summer of 1934, Edgar Osborne attended the conference of the American Library Association, which was held that year in Montreal. Before returning home, he and his wife Mabel visited Toronto for the first time. They met Lillian H. Smith and were deeply impressed by the high standard of children's library service that she had developed and was directing at the Toronto Public Library. They realized that Boys' and Girls' House was a unique center for the study of children's literature, and it occurred to Mrs. Osborne that someday this library might be a suitable home for their growing private collection. After his wife's death Dr. Osborne wrote to the chief librarian offering to give his collection of about two thousand children's books as a tribute to Miss Smith and in memory of his wife—on condition that the library would promise to add to it, maintain it, house it adequately and accessibly, staff it with a children's librarian, and publish a printed catalog within a reasonable length of time. He presented the books on November 14, 1949.
>
> * * *
>
> Dr. Osborne set out to make a representative collection of successful children's books published in England, going backward in time from the days of his boyhood. He was born in 1890, and if twenty-one is accepted as the age of majority, his boyhood ended shortly after 1910, the year of King Edward VII. Miss Smith had been appointed Toronto's first children's librarian in 1912; and in celebration of this event fifty years later, the Library Board established the Lillian H. Smith Collection to be made up of the best children's books, from a literary and an artistic point of view, published in English since 1910 and exemplifying the principles set forth by Lillian Smith in *The Unreluctant Years* (ALA). Along with these collections, which now span six centuries of time, are the Canadiana Collection and the Jean Thomson Collection of Original Art, which was designated to honor the wise and beloved successor of Miss Smith, who had retired in March 1952. . . . Volume I of the catalog, *The Osborne Collection of Early Children's Books: 1566–1920*, was published by the Toronto Public Library in 1958. It was reprinted with minor corrections in 1966 and again in 1975 to coincide with the publication of Volume II.
>
> Dr. Osborne and his second wife visited Toronto in the autumn of 1965. A memorable colloquium was held in their honor, and fourteen book collectors were invited to attend. They included the late Elisabeth Ball, whose books are now in the Pierpont Morgan Library in New York and at Indiana University, the late d'Alte Welch, who was then compiling his bibliography of American

children's books printed before 1821, and the late John Shaw whose Childhood and Poetry Collection is at Tallahassee, Florida. Casually structured meetings when everyone had a chance to recount book-collecting adventures left plenty of time for conversation and for viewing our special holdings.

A significant result of the colloquium was the formation of the Friends of the Osborne and Lillian H. Smith Collections, initially suggested by the late Ludwig Ries, the New York collector. . . . By 1980 the membership had grown to over seven hundred people from eleven countries and includes the active British branch organized by Brian Alderson in 1969 . . . Members receive an annual gift of a facsimile from the Osborne Collection or a book pertaining to it. In 1975, their generous contribution made possible the publication of Volume II of the Osborne catalog which otherwise would not have been published. (p. 652–60).

|| USING SPECIAL COLLECTIONS

Now we ask "What's in all this for us? And come to the answer—the ability to know and follow successful collectors and to use the fruits of their endeavors as collecting aids. If each generation of scholars can be said to begin its work by using footnotes as shoulders upon which to climb, then institutional holdings can be said to rest upon the shoulders of those individual collectors whose treasures they now store—and share. Since items in these special collections are special, so must be the conduct of their users. Preserving books is a goal not compatible with unlimited access. Understanding this should help researchers accept policies that seem restrictive. When an entire group wants to handle a book, the wear is multiplied to a degree far beyond the bounds of good collection management. I asked Dr. Donald Farren, then Associate Director of Libraries for Special Collections of the College Park Campus of the University of Maryland to set down his advice:

Fundamentally, researchers who want to use rare children's books should, to get the most out of their research:

Do their homework before contacting a respository in person or in writing. This means knowing the literature of their field and learning as much ·as they can about the holdings of the repository from guides to library collections.

Expect to have to go through a certain number of preliminaries before they can use collections. That is, register who they are and explain to the responsible librarian what they want to work on.

Expect a certain number of restrictions and delays such as: working in a secure reading room under surveillance; using a limited number of pieces at one time; not doing their own photocopying or being able to order any photocopies of fragile pieces.

Expect the need to learn about the holdings of a repository in ways other than through a card catalog, such as using guides, inventories, and other finding aids—and even online catalogues. Despite the above, or, especially in light of the above, expect, once settled in, to enjoy using the splendid resources to be found in libraries, supported by knowledgeable and enthusiastic library staff.

The introductory material for the revised edition of Carolyn Field's *Special Collections in Children's Literature* offers these additional suggestions:

> Researchers interested in a particular collection should contact the institution concerned for specific information. They should provide, in writing, the Librarian or Curator with a statement of credentials, (letter from a sponsor helpful), the nature of their project, previous steps taken and collections investigated, date and approximate time of visit and how to be reached if date and time are not convenient. . . . Individuals should be familiar with the proper handling of rare materials. (p. lx)

Moving through the looking glass to the concerns of collection managers, Blanche Ebeling-Konig, Curator for Special Collections at the University of Maryland, offered these thoughts:

> The first gift to us is the user's expressed appreciation for the treasures put into their hands. After that, our needs are more demanding—but can offer palpable rewards to participants. If you live near a collection of special value to you, consider taking the time to discuss its needs with the curatorial staff to ask what assistance you might offer—either tax-deductible financial support or behind-the-scenes time to catalog, search dealers' catalogs or perform other related "Friends of the Collection" tasks. Rare material is usually given, not purchased, often as a memorial to a family member who died young or to the collector, often with a bequest for maintenance. But the ogre of rising costs cuts away at that more and more successfully.

Colleges and universities seldom give first consideration to spending money on juveniles, both because the majority of administrators have not made it a high priority, and donors have been generous with books and funds. The collector's motives, expressed in deeds of gift, are to keep treasured acquisitions together as a significant collection and to ensure their proper care. Some donated collections have been systematically enlarged as support for particular courses in the history of children's literature, taught either in a graduate library school or a department of English or education. We inherit the fruit of those who put their time and money where our interest lies and, therefore, it behooves us to let our giving support our hobby.

‖ PRIVATE, MUSEUM, AND HISTORICAL SOCIETY LIBRARY COLLECTIONS

Private society libraries hold a variety of wonderful juveniles. They are often small and quite specialized, with low budgets for publicity. But ones that match our interests, when found, can offer very rewarding collecting connections.

The library of the American Antiquarian Society in Worcester, Massachusetts includes d'Alte Welch's personal library of Americana, containing more than 2,800 items, representing two-thirds of the total number of titles printed in America before 1821. The latter time period has been extended to include a gift of the McLoughlin Brothers' publications.

The Pierpont Morgan Library in New York is a researcher's mecca. It holds a wealth of treasures from ancient times to the present. An introduction to the very small part of the Morgan's holdings which are children's books may be found in its publication, *Early Children's Books and Their Illustrations.* As with most institutions of this caliber, their exhibition catalogs are elegant and scholarly and their exhibitions—for example, the 1988 Beatrix Potter extravaganza—often the most exciting book show in town.

For any lover of childhood the two Gainsborough portraits, "The Blue Boy" and "The Pink Girl" are reason enough to visit The Henry E. Huntington Library and Art Gallery in San Marino, California. What a delight to find that they have important holdings of American and English children's books from the 19th century into the past. Their deserved fame makes this a good place to reiterate the caveat that you need special permission and a good reason to use materials in research libraries.

In 1803, when the Boston Athenaeum opened, children's books were part of the general collection; by 1898 that collection was large enough to merit relocation to a separate room. Strongest in Victorian and Edwardian children's books, the collection represents almost two centuries of book publishing.

The libraries of historical societies are another fertile resource for us. In Hartford, the Connecticut Historical Society holds a valuable early children's book collection that features the personal library of historian and librarian Albert Carlos Bates given in 1953, as well as the book and periodical collection of Caroline M. Hewins, first librarian of the Hartford Public Library. It is natural to find important Lincoln material in the Illinois Historical Society such as a collection of juveniles that includes Horatio Alger, Jr.'s *Abraham Lincoln: Backwoods Boy; or A Young Railsplitter Becomes President* (1883); and James Baldwin's *Story of Abraham Lincoln for Young Readers* (1896).

An important picture book collection can be found in the American Life Foundation in Watkins Glen, New York. The collection, begun in the 1930s by nursery education pioneer Ruth S. Freeman and her husband, contains early periodicals, reference books, juveniles from several periods, and publishers' catalogs, many of which are described in two publications: *Children's Picture Books Yesterday and Today* and *Children's Books: Their Illustrations and Decorative Art.*

A sharp-eyed tourist can locate juveniles used to animate historical accuracy in historic sites. In houses and schools within reconstructed villages such as Greenfield Village, the Henry Ford Museum in Dearborn, Michigan, and Old Sturbridge Village in Sturbridge, Massachusetts they can be seen beside a bed or a favorite reading chair. Orchard House in Concord, Massachusetts, the home of Louisa May Alcott, contains her works and those of family members. Alcott manuscripts, letters, and first editions are housed in the Houghton Library at Harvard.

Nook Farm, Mark Twain's home in Hartford, Connecticut holds his own books, and members of the Mark Twain Memorial Association are searching for titles he is known to have owned. About 400 juveniles are in the Franklin D. Roosevelt Library in Hyde Park, New York. Roosevelt (1882-1945) built on books that were childhood possessions or belonged to his mother or children, including a first edition of *The Last of the Huggermuggers* (1856) by Christopher Cranch, inscribed by Roosevelt: "This and its sequel I read at least a dozen times."

More institutions are now adding juveniles to their collections, convinced that they reflect historical importance beyond the reading enthusiasms of passing generations. If you learn of a home in your geographical area being established as a historical site, consider contacting them to offer assistance toward making an appropriate juvenile collection part of their planning. Support for relevant special collections is surely wisdom for us all.

‖ THE LIBRARY OF CONGRESS COLLECTIONS

Because its constituency encompasses all Americans, the Library of Congress merits a longish story. Its holdings exemplify the two kinds of special collections available to collectors in institutions both private and public. Broadly defined, these are ones with limited access within the general collection, and those in rare book rooms where, as at LC, users must place all personal belongings but note-taking paper into a locker. Talented thievery demands tightened security.

There were no children's books among the contents of the eleven hair trunks and one map case that arrived from a London dealer in 1800 to constitute the original Library of Congress. In 1815, to replace the books burned by the British during the War of 1812, Congress purchased Thomas Jefferson's private library which included five different editions of Aesop and a collection of La Fontaine's fables. These books began the juvenile collection at the Library.

The copyright law of 1870 is central to the collection because it required two copies of every copyrighted book in the United States—juvenile as well as adult—to be deposited first with the clerk of the United States District Court, and after 1871, with the Librarian of Congress. The law does not require the Library to add them all to its collections, and it has not consistently done so.

The initial deliberate effort to collect historical children's books began with the 1927 appointment of Valta Parma as the first Curator of Rare Books.

Parma saw the significance of children's books as social history and thus of their importance to a national library. In pulling together about 7,000 books the earliest American juvenile Parma found was Cotton Mather's A *Family Well Ordered, or an Essay to Render Parents and Children Happy in One Another* (1699) containing the typical Puritan admonition, "The Heavy Curse of God will fall upon those Children that make Light of their Parents." Now, the Library holds one of the most comprehensive research collections of post-18th-century American children's books.

It was a long struggle to develop the services that would enable proper use of the children's books scattered throughout the Library. These are the "story" books that can be requested from the stacks and used in the Main Reading Room, and the reference materials, most of which are kept in the offices of the Children's Book Center. In addition, their offices constantly overflow with brand-new books sent in by publishers for the use of staff in compiling their annual best books lists that are available for patron use. There is no public circulation of any of the library's materials. In 1944 a joint committee of the Association for Childhood Education International and the American Association of University Women was formed to retain a staff children's literature consultant. Money was raised to finance a survey of juvenile holdings and develop a plan for service.

In 1952 Frances Clarke Sayers, then of the New York Public Library, conducted the study and reported:

> Children's books and reading constitute an area of research in their own right and as such have just claim to the service of the Library of Congress since interest in books and reading for children and young people is the major concern of librarians, educators, sociologists, anthropologists and everyone concerned with the future. (Sayers, p. 34)

Ten years later, the Library still lacked funds, space, or staff for children's books. During that time, Dr. Irving Kerlan, as Honorary Consultant on the Acquisition of Children's Books, did much to enrich the collection. Finally on March 4, 1963, the Children's Book Section in the General Reference and Bibliography Division of the Reference Department began operations with the appointment of Virginia Haviland as its head.

The primary purpose of the "proposed Children's Book Section was to provide reference and bibliographic services to government officials, children's librarians, publishers, writers and illustrators, and the general public, but not to serve children." No one disagreed. It is a testimony to Miss Haviland's resourcefulness that she was able to capture the essence of the negative warning and turn it around to conceptualize a new vision for her office as "serving those who serve children" (Huthwaite, p. 480). In March 1978, the Children's Book Section of the Library of Congress was renamed the Children's Literature Center to more accurately reflect its special mission. Currently Dr. Sybille A. Jagusch is Chief of the Center.

‖ A HUNT FOR SPECIAL COLLECTIONS

It is of immense value to today's collectors to know where a desired book can be found. The benefits of personal, hands-on access to items of special collections quality seems twofold: one, the spine-tingling excitement of holding a book long dreamed about, and being somehow transported to the moment when it was newly published; and two, the practical knowledge best gained from hands-on learning. The first feeds our spirit; the second trains our eyes and hands.

In Chapter 10, "Printed Helpers," finding guides to material in collections are listed. These are not as current as everyone wishes. It is too costly to publish (or purchase) updates every year. Although the bulk of the great collections stay where they were put by their donors, you cannot depend upon spur-of-your-visit availability for any specific book known to be in a collection. Materials travel and also require "down time" for conservation. Permission to visit and rules about collection use should be ascertained ahead of time whenever possible. All libraries reserve the right to vary hours of opening, and academic and museum libraries are especially subject to fluid scheduling.

The great American collections are known—and known to be mainly on the East Coast. But what of lesser knowns? In the hope of finding these and adding new personalities to information already available, I cast a nationwide net for new collections. After placing notices requesting information about special institutional or personal collections in book trade and book collecting journals with no response, I asked Arthur Plotnik, then editor of *American Libraries* magazine, to request the same thing of librarians. His gracious cooperation brought twenty-two responses, a sample that seems small, unless you contrast it to several previous zeros. By far the largest number, twelve, came from academic libraries. Some who wrote described a personal collection, and others wanted to share their institutional holdings with a national audience of appreciators—you. The results of this informal survey reinforced two personal beliefs: the existence of a collecting network with research potential and the existence of an ever-growing number of juvenile collections across the country.

Pinpointed on the map, this network displays resources varied in depth, focus, and usefulness to us spread across the U.S. and Canada. If one of them is close to you, seek it out. Otherwise, again, consider them as examples to demonstrate that searching through directories of special collections to develop a personal resource network should prove a worthwhile use of your time. Somewhere in this network lies just what is wanted to satisfy your next need for "hands-on" learning: information about an illustrative process; book paper; a binding comparison to establish edition; or help from secondary research materials for tracking down imprint data from a bibliography, or locating an author or illustrator reference from an old periodical. Since we librarians classify everything, I choose a geographical order as being more illustrative of my intent. Here are their invitations.

The roster begins with the Education Resource Center of the Harriet Irving Library of the University of New Brunswick, Canada. Dr. Andrew Pope, Head Librarian, replied promptly in November 1989, describing their collection. "While it was only established about a year ago, it has grown quickly and now consists of about 5,000 books."

The assistant librarian of Williams College's Chapin Library in Williamstown, Massachusetts, Dr. Wayne S. Hammond, responded thus: "The collection is growing slowly, principally by gift. Though Williams College does not offer regular courses in children's literature, we have found that there is interest in the subject among our students which we are happy to encourage. An adjunct to our children's literature collection is our archive (approximately 300 pieces) of the books, proofs, and original art by C.B. Falls (1874–1960), the American artist and illustrator best known for his *ABC Book* (in print from Doubleday 1923–1982)." Dr. Hammond also describes himself as "someone with a personal interest in (and a very modest collection of) children's literature." Dr. Diana L. Spirt of the Palmer School of Library and Information Science (C.W. Post campus of Long Island University) at Brookville, New York wrote me about two collections: the Christine B. Gilbert Collection of Children's Literature and an American Juvenile Collection.

From the main library at the University of Albany, New York came a brochure titled "From Pilgrim's Progress to Pinocchio," the catalog of an exhibition of items from their collection held in the University Art Gallery in the fall of 1987. From Pennsylvania came a letter from Sister Mary Dennis Lynch, SHCJ, Director of Library Service at Rosemont College, Rosemont. "We have a special collection of early Catholic children's books in the English language, whose authors' major works appeared prior to 1940. We are most interested in knowing of Catholic schools which are either closed, closing, or weeding collections. So much has already been discarded. Some parish libraries may also be trying to remove this type of material from their collections—or their belltowers." Sister Mary Dennis Lynch had seen the *American Libraries* notice as a way to advertise her specialty and thus improve her chance for collection building.

Such networking was part of the response I sought. From Mary Catharine Johnsen, Special Collections Librarian at Carnegie Mellon, came word of the "Anne Lyon Haight Collection of 'T'was the Night Before Christmas' and the Frances Hooper Collection of Kate Greenaway—the collection used in Rodney Engen's bibliography of Greenaway—and fine examples of significant children's books such as F.H. Burnett's *Little Lord Fauntleroy* with an original watercolor laid in." She concluded, "I hope you will be able to visit us and also see the Elizabeth Nesbitt Room Collections at the library school of the University of Pittsburgh."

On your "someday" travel map, make a notation for Transylvania University in Lexington, Kentucky. The special collections curator, Carolyn D. Palmgren, enclosed a sheet on their Marcia L. Owen Collection. This material connects to the Kerlan Collection, described earlier in this chapter. "Dr. Irving Kerlan, a close Washington, D. C. friend of Miss Owens, was instrumental in acquiring this gift for the University. . . . Dr. Kerlan supplemented the collection himself until his death." It resembles the material in the Kerlan, being "nearly all first editions . . . Many of the volumes have original drawings and woodcuts laid in."

There was a reply from the deep South, from Anne H. Lundin, Assistant Curator of the justly famous de Grummond Collection in the McCain Library and Archives of the University of Southern Mississippi. Reading the brochure that Ms. Lundin sent, I felt a connection between Lena Y. de Grummond who founded that collection in 1966, and the late Ruth Baldwin, whose collection is described earlier in this chapter. Both were professors of library education who shared somewhat the same time period for collection building. "The Collection is especially strong in its holdings of Aesop and other fabulists, having over 170 editions including thirty pre-1750 imprints." The so-frequent appearance of Aesop's name reinforces the folk power held within each of these timeless pieces of literature children have adopted.

Moving west brings us to two of the three replies from curriculum librarians. Leslie Bjorncrantz, Curriculum Librarian of Northwestern University in Evanston, Illinois, wrote of their collection "of approximately 12,700 volumes." Professor Doris Dale of the department of curriculum and instruction at Southern Illinois University at Carbondale described a personal collection of "Spanish/English bilingual books, publications of Lollipop Power, a small press in Chapel Hill, North Carolina, and Paul Goble's books." These responses alerted me to the value of investigating schools of education as we search for hands-on experience and networking with knowledgeable fellow collectors. Laura Gowdy, Special Collections Librarian and University Archivist at Milner Library, Illinois State University in Normal, Illinois wrote: "We have a historical collection of about 3,500 titles, chiefly 19th century, but including a number of mid-20th century imprints."

A few public libraries heeded my information request. Shirley Shisler, Head of Reference at the Public Library of Des Moines, Iowa, sent me this press release which included a current listing of the authors held.

The C.E. Rohm family has announced a gift to the Public Library of Des Moines to set up the Elizabeth Anne Rohm Memorial Fund which will be used to develop an Iowa Children's Book Collection to consist of first or early editions of the children's books by Iowa authors or about Iowans. . . . The books will be a part of this library's Iowa Collection and be available to users in the reference department of the main library.

From Missouri came word of the Schmidt Storytelling Collection, coordinated by the Children's Services Round Table of the Missouri Library Association. It honors the memory of Thusnelda Schmidt, who served as the first children's consultant for the Missouri State Library. According to Connie Adams Bush, CSRT First Year Committee Member, "The Collection provides specialized resource materials and includes both professional materials and collections of good stories to tell. . . . It is currently boxed up, waiting for relocation to its permanent home . . . where it will be available for use by anyone interested in the materials."

Texas comes next with a letter from a children's librarian in Austin, Dorothy Brand Smith of Galindo Elementary School. Her special collection is a personal one. "I own a collection of over sixty books which consists of children's picture books in the language of the countries where I travel. . . . My criteria for selection is to see if I can tell what the story is by looking at the pictures. Being a children's librarian gives me a resident audience with which to share my growing hobby."

In Oregon, we "caught" another teacher of children's literature, Rosemary Allen Nagel of Eugene. One of her special collecting areas is Roman Catholic readers. "I was in Cambridge, England this summer, talking to a bookseller about the various publishers, and he said, 'Oh, yes, those are the books we keep throwing out.' He advised me to look at Oxfam and such resale shops." This response provides a network match for Sister Mary Dennis Lynch of Rosemont College.

From California came three replies—two from public libraries and one more from a university. Anne Osborn of the children's services department of Riverside City and County Public Library told me another memorial gift story, that of the Dorothy Daniels Collection which "was established in 1931 by Joseph Daniels, City Librarian, as a memorial for his daughter, Dorothy, who had died that year. The Collection began with the donation of Dorothy's historical children's books, toy books, hornbooks, chapbooks and eighteenth and nineteenth century imprints. It has been expanded through gifts and purchases from the fund established by the Daniels family and friends. . . . Daniels specified that it be a display collection. . . . But it may be used for protected display outside of the library if the stipulated lending conditions are met." From the city of Beverly Hills, Michael Cart, Director of Library and Community Services wrote, enclosing a 1988 copy of a thirty-nine page catalog, "From the Enchanted Woods: A Catalog of Special Collections." The bibliography is excellent with the form of entry modeled loosely on the style used for the *Osborne Collection of Children's Books*.

James Davis, Rare Book Librarian of the University of California at Los Angeles, replied with his card and a brochure describing the holdings of their department of special collections on which he had invitingly marked the section on children's books. From the October 1975 issue of the *Wilson Library Bulletin*, I've culled part of the story of the treasures that Davis manages. The Olive Percival Collection at UCLA was bought from Dawson's Bookstore in Los Angeles in 1946. Percival was guided by F. J. Harvey Darton's *Childrens' Books in England* in making her selections. While there had been staff discussions about its cataloging, and even a tentative start in 1948, matters of higher priority had deferred the project. The 540 books of the modest Percival Collection were tucked away in shoe boxes and locked in a closet in the then-newly established department of special collections. It seems that there were ambivalent feelings regarding the value of children's books in a research collection. Yet when the curator of rare books asked that the cataloging go forward, there was ready approval.

The year 1956 saw UCLA buy the magnificent 2,100 volume collection of Elvah Karshner of Los Angeles, thereby providing the university with its first important addition of 18th and 19th-century American books. Roughly 300 of these books qualified for inclusion in Welch's *Bibliography of American Children's Books Printed Prior to 1821*. Theodor Giesel (Dr. Seuss) also selected UCLA to receive his personal archive of books, manuscripts, and original drawings, and, like Topsy, it "just growed"—a typical story of a collection of collections.

Our journey will end where it began, in Canada. The third curriculum librarian I heard from was Josie Tong of the University of Alberta at Edmonton. Her fact sheet describes a collection of "approximately 15,000 titles . . . with emphasis on Canadian children's literature. Books from the U.S. and other countries are acquired based on 'best lists'. . . . Although the emphasis is on post-World War II material, some historical children's literature of research value is kept. The primary language is English, although French and other languages are represented."

These *American Libraries* responses tell us that, regardless of personal geography, we are surrounded by libraries with collections to be enjoyed and, someday, honored with our treasures. The collections—the very personal autobiographies that move memory to rememory—have been gathered and assembled into collections of collections, and we've been invited to come and share. We understand what's in all this for us. We properly value both role models and their books, magazines, letters, and artists' originals that serve our research goals. Now it is time to look up and find ourselves on center stage. Ours are the doings that will continue this story. We are the ones who will face opposing desires, make choices, and assess treasures all the while agreeing with Hugh Walpole that good books "like to be close to suitable companions." Our autobiography in books can then find its own transition way into the special libraries of the future.

5

A good hobby must be a gamble . . . The possible debacle is an essential element in all hobbies, and stands in bold contradistinction to the humdrum certainty that the endless belt will eventuate in a Ford . . . It may be a solitary revolt against the commonplace, or it may be the joint conspiracy of a congenial group.
—Aldo Leopold, A *Sand County Almanac*

Practical Acquisition Knowledge

The value of practical how-to knowledge about various acquisition sources varies directly with a collector's personal time, money, technical expertise, storage space, physical location, and mobility. All attempts to provide worthwhile how-to guidance illuminate the inherent anomalies between it and the application of valid particulars. Both guidebooks and Cinderella advise us: "If the shoe fits, wear it." Helping you fit yourself with a successful acquisition scheme, cobbled to fit your size, is this chapter's objective.

To determine a personal acquisition plan you must analyze and weigh each of the variables. A comfortably fitting acquisition plan depends upon proper analysis of time, money, and place components. If you elect to spend a good deal of money and little time, geographic location is not important and your plan probably specifies a dealer, and possibly a personal librarian, to care for your collection. For the person with abundant time and energy, available transportation, and little money, the recommended plan would be to "shop" the bargain spots within a wide local range. All successful plans depend upon a knowledge of the edition points of the books sought, and a solid personal database will allow your choices to be mixed, creative, and variable over time.

‖ COLLECTING SOURCES

Your range of possible sources is given in an order that puts the most money and the least time first, and goes on to decrease cost and increase time. These are an exclusive dealer; catalogs; a variety of dealers; large antiquarian book sales (sponsored by dealers); auctions (by either professional or nonprofit groups such as schools); large "used" book sales (sponsored by public libraries, colleges, or other nonprofit organizations); used book stores belonging to nonprofit organizations (such as the Lantern Bookshops run by Bryn Mawr college alumnae in various cities); fellow collectors, church bazaars; ongoing public library book sales (from donated or de-accessioned books); thrift shops run by nonprofit agencies; garage and tag sales; and attics (yours or other people's).

Beyond time and money, each of these acquisition methods has attributes or givens to be considered. Each method requires appropriate interaction with a variety of people. Among these are dealers, the army of volunteers that empower the nonprofit money-making book sales, those individuals who put on personal possession sales, and fellow collectors. The fact that you need to develop successful bargaining skills may sound almost melodramatic, but it's not. One doesn't actually need to "dress for success" on these differing stages (as did a mentor of mine), but in all of these markets, you're competing for what you prize, and personal style and conduct can help or hinder.

‖ DEALERS AS COLLECTING SOURCES

Visiting dealers in person permits a balance in investments of time and money depending upon what dealers are within your shopping range, since prices do vary with geographic location. Rent is an important cost of overhead for dealers who maintain an open shop; thus low-rent areas should mean lower book prices. In-person rather than by-mail shopping can also affect prices if one forms the habit of politely inquiring, "Is this your best price?" The increased interest in antiquarian children's books means that most out-of-print dealers will stock them. But as interest grows, easy, well-priced availability diminishes. Financially able dealers respond to the "buy signal" of increasing value with wallet-stuffed scouting expeditions for important titles in top condition. Their success depends on finite sources that range from neighboring attics and estate sales to fellow dealers. Our books are children's books—remember? Many have been loved by the first possessors into either tatters or reader-illustrated condition.

Working closely with a dealer creates a relationship similar to that with a long-term stockbroker or short-term real estate broker. Anything so highly one-on-one asks for open-agenda communication, agreement on business methods, mutual understanding, and trust. Our hobby operates through commercial transactions—buying and selling. Listening to an experienced juvenile book dealer describe this complex process will enable you to move to the other side of the looking glass to see the process of "dealing" from both sides—whole.

‖ AN AMERICAN DEALER SPEAKS

This personal communication from the distinguished McLean, Virginia dealer, Jo Ann Reisler, invites us through Alice's mirror.

"I'm sure you, the collector of children's books, have heard elaborate discussions about how to define your collection, discover its inner meaning and its relationship with the cosmos. How can you elicit the most benefit and enjoyment from the process of collecting? My answer comes from the perspective of the specialist dealer in children's books.

"To understand where you are going, it may be helpful to recognize several categories of collectors, each with their own set of goals and objectives that drive their interests and passions. I can identify at least the following broad groupings. Do you recognize yourself in one of them?

1. Occasional collector who buys for recreational purposes. He sometimes buys nice books but is usually too whimsical and unpredictable for the typical dealer. We don't know how to treat a person who isn't focused.
2. Passionate collector who spends all available moments hunting. These are great people to work with early in their collecting, but they often burn out or get everything they want and then search for the most obscure items that you can't ever stock in quantity. Frustrating involvement for all.
3. Collector who is building a complete collection. They can be great to work with because you feel that something good is being built.
4. Collector who is organized, has lists, cross-indexed and cataloged several different ways. This person should be appreciated, wondered at, and sometimes viewed with frustration because we'd like to be that organized.
5. Collector who has amassed many, many things and is just about ready to get organized. In a few weeks the books will be out of bags and off the kitchen table. Frankly, I relate to this person, since I'm sure I can do the same thing by the end of the week.
6. Collector who uses the collection in conjunction with work. These include teachers and other persons who can provide insights and different and exciting perspectives on the books we thought we knew.
7. Collector whose chief aim is recapturing a good feeling from an earlier time in his past or another time in history: "It was just exactly like that"; or, "If only I'd been born when Galileo was around; oh, the conversations we could have had." Requires a sensitive dealer.
8. Collector for whom getting something at a great discount is paramount. What can I say? I love the books and the hunt is a means to an end, not an end in itself. These people have their own kind of fun, and it's not enough for me.

"Now, how can you find your way to the elusive species *Dealer Correctus*? First, you have to go where they are typically found—shops, book fairs, and shows. The distribution of dealers is not uniform geographically and there are definite collecting advantages to living on one of the coasts near a big city. Alas, dealers do not typically make house calls unless they are lured by a significant collection. There are two primary differences between a collector and a dealer. First is the amount of the dealer's time and effort required to read, think, talk, search, and travel in order to learn his profession and accumulate his stock. The second is the fact, sad for the dealer, who must buy for less than a selling price or cease being a book dealer. He must buy with a differential sufficient to cover all expenses plus make a profit.

"During my countless hours at book fairs, I have observed the different styles collectors use in approaching a dealer. There is the sneak attack practiced by waiting until the dealer isn't looking and then rushing into the booth to look around. If asked, "Can I help you?" he snaps, "No, I'm just looking," and quickly re-buries his head in a book to avoid conversation. Dangerous, these dealers! The direct attack involves a friend who doesn't know anything about books and is waiting to be impressed by the collector's knowledge. It is begun by asking, "You don't have a copy of *Xanfrancis Trilogy* in large paper with green stamping, do you?" The desired and usual response from the dealer is, "No, what else do you collect?" The attacker, now satisfied, turns to his friend with that knowing smile and says, "I didn't think they'd heard of it. Boy, dealers don't know what they did when I started collecting." Score two points for a direct hit. Both approaches make great hobbies—for collecting experiences, but not treasured books.

"Pick your hobby. If you want to demolish dealers, we are vulnerable to such sorties, although I do happen to have a copy of Xanfrancis's work in the earlier version that was released first in a magazine in prepublication format. If your goal is to acquire great books that are enjoyable to see, handle, smell, and even, sometimes, read, then do let me talk to you. Does the booth or shop look like the way your own books are stored? If you are really organized, how can you like a dealer whose stuff is a mess? Conversely, if you find neatness an illusion, then an ultra-careful dealer will grate. Dealers focus differently—some on condition and perfection, or titles and editions, or tactile aspects of the books. Some emphasize historical importance. None is abstractly right, only concretely correct for you.

"Find a dealer the appearance of whose booth pleases you, and when she's not talking to someone, start a conversation. Tell her, broadly, what you collect. Shape your conversation so that it is directed toward letting the dealer know what you want. If she has something related, she'll tell you. We know most of what we have and we certainly know what we are looking for. If you really like *Alice* books and I love *Alice* books, then great, you're in the right place. If I sneer and say, "We don't carry books like that, we carry *raaare* books," move on. If the dealer shows knowledge and a passion for your interest, stick around and talk some more. Look at what you're shown and respond. Eventually, you will understand something about each other's focus and interests, to say nothing of personality.

"Your ultimate goal is to find a dealer who likes what you like and behaves in a way that you find pleasurable. When you have identified these people, concentrate your purchases there. You want them to contact you when they get what you're seeking. If I call you repeatedly and report wonderful books and you say, "Great, thanks, I'll be on the lookout for that book at a better price," what do you think will happen next time? We're neither brilliant nor stupid. Convince me that you're serious, then I'll quote things to you. When I'm buying, I'll buy with you in mind. I'll show you unrequested things that might appeal to you. That is what we do that is helpful and fun. You don't need to buy everything we offer. Just be reasonable. Depending on the size of your budget, concentrate on a few dealers. It will be more efficient, more fun, and your collection will have better scope than if you rely entirely upon your own expeditions to locate what you want.

"Let me convince you to view the dealer as a person with a particular eye for certain items that may appeal to you. Since the dealers will spend all of their time looking, while you will not, rely upon them to be your eyes in absentia. A dealer's stock reveals a special focus, style, and view of the world. You want to find those whose feel for a particular book or genre matches yours. This shopping arrangement gives you a chance to see things you didn't know existed but which you will probably like because we both enthuse over the same things.

"How can you tell if the dealer likes what you like? Easy, look at their books and how they are arranged. Look into their eyes when they talk to you about the books. Do you both sparkle and get a thrill about the same books and illustrators? Hunt down a dealer with a large number of books that you like. That means he really likes them too. The only real counter-example is when a dealer stumbles upon and purchases a collection of items about which he has no knowledge or fire.

"There are two broad ways to work with a dealer. This first scenario is played out when the collector finds something she's been seeking in a particular booth and says, "Oh, what the heck. I've been meaning to pick up a copy of this book and here is a nice copy at a fair price, so why not now?" In this case, the collector views the dealer as an invisible person who happens to have carried that book into his sight. In the second, the collector believes that the dealer will provide a continuing service and there is also a certain sense of "we are building the collection"—a combined effort. I recommend this approach because it enlists the dealer as part of your collection building and something in which to take pride.

"There is yet another aspect to designing the perfect collection. You must carefully choose a level of collecting rarity that is commensurate with your personality, your available time, and your wallet. It isn't much fun to be a collector who finds one item to add to the collection every year or two. The rewards are too few and far between. Conversely, there is inadequate excitement and feedback if you collect something that shows up ten times each hour. Normal people who collect each day's newspaper quickly tire of the thrill. If you can only spend an hour a month, make your search for something easy, so that you'll have success. With more time, you'll naturally gravitate to more elusive prey to keep you amused and motivated.

"Make sure that this aspect of collecting dovetails with your budget. If you can only afford to buy something that is grossly underpriced, you will be frustrated since you will see desirable items but will be barred from adding them to your collection. If you are amassing items available in a range well below your budget, then you'll lose the thrill of finding special items at a fair price. If you are collecting grains of beach sand, you'll bring home a lot, but it won't stay exciting. Balance leads to long-term happiness.

"Your choice of the payoff frequency—how often you get something to add to your collection—also depends on your personality. Some people prefer the puritanical approach: too much is wrong and has an evil feel. Some people love lots and lots. Do you remember Scrooge McDuck in the Disney comics? More was better and much more was much better.

"Investment is a topic that most new collectors discuss before the passion has grown to become sufficient justification for the money they are going to spend anyway. Traditionally, high-quality books have been a good investment. Will they continue to be? Hey. I'm a children's book dealer, not a sage. Collect what you want to have around your home. Collect relatively wisely and the books will most likely go up in value after some years have elapsed. That is the track record. If you need to get permission from someone to spend so much on wonderful books, then by all means tell them it's a great investment. It might be a lie, but they're great books and you want them.

"Quality in books is similar to quality in other investment areas. The best is the best for one of two reasons. It really is great in the long-term sense or it really is a fad. When does a fad become really great? That's too hard. Ask me another question. To the extent that long-term value is important, focus on the best copies in the best condition you can possibly afford and you will probably be happier. This is a serious distinction. Some people want to read their books. They don't want valuable books. Some people want to look at the illustrations to inspire their own artistic work. Forget the great condition, just show me that the pictures aren't damaged. Some people want to have great-looking bookshelves. Forget the paper ephemera, get me great leather bindings with lots of stamping, thick gilt on all edges and reeking with prestige and impact. Peculiar? Not at all. Among book collectors all kinds of preferences have their own validity.

"Where does this leave us in providing counsel for you, the collector? Chiefly, find books to collect that you will enjoy. Find a dealer who blends well with your needs. Find a few dealers and concentrate your purchases among them and keep them inspired to work for you. Go crazy, buy that first book, and start a collection."

‖ THE ENGLISH PERSPECTIVE

To describe this as a book dealing with children's books in the English language acknowledges two things: that our universe of collectibles began in England and that, in truth, England still sets the tone for the field. As Milton Reissman of New York's Victoria Book Shop said to me, "All forms of tradition go deeper there. It remains the book center of the world. Perhaps that is because it occupies a geographically small, island space and 'everyone' goes to all the sales." Now it seems appropriate to cross the Atlantic and hear the comments and the counsel of someone from Alice's native land.

Once a children's bookperson enters Charing Cross and Cecil Court and asks the way to Mecca, all roads lead to Peter Stockham. And most properly so. In 1989 he could be found in his own Cecil Court shop, Images. For a time he owned Images and the Staffs Bookshop in Litchfield, north of London. However, he has now sold the London shop to Marchpane, and has incorporated Images into his much larger Staffs Bookshop, still retaining his highly specialized and vast stock—illustrated & juvenile books, fine printing and books on dolls, miniatures and crafts. Stockham's special communication, a letter to me titled "The Trade in Children's Books," adds the English market to Reisler's purview and provides another important dealer's perspective on the field.

"This market is supplied by various types of booksellers mostly concerned to satisfy particular types of collectors.

1. Top-of-market dealers—a few are less in the market than they used to be (i.e., Maggs, Quaritch), who act as agents for rich collectors, or for U.S. or Japanese dealers. Their market is for famous books, plus the earlier books before, say, 1830, and richly illustrated books from later periods (i.e., Rackhams, Robinsons, etc.). They also serve collectors interested in the original artwork of named illustrators. These books tend to be expensive, rare, and of high quality. At this level, it's a bit like stamp collecting, with some idea of investment, but also a strong collecting instinct.
2. Second-string dealers, plus those described above, are satisfying a need for fine illustrated books, Rackhams, etc., in fine bindings, but of more recent vintage—say, from the 1880s onwards. These books are cheaper and more easily available, although their condition can be very varied.

3. The market for fine copies of school stories (booksellers tend to be good at boys' or girls' stories, but rarely both) and books from the thirties and forties (i.e., from the childhood of the collector), or for ordinary copies (any copy will do, not necessarily first editions) of books to read. Thus the collector can relive childhood. Curiously, the same dealers serve both markets. Books are getting scarcer, particularly those in fine condition with dust wrapper, because of World War II and time passing. Books of the thirties and forties in fine condition are probably as scarce as books of the 1860s. This also applies to other antiques for children like dinky toys.

4. The science fiction/comics market is satisfied by specialist dealers and rarely satisfied by legitimate second-hand booksellers. But do see *Book and Magazine Collector*, which has done a lot to create markets for numbers 3 and 4 above. The effect of the *Antiquarian Book Monthly Review* and *Book Collector*, as of *The Library*, etc., is towards the top end of the market, however popular the approach is.

5. The collecting market is supported by new magazines—one is *Books, Maps and Prints*, of which Volume 1, issue 8 was for November 1989; by the older ones mentioned above; by a specialist book trade; and by some dealers who specialize in a single author or group of books. However, the main support in recent years has been the publicity for the history of children's literature. The Children's Books History Society with its regular meetings and newsletter has contributed, as have author societies such as that for Elinor M. Brent-Dyer, and older societies for Lewis Carroll, George MacDonald, and others. Some of these have made efforts to publish bibliographies of their author's works.

6. A great deal of publicity resulted from the appeal for one million pounds for Bodley's Library in Oxford to buy the Opie Collection. Iona Opie had offered to give half the sum provided the other half was raised by a public appeal. It was raised and the collection is now at the Bodley being catalogued. Cataloguing is also being done at other public collections. Tessa Rose Chester is continuing work on the Renier Collection at the Museum of Childhood at Bethnal Green, London, which is currently half completed. The Wandsworth Collection of books, which includes a famous Henty collection, has been recatalogued. By clever purchasing around known authors and illustrators and gap-filling within older collections, the Manchester Polytechnic has formed an interesting collection with a good, recently published catalogue.

7. The Opie Collection has received strong publishing support. Fall 1989 saw the publication of *Children and Their Books: A Celebration of the Work of Iona and Peter Opie*, and the beautiful *Treasures of Childhood* by Iona and Robert Opie and Brian Alderson. This includes a very good introduction by Alderson which describes the collection and the Opies' methods of working and collecting. It includes abundant color photographs, dealing with half of the book collection and half of the toys and games which were not sold to the Bodley. In addition, Iona Opie and Moira Tatem have added *A Dictionary of Superstitions* to their Oxford collected works. All this publishing will, we hope, attract academic support, particularly at Oxford University. In addition we look hopefully for real research to be carried out in this country on many aspects of childhood history of which total, picture books are part. Opie-related conferences are being held, one by the Folklore Society in the fall of 1989. The Opies were, of course, great supporters of the Folklore Society. Peter was its president and much of their work borders on aspects of folklore.

‖ SELECTING YOUR DEALER OR DEALERS

According to the November 1989 issue of *AB Bookman's Weekly*, the Association of Booksellers for Children (ABC), which was formed in 1985 "to foster communication among those concerned with children's books," has a flourishing membership of 750. The periodical *Book Source Monthly* also publishes lists of children's book dealers. One way to secure the highest standards in dealership is to restrict your choices to members of the Antiquarian Book Dealers Association, a self-regulated group. Most states have an antiquarian book association which publishes lists of its members with addresses and subject specialties. Rare book and special libraries and dealers will have these, general libraries will not.

The least expensive, easiest to acquire, single resource for dealer listings is that often-commended November children's book issue of *AB Bookman's Weekly*. Not all the dealers important to your goals will be in any one year's issue, but responding to those who are will more than get you started. There are specialized journals such as Gil O'Gara's *The Yellowback Library* and Fred Woodworth's *The Mystery and Adventure Series Review* for series collectors; and Martha Rasmussen's *Martha's Kidlit Newsletter* whose title reflects Rasmussen's attempt to change the pejorative aspect of the term "kiddie lit" by meeting prejudice head-on. Beyond these institutional reference points, wise selection rests on your shopper's ability to judge performance, buttressed with whatever background information can be gained from the community of local bookpeople.

‖ DEALER RELATIONS

Establishing a money/time balance without an exclusive relationship requires friendly detective work. Get to know many dealers to discover their buying habits and what they personally collect. Most will shop the market for serious customers, and some offer special discounts for limited time periods in slack selling seasons. In Washington, D.C., that time is torrid August, when, as in Paris, all who can, flee. One summer being there got me a 30 percent discount on an already fair price for the MGM movie edition of *The Wizard of Oz*. Most dealers maintain regular weekly days away from their businesses to shop local nondealer sources. You'll find it worthwhile to learn their habits and thought processes—when they go on buying trips, when they expect a sought-after estate to become available, etc.—and record them in some form of organized dealer-listed information resource along with a list of the big dealer-sponsored shows they regularly attend. The payoff you seek is the opportunity to be among the first to see the shop's new arrivals. If you live in an area where there are several shops dealing solely or partly in children's books, shop them all on a regular basis. Persistent visiting increases your chances of finding a mis-priced item. Catching a human error can equal winning a lottery. It almost "gave" me a first of E. B. White's *Charlotte's Web* (1952) in mint dust jacket for $5 (1992 retail $350). Remember, whatever the level of your current information technology—computer or 3x5 index cards— decide on your information needs and the sequence in which data will be used before you set out to create your personal dealer file.

|| SHOPPING BY CATALOG

Purchasing from catalogs involves two steps: getting them and shopping from them. Putting your name on suitable lists can absorb considerable time. Some catalogs are for sale, with the price to be deducted from any purchase. Unless you order, most dealers will keep you on their list for only a couple of issues. They don't deem it good business to finance your catalog reference library. If you are able to indulge in some in-state travel, attending your state's usually annual antiquarian book fair is an excellent method for getting onto suitable catalog lists. Unless you amass your own you must find ways to make use of someone else's catalogs. Dealers, acquisition librarians in libraries that maintain special out-of-print and rare collections, and fellow collectors are good sources. Which of these might be receptive to letting you use their catalogs? I would bet on the acquisition librarian. Though they are also your competitors in collection building, they serve nonprofit institutions whose tradition is one of public service. Dealers do not date their catalogs, though most use a series notation similar to that of periodicals. Milton Reissman of Victoria Book Shop answered my question:

> Let's say my catalog comes when you're away for a week or so. If there is no date, you quickly pull it from the pile of mail, study it, and order at once, hoping you are "in time." If you see a past date, you hesitate making the effort to order, feeling that all the best bargains and rarities went at once, and surely what you are about to order is one of these. So, we don't date our catalogs, but savvy collectors do, at once.

Therefore, wisdom recommends immediate perusal and ordering for anything on your purchase list. Once catalogs start to come, your task is to view them as reference books. Study each to understand its specific arrangement, either alphabetical, by subject, or both. The important front matter gives precise ordering instructions. Catalogs, other than series, rarely list items priced under $15 and, as prices rise, so will the sum dealers deem adequate to cover the cost of catalog inclusion. Do remember that to remain on a catalog list you must be at least a sporadic purchaser.

|| BUYING AT AUCTION

Buying at auction can take little time if you place absentee, adequately high bids for topflight, "glowing" items. Directions for doing this can be found in the front matter of each house's catalog. Faithful attendance at local auctions increases the time factor, but lowers your costs and increases your chances of acquiring lesser yet worthwhile items at bargain to fair price. Being present allows you to bid on bargains and to observe prices explode when two bidders fight to own an item. For some expert advice in this tricky marketplace I asked the help of another valued member of my collecting network, Dr. Dale A. Sorenson, President of the Waverly Auction Galleries in Bethesda, Maryland. He counsels us thus:

> We need to define the three entities that compose an auction: the type of auction; the category of material being sold; and the cachet and clientele of a specific auction house and/or collection to be sold. The first auction specific is whether the material is cataloged or uncataloged. That a sale is cataloged tells us two things: the material is of somewhat high quality (price) and it has been researched by the auction house and found to be exactly as their catalog states. Any house worthy of your trade will stand behind its descriptions. These include the crucial condition note and any known edition points. The geographical location of the auction house gives you needed general information about its probable clientele and, therefore, its potential prices. These rise with the sophistication and disposable income level of the probable bidders. The buying of dealers is, naturally, consistently more businesslike than the impulse reactions of collectors. Bidding wars that may escalate a price beyond current market value usually occur between collectors, unless the dealers are bidding with specific clients in mind who have said, "Buy it."
>
> Glamor books do well at auction. The mundane and the esoteric do not. Collectors will pay top prices for quality material and probably don't even want the particular book in poor condition unless rarity enters in with a copy being unique (i.e., they may never see another in their lifetime of collecting). Conversely, the ordinary, the average, the common, does less and less well at auction, at least at planned, cataloged sales. Such material might do slightly better at estate or country auctions because the audience is more diverse, less sophisticated about the prices and the commonality of the items being sold. A glamor copy may sell at $100 and a read and worn one for $20. It takes the auction house exactly as long to research the poor copy as the fine one and their profit—the 10 percent buyer's fee—is proportionately less. The buyer will find that the $100 book will perhaps increase in value at the 10 percent annual rise, but at least will not need to be sold at a loss; whereas he will be lucky to get $5 for the reading copy. For the dealer, making a good buy of a "glower" for $50 that can be re-sold at $125 makes real economic sense. Re-selling is always uncertain and the profit margin is small. Over time, much of the cream of this finite quantity will go into institutional collections, making known books ever scarcer. Therefore, a good copy should, probably, enable you to get your money back, but over some uncertain period of time. Remember, too, that book condition can never improve. The internal, the essence, the content of the book to which a collector is drawn, remains the same, unless plates or pages are missing; but any change in externals, in condition, can only be downward. Like Alice, keeping care can mean only running to stay even. Monetarily, if your "at least" implies the goal of designing your collection for short-term, in-the-black liquidity, buy only the finest.

The speed of auction decisions dictates your taking full advantage of the exhibit days provided by a gallery just before the sale. Bring your own marked catalog or use one provided for patrons' convenience, and examine and make notes of anything of interest. Auction pace also emphasizes the special problems collectors of children's books have in relation to issue points. There is still a sad scarcity of truly complete juvenile bibliographies. Why? Perhaps too few collectors have been and are scholars, interested in making the commitment of time and money necessary to ascertain full bibliographic description. We really don't know. What can be said is that the field is wide open for current collectors to add to the record. Look to Chapter 10, "Printed Helpers" for guidance to available sources. According to Allen Ahearn, production of a definitive general reference needs the cooperation of dealers in supplying the broadest range of their current catalogs as the best available source of edition description.

Here is an example of the complexity and precision of issue points in a description of Wiggin's *Rebecca of Sunnybrook Farm*. The following are notes Dr. Sorenson had taken on 3x5 index cards (prior to computer input) from various general bibliographies that include some important children's titles. These were done while he was researching *Rebecca* to prepare his catalog entry:

Boston, N.Y., Houghton Mifflin, 1903, c. 1903, Publ. 1903 [showing all places the date appears to let us understand what each implies about this particular book], 8 vo., with pictorial front cover and spine; 1st issue with $\frac{1}{32}$" 'Houghton Mifflin & Co' on spine. First edition, first state, v.g. $45.

Another source gives: "With publisher's spine imprint in letters only $\frac{1}{16}$" high, signed, else an unusually clean & excel. copy, $50."

Dr. Sorenson's final admonition is:

If you are paying a few dollars for a good to fine copy of something you want, such precision may not be of import, but if you think it is a true first, which could be, say, $150 in glamor shape, and the bidding price is up to $50—you jolly well better know your issue points before you keep your hand up. The time to do this is during the auction preview days that precede each sale. Knowing the points important for you implies the homework needed to have them in mind or in hand in order to make the quick but sound decisions appropriate to the auction flow. Auction buying also re-emphasizes the value of your carefully built network of dealers and collectors because it can help you identify and thus properly evaluate other bidders in the audience.

|| IMPORTANT AUCTION SALES

What is implied by what Dr. Sorenson calls "cachet and clientele?" The January 1990 sale of Martin Bradley's collection at Sotheby's in New York brought a price of $5,000 for a mint first of *The Wind in the Willows* with a letter enclosed. (Bradley's grandfather was a partner of Andrew Carnegie who shared the latter's interest in books and success in business.) There is prestige attached to owning a "Martin Bradley" copy, but the sale was also limited to children's books, which traditionally generate higher prices than do juveniles within a general sale. The conjunction of these factors produced a national audience of avid, wealthy collectors, which resulted in prices dealers describe as outrageous. In conversation Peter Baughman, owner of the Toledo, Ohio, Antiquarian Book House, gave a "for instance" of this: "A fine first edition of the first Mickey Mouse book sold there for $5,000, yet after the sale I still made money selling the identical book for $700." Such an inflated price may be the result of a bidding duel and not representative of the overall price level for the sale.

Another facet of "cachet" is being part of the audience for a big sale. Some of these are by invitation only. A gathering of "important"—translate wealthy and prominent—people and its attendant hype creates a situation in which the very air to be shared with these jeweled and costumed creatures seems to solidify into money. In this atmosphere, the state of personal finance ceases to dampen anyone's acquisitive urge. Such events cause prices of record to soar.

‖ NONPROFIT BOOK SALES

Place—geography, distance, space—keeps appearing as a determining variable of collecting. Large annual or seasonal nonprofit book sales exist only where a population center can supply the necessary ingredients: surplus books; a literate, motivated reservoir of volunteer workers; and a potential market. City size alone can be surmounted. The small Florida town of Dora sponsors a famous, annual two-day art fair during which the public library holds a matching used book extravaganza. These sales provide us with five-star hunting grounds. If our hometown has them, jolly good, done. If it doesn't, maybe we can learn from Dora and start one ourselves.

The limitations of place can be extended by combining travel with book hunting. Being a good shopper on trips afield by car does require a driver sympathetic to quick stops or Detroit left turns in order not to miss a surprise small library or storefront. For instance, if you're researching a driving trip to explore your state or region, learn about the locations and dates of monthly, seasonal, or annual special "markets" and schedule your trips to coincide. Sponsoring organizations can include public libraries, public schools (although they tend more to new book sales and author autographings), colleges and universities and their alumni groups, and charitable organizations such as Goodwill Industries and the Salvation Army.

If you really want an insider's track, become a "friend" of your own public library or a worker for any similar group. Work at these sales—toting and sorting, advising, or being a cashier. Volunteer helpers often have fringe benefits such as the privilege of a restricted buying preview and the opportunity to strengthen their collecting network. Prices should be in the fair to "lottery find" range. Condition is the big negative. "Glowers" may be for dreamers, but dreams do come true and good copies abound. If you're an active parent, you'll at least be able to keep your children's bookshelves stocked with titles appropriate to their developing needs. Locating and attending these sales draws down your time budget. Working at them will, of course, absorb many more hours, but offers potential compensation in "first choice" privileges.

‖ NONPROFIT BOOK SHOPS

The nonprofit antiquarian book shops I've known are located in metropolitan areas, run by alumnae of what are or used to be women's colleges or organizations like the Junior League or American Association of University Women. People who have unpaid time to give in support of some cause still exist—seniors of either sex, currently nonworking mothers, or mothers of college students or alumni. During my book hunting travels, I've found small-town shops that combine books with high-quality recycled clothing and art objects with apparent success. To more than mention the huge advantages to any collector who could encourage the establishment of a similar shop in his or her own town belabors the obvious.

‖ BAZAAR SHOPPING

America's fall season in my part of the country brings varied delights—apples, cider, dazzling leaf displays, and October with a Columbus Day long weekend, Halloween, and church bazaars. For devotees, the latter takes planning time—short- and long-range—and most of the season's Saturdays. The librarian in me begins this discussion with the admonition that good groundwork helps guarantee good results. Groundwork implies gathering the information needed to organize your visits. Each church that offers us such happy hunting establishes and maintains a somewhat regular festival date. In my area, the *Washington Post* provides a weekly scoreboard in its "Weekender" section, headed helpfully, "Bazaars." This comes out on Friday, giving only one day's warning. That is why a seasonal, year-to-year schedule is needed. Even though bazaar features are pretty standard, individual festivals vary as to abundance, excellence, and enthusiasm. Versions of "Granny's Goodies," "Santa's Workshop," "The French Room," or "Book Nook" need to be seen to be believed. You can organize your bazaar notebook alphabetically by church or geographical area. You will need to enter the address with directions, transportation time, quality of books available, location of the "Book Nook" within the parish hall, and bazaar date for each year you attend. Whether you add a listing of items purchased depends upon how you organize your acquisition recordkeeping.

‖ ONGOING PUBLIC LIBRARY BOOK SALES

Dealers consider it professional treason to publicize the existence of ongoing public library book sales. Plank-walking is deemed suitable punishment. But in the flush spirit of an author telling all, full disclosure means that these must be acknowledged, with the caveat that many of the copies they sell are "ex-library" with intrusions that vary with the practices of each library. It is the unmarked, unwanted gift books that the collector hopes to find. Within your own town, or on the road, seeking out these sales requires the usual conjunction of research skills, persistence, time, and luck. In 1988, I found an unmarked fine copy of *The Jolly Jump-Ups Vacation* by Geraldyne Clyne (1942) for $1 at the Concord, Massachusetts, Public Library and saw an identical one priced at $50 at the Beltway Book Fair in Silver Spring, Maryland, in the fall of 1992. Other nonprofit institutions also hold such continuing sales to dispose of unwanted gift items. One such I've shopped is at the Lauinger Library of Washington's Georgetown University. Universities are less likely to have children's books, but if such a source is on one of your routes, making regular drop-ins possible, why not add it to your list?

‖ THRIFT STORES

Practical information for shopping thrift stores varies little from that for shopping continuing book sales at nonprofit institutions and libraries. Not all of these accept books. The one variable that is beyond short-range control is geographic access. The telephone *Yellow Pages* is the best resource for locating these stores. Listings can be found under both "Thrift Stores" and "Secondhand Stores." Equipped with name, location, and a city map, the obvious next step is to go and see the kind and quality of the donations that form their stock. My recent experience in these shops does not give them high marks as collecting sources, but someday, somewhere, there'll be the rainbow's end for you or me.

‖ ANTIQUE AND COLLECTIBLE STORES

A related but variant source is the growing number of antique and "collectible" stores that stock some form of out-of-print reading matter—magazines, comic books, illustrations from "breaker" books (ones taken apart), and books themselves. The subject matter and format differ from shop to shop, based on the interests of the owners and the availability of stock. You shop these in the same manner as the thrift shops. Locate them with listings in the *Yellow Pages* under "Antiques" or "Collectibles," get directions, and go to look. Recordkeeping for these shops will also reward your time and effort. Note owners' names and develop your best shared-enthusiasm relationships with them. You may make finds in areas where they personally collect, and passing along your luck should encourage them to return the favor.

|| GARAGE, ESTATE, AND TAG SALES, AND OBITUARY READING

One way to establish your local network is through someone who makes going to garage sales a major hobby. Most newspapers—city, suburban, or giveaway neighborhood—list them. The *Washington Post* does on Thursday and Friday, under the heading "Estate Sales." A dealer within my network, who does not keep an open shop, entertained me at a Washington Rare Book Group luncheon with an account of a recent Friday.

> My alarm goes off at 3 A.M., I go by Seven-Eleven, pick up hot coffee and go on to the first address. There are eleven people there when I arrived at four, eight of them dealers. The first or second person there distributes informal number chits. With mine, I doze in the car and watch for lights to go on in the house. It is crucial to hit the door at the moment real tickets are available otherwise you go to the back of the line. Once that real number is in hand, we all go to a nearby eatery and have breakfast like the colleagues we are. But the hunt is not friendly. Afterwards, we pass around our finds, and sometimes sell or trade before moving on where, arriving late, we must count on finding something overlooked.

Since such events are almost always one-time occurrences, there is no way to keep records on them. Prices should be low. "Glowers" may appear, and books useful for current children surely will. When you're out of your car and looking, the once-over should take little time. A warning: Don't let your budgeted amount for book collecting ooze away into other great finds when your book search leads you into other forms of temptation.

Is it too crass to expand these comments on collectibles from personal sales into a short note on "hearse-following" or obituary-reading? Specialized as is our estate interest, the general obituary is of no help, but such newspaper-scanning can alert us to the death of any known collector whose heirs may not be interested in books. If the established collection is small enough, it could be purchased *en bloc*. If it is too large for our purse, we might offer our knowledgeable assistance to the heirs as they struggle to make intelligent disposition of unwanted assets. Profitable brokering of the majority of the collection might enable us to obtain a "glower" or fill a gap.

‖ COLLECTOR NETWORKING

Trading with or buying from fellow collectors offers chances for less cash outlay, good ability to prune a collection or alter collecting direction, and a challenge to develop a vital information network either locally or by mail, anywhere and everywhere. The time factor will be great at first, but will diminish as you build your network and use it knowledgeably. Our foundation for this includes knowledge of competing collectors with whom to exchange information and, someday, possibly, books; and also bits of information such as learning when bookish folk are moving away (garage sale to come) and when (forgive us) someone's antique-bookish relative has left this world, and her unwilled book collection. Done well, your efforts will reward you with the identity of your competitors. Forewarned, plan to handle any difficult human encounters with all the gentility of which people of the book take pride. Sharpies exist, but rarely, and they are scorned. Perhaps our honor and integrity, our special form of "old-school-tie-ness," derives from the book's very, very ancient and distinguished heredity. Sharing the genealogy of the family of bookfolk gives us a special place among the literate, to which all but a few of us add continuing luster.

The article "The Accession Diaries of Peter Opie," from *Children and Their Books*, includes this English story about a book hunt in a room that the owner did not know he possessed.

> The owner had recently inherited the property and could no longer pay his gambling debts. He rang Westwood (a dealer) and asked him over. The rooms were lined with books. He would pick a book off a shelf and ask Westwood how much he would give for it. Westwood would give a price. The man would say, "Chickenfeed, not worth selling," and put it back . . . They came to a room which the owner said he did not know was there. In this room was a cupboard stuffed with grocery cartons. "How much for this?" . . . "A hundred pounds" said Westwood. "Right," he said, "clear it out." . . . Here were the unbound books, magazines and ephemera that, over the course of a hundred years, a country family of landed gentry had stuffed into a cupboard instead of throwing away. They had been hoarders, but not embellishers. Every article was in the state in which it had been issued or purchased. And, judging by the dust, it seems that nobody had looked in this cupboard for 200 years. (Avery, p. 35)

In America, such a story ranks as a fairytale, but allowing for the different English historic time scale, the knowledgable eye, hand, and keen fervor of Peter Opie makes him an inspiring teacher as we carry out our personal acquisition plans.

6

But where there is no menial to do the dirty work, no specialist at hand, and no custom debarring one from doing work oneself, what a secret joy it is to do it, and what a satisfaction when it is complete, to feel that it has been done properly by one who understands.
—Ralph Alger Bagnold, *Libyan Sands*

Collection Maintenance
and Development

As collectors of children's books we have weighed and resolved many choices—decisions for and against. The results map personal versions of the crossroads Robert Frost made memorable in his poem "The Road Not Taken." Our "taken road" displays two sequential decisions: to be a collector of some kind of "thing," and then that this "thing" will be books—antiquarian (and/or out-of-print) children's books. This chapter addresses several immediately subsequent collection crossroads: housekeeping for what you now possess; space planning for future acquisitions; and resources for collection development.

Begin by confronting the physical results of earlier decisions. Sit down with these embodiments of your past, and ask yourself and your books a few questions. Is each comfortably housed, or is it threatened by some indoor equivalent of being a street person? Should you worry that some comfort-seeking guest may want to sit on its home—that chair in the corner—and before you can intervene let the precious volume slip to the floor? Is its skin, the decorated paper cover or dust jacket, safe from jostling by its fellows or human approach other than yours? Do you believe that its skin can profit from the sun? Could one of your "glowers" thrill as you praise it to a visitor, only to rage at you as you search for it in vain? Become your collection. Change identities and reply to your own questions. Next, face the key consideration. Do you have plans for future acquisitions? Then you're ready to utilize this chapter's content.

Plain speaking can be risky, but to discuss the topics of organization, storage, access, maintenance, preservation, and recordkeeping inescapably raises the issue of personal housekeeping style. Experience has shown that collection care can differ markedly from general domestic practice. Most adults—whether believers whose credo links cleanliness, motherhood, and apple pie, or those others who see physical order as an unnecessary thief of time—have watched two maintenance systems operate under the control of one person. Therefore, whatever your general level of orderliness, as a collector you must understand the need for correct care of what you own. If this sounds obsessive or compulsive, remember that except for condition, retrieval is the *sine qua non* of possession.

If you are unclear about the physical requirements of your collection, how can you handle the "choosing" parts of the collecting process? Answer: with difficulty. Start, then, by taking stock of the physicalities of your accumulation or collection as it now exists; confront and count it, noting all formats. If you are cross-collecting from, say, Batman, *Oz*, or Beatrix Potter, you either already have planned or need to plan for comic books, tapes, records, books, and possibly even (if you really think ahead) advertising posters. So survey what you have, count what money you have to spend within a reasonable future, and then compute (allowing for price rise) what that should buy for you. This exercise will demonstrate the state of your recordkeeping while giving you current numbers for each planned acquisition and thus for storage space, including requirements for the special shelves or cases needed for fragile or outsize items. Your survey needs to be quite specific. The function of broad technical advice is to present options and illuminate any possible unfamiliar crossroads ahead.

‖ COLLECTION STORAGE

Access forms a small but decisive component of collection storage. What can't be found is only a less bearable frustration than what can't be acquired. Time and money spent—for naught. Simply stated, the "lost" volume lacks value. Successful access includes not only recordkeeping (knowing what you have bought) but also proper storage and housekeeping (knowing where you've put what you bought). The topic of security is corollary to access. Vermin, flood, sunlight, and fire as well as misuse or theft are the kinds of preventable risks that can overtake pieces or the whole of your collection.

Informing yourself and, in Hamlet's words, taking "arms against a sea of troubles" is obviously necessary.

‖ CATALOGING: BIBLIOGRAPHIC DESCRIPTION

A recordkeeping design will take into account the specifics of the items to be cataloged. Each book description should include author, illustrator, title, place and date of publication, publisher, size, and number of pages—to which you'll be adding information on price, place of acquisition, variant edition points, etc. Since the basic bibliographic data you will be recording matches that on a library catalog card or in a dealer's catalog, why not approach it in one of those forms, thereby mastering or improving mastery of your skill at reading those standard reference tools? This knowledge is also a prerequisite to using those online systems that hold the same data in a similarly structured arrangement. If your collection holds posters and ephemera, it would be wise to ask a librarian to locate those variant notation systems for you.

The appendix here includes simple guidelines for cataloging children's books. To bring out the details that make juvenile collections special, pay attention to the characteristics that distinguish them from the majority of adult books, such as the fact that they are better known by title than by author, often issued without a publication date, and are usually of illustrative importance. Once you have designed your own bibliographic citation "blank" for each format in your collection, the physical form for recording the data need suit only your inclinations and abilities. The finite space within a bound ledger eliminates the possibility of interfiling but surely satisfies our innate "book-in-handness." Computers do sometimes go blank, but they can produce printouts that eliminate note-taking for information needed on shopping expeditions. Many prefer using a file of 3x5 cards. Do try to foresee your needs as far as is comfortable, because reentering information in a new system is a painfully labor-intensive and boring task.

‖ CREATING YOUR CLASSIFICATION SYSTEM

Another useful bit of "libraryese" exists within collection development and stocktaking—classification. This helps arrange and retrieve items in your collection by subject groups. Most larger libraries, either academic, public, or school, use one of two dominant established systems for classifying library collections: the Library of Congress and Dewey Decimal classification systems. There also exist a variety of hand-tailored systems (often in words only) for highly specialized, small-to-medium-size libraries such as those of museums, churches, or historical societies. All classification schemes serve the common purpose of making materials in each subject area systematically accessible for browsing on "open" shelves where the collection user has direct access. Having the patience and persistence to acquire an intelligently conceived system provides us the satisfaction of being ·in step with other collectors and dealers. Wholeness exudes its own beneficence.

Otherwise, any retrieval system that works for you will do—chronology of acquisition, size, color of binding, etc. You, as sole collection developer, can establish a distinctive classification system that both tells you how to arrange materials already in hand and helps lay out your collecting path. To do this, set down your collecting subjects—author, illustrator, historical period, geographical area, etc.—with their subdivisions. Now there exists your own word classification system—a visible sign of your collecting strategy.

‖ PROCUREMENT OF STORAGE FURNITURE

This is a good place to suggest that you acquire catalogs from the major library supply houses, most of which sell furniture, and relevant specialized furniture manufacturers. Wherever you purchase such storage items, the only better way to comparison shop than through these catalogs is to attend a library convention, where catalogs come to life. Chapter 10, "Printed Helpers" has the names and addresses of the major firms as well as dates and locations of major library conventions where, for a nominal sum, you'll be able to procure a pass to wander the exhibit aisles. An additional benefit of browsing the convention exhibits is the ability to see exhibitors' displays for new and forthcoming children's books, as well as children's authors, illustrators, and editors on duty "live."

Prices of furniture for storage vary from garage- or estate-sale level to standard three-foot shelving of particleboard (enameled or covered with wood veneer) to the wide range of quality and price displayed in the library catalogs to custom installations. For bottom-priced, very satisfactory thirty-six-inch shelving in a variety of heights, let me recommend IKEA, the Swedish firm located on the East Coast, and Conran's, the furniture store which has a wider geographic range. Both of these firms issue catalogs. As usual, catalogs save time, while garage and bargain-store sales spend it.

A Mellon can throw up a wing on his home—or, with help from the architect I. M. Pei, the East Wing of Washington's National Gallery of Art, which houses its magnificent fine arts library. A triumvirate of Beineckes built their own multimillion-dollar library at Yale. But for·most of us, our domestic roof defines our boundaries for space available. Some of us, equipped with measuring tools and collection inventory, can produce a scale drawing of available space to take to a supplier. Most of us, however, armed with a yardstick and the useful rule of thumb that thirty-five books fill a three-foot shelf, can provide properly for our own collection. For truly fine things, special storage, such as book boxes and properly sized or perhaps glass-doored shelving, is a must. You have paid for top condition and your task (and pleasure) now is to keep it that way. The extremely spontaneous housekeeper had best confine purchases to reading copies that have already met some trauma—if not strawberry jam, then amateur illustrators!

‖ COLLECTION PROTECTION AND PRESERVATION

Startling as it may be, collection protection lies in not reading that mint copy for which you probably just paid top dollar. All the experiences that brought me to write this book cry out against such advice. What good is an unread book? Yet after this advice has been given several times, its wisdom becomes clear. Even a careful adult, savoring the spirit of the text by slowly turning page after page and holding the book open at each double page, takes away from its "as new-ness." This does not apply as firmly to illustrated books, because even the finest editions of Dulac and Rackham, with tipped-in plates protected by tissue guards, were bound to be opened to be appreciated.

The Bible warns us of thieves that steal and elements that corrupt the treasures of this world. Protection against loss or damage from deterioration, fire, water, sunlight, or theft are backbone considerations of collection maintenance. Prevention includes both preservation and insurance. Preservation quality depends on the microclimate of your storage area and the condition of the paper in your collection. Remembrance of the desert climate's role in preserving the Dead Sea Scrolls can serve as Lesson One. Paper, leather, and cloth endure best in areas of constant low humidity, roughly 70-degree temperature, and storage free of direct light. Since such an interior environment now can be a domestic norm, fine-tuning our collection storage areas is probably all we have to do. If we have no room devoted simply to housing our collection, we must make provisions to deflect direct sunlight. A draw curtain to cover bookshelves offers one practical solution.

To establish truly state-of-the-art guidance for collection storage, here are the suggestions of two professional conservators from the Sackler Gallery, Smithsonian Institution. Martha M. Smith, Paper Conservator, advises:

> Books written for children are often made of inherently self-destructive materials and are deteriorating. Restoration and rebinding are expensive and time-consuming. Proper housing and storage will keep all the parts of a book intact and help protect it from light, dust, fluctuating temperature, and humidity, thus prolonging book life. Store your books in the middle of buildings, as attics are hot and dry and basements and outside walls are damp. Air-conditioning in the summer and humidification in the winter help maintain even temperature and humidity.

Scott Husby, Book Conservator, wrote:

> Put your books in boxes made of acid-free buffered paperboard, which will absorb acidity from the book materials. Books should fit snugly in their boxes.

Fill up spaces with acid-free tissue paper or shims of acid-free paperboard. If boxes are neither available nor practical, wrap books in acid-free, buffered tissue or heavy paper or in unbleached muslin and tie them with unbleached linen tape.

Such advice may seem to be going too far, but being aware of this ultimate, museum-level protective security should at least encourage a realistic appraisal of our own current practices and preservation objectives.

‖ INSURANCE

The kind and amount of insurance protection you will need depends on the size, value, and storage conditions of your collection. Your current carrier is the one to provide technical guidance. The most economical coverage is usually linked to your homeowner's policy. Most of these policies have a limit on collectibles, so you may need to purchase a special rider to cover your books. Beyond obtaining coverage, there is some generally applicable insurance wisdom. A first consideration should be the rubric that appraisal must precede obtaining coverage. This procedure is standard for all listed items, such as art, jewelry, furs, or books. How to locate an appraiser? There is not a separate association for book appraisers, but they can, and many do, join either the American Society of Appraisers or the Appraisers Association of America. The local *Yellow Pages* may lead you to someone listed under "Appraisers"; otherwise, turn to a book dealer, most of whom will appraise. Select yours carefully for both general reputation and knowledge in your collecting area, for these credentials are what will make an appraiser's figures valid to insurance carriers and the IRS. One dealer's personal comments follow in Chapter 7.

Dealers appraise for several good reasons, including identifying potential purchasable items or collections, and building customer goodwill. The flip side of this, for us, is the immutable rule: "Never sell anything to anyone who appraises it." Or, "Lead us not into temptation." Value must be established by a qualified, dispassionate professional. Another rule to write large is the one for appraisal fees. Always establish these on an hourly basis, with at least a firm estimate of the number of hours required. This saves you from the sharpie who, if paid a percentage of the collection's value, will inflate that in order to improve a fee.

Should you suffer a major loss, your personal recordkeeping is the best means for convincing the insurance company that you actually possess, or possessed, the insured items. Log in each purchase, including price, with complete bibliographic descriptions, to document your ownership of each item listed. Then you will be able to establish the precise identity (by edition points) of each item in order to establish current market value and be fairly reimbursed in event of loss. Photography offers another normally available means of documenting ownership. Take pictures of the bibliographic information on each spine and/or the title page. Ephemera may require more difficult research, but proper documentation will multiply the fabled "time well spent" should the need arise. You have no need to establish ownership by insulting your bookmanship with obvious markings. However, putting a *light* pencil notation inside the front cover of each book with price, place of purchase, and classification will save the time of pulling out the information from another record. If you don't object to an extra step, noting this same data on a bookmark-shaped piece of acid-free paper will allow you to access the data without handling the book. Dealer's do this to limit book handling at fairs. Do not put or leave oddments in your books. Over time, newsprint or other highly acetic wood pulp paper will damage any paper it touches.

‖ SOURCEBOOKS FOR GUIDANCE IN COLLECTION DEVELOPMENT

After all this organizing and stocktaking, you should truly know the whereabouts of the collecting you. Now, what next? Where do you want to go from here? These queries direct us back to the three prime collecting ingredients: money, time, and place. How much of the first two do you want to put into your hobby, and what collecting constraints does place exert? In truth, a balanced budget of time and money describes reality for most people. Next, add your broadest discernible opportunities of internal space and location. With these basics settled, it's "fun choice" time. Do you want to complete a "run" of what's been started—author, illustrator, publisher, historical or geographic period, etc.? Or do you want to begin investigating possible connective fields?

The success rate in any new direction can be improved by seeking out and using additional supporting scholarship. To obtain assistance go to your public library, grateful for access to very expensive sources such as the $495 *Fiction, Folklore, Fantasy and Poetry for Children, 1876–1985*. Beverly Lamar is managing editor for this two-volume, 2,563-page set that is a bibliography arranged by author, title, illustrator, and awards. Entries include: author/editor(s); primary author dates; pseudonyms; illustrators; primary illustrator dates; variant forms of author's name; title; subtitle; series; pagination, size; publisher and publication date; any other edition information; Library of Congress (LC) card number and International Standard Book Number (ISBN)—in short, most of the points needed for identification. It has no prices, however.

Do begin your use of any new reference source with a thorough study of the introductory front matter designed to answer "how to use it" queries. If you're stumped, don't hesitate to turn to the reference librarian, whose professional pleasure is to help you use the collection. All reference books should give full directions for their use, but not all do—at least to the uninitiated. Full information about the wide range of journals, bibliographies, and other tools that will help you shape your collection can be found in Chapter 10, "Printed Helpers." Read, learn, mark, and inwardly digest as you plot collecting direction.

Your own collection of dealers' catalogs is probably still the best print source for out-of-print prices, but you'll also want to consult *American Book Prices Current*. This quotes auction records and the most recent edition of *Mandeville's Used Book Price Guide*, which publishes prices from "Used, Scarce, and Rare Books from Hundreds of U.S. and Canadian Used Book Dealers' Catalogs." The introduction identifies the dealers' catalogs quoted as sources. Both of these sources have proportionately few children's listings. One dealer who went to *Mandeville* to solve a pricing quandary found the title he sought, but the recorded price came from his own catalog! You should be able to find the standard out-of-print price guides in at least the central library in small towns and many sizable libraries in larger places. The first price guide for children's books, *Price List for Children's and Illustrated Books for the Years 1880–1940*, prepared by E. Lee Baumgarten, appeared in 1990 and was revised in 1991. These are paper-covered publications that you will want to buy as important desk references, especially so since their format will make them low-priority purchases for budget-crunched public libraries. Remember, too, that these quote prices asked by dealers, not prices we can be sure any buyer actually ever paid. Auction prices, however low or high, were paid. Computer activists should check libraries for details on the new online out-of-print database, "BookQuest/SerialsQuest," for dealers and collectors. Almost all libraries have *Children's Books in Print*, which prices in-print items with author, title, illustrator, and subject access.

‖ BRIEF NOTES ON AVAILABILITY

For all of us medium-budget people, there still exists a wide range of antiquarian children's materials worthy of our attentive effort. Even a less than leisurely "walk" through the "Classified Books for Sale" pages of the annual November children's book issue of *AB Bookman's Weekly* can reassure us of the wealth of medium-price-range ($15–$25) books awaiting acquisition by a knowledgeably focused collector. *AB Bookman's Weekly* publishes a column of definitions called "Describing Condition" that you might profitably photocopy and post somewhere in your acquisition recordkeeping material. Such information should be in your head, but even more it should be at hand as you study dealers' catalogs. Collecting wisdom recommends that you structure your purchases around fine copies of the more easily obtainable titles, reserving bigger money for the rarities also in fine or as-new condition. These "glowers" make good items to put on your Christmas or birthday want lists, too.

If bought at an appropriate price, any book worthy of the knowledgeable collector will appreciate in value in the short term. Ten percent a year is the current conventional wisdom. All that the best informed can honestly tell you about the long term is that many things of seeming, gilt-edged, forever, literary merit are subject to fashion. However, my hunch is that this is true more of the adult than the juvenile market. The most expensive collectible children's books are illustrated, and time seems to stand still longer for these affective art objects than it does, say, for the novels of John Galsworthy. If you adopt such a plan for collection development, and your time and temperament allow for searching low-budget outlets, allot some money for buying reading copies if they are truly cheap. Your collection may assume a rounded form earlier this way, allowing you the pleasures both of wholeness and familiarity with more of your selected works. But beyond small money— no.

There was a reading copy first edition of the 1911 Dulac-illustrated *Stories of Hans Christian Andersen* priced at $82 at a 1990 book fair. A good to fine copy is in the $200-to-$300 range. I asked dealer friends, "Should I buy it?" The cry of condition, condition, condition gave the answer: "Not unless you are desperate to have the color plates." I will, however, forever mourn a $5, really raggedy Rackham *Mother Goose*, held tucked under a table at the 1989 Vermont Antiquarian Book Fair, which I lost because I delayed too long in returning for it.

In no way, repeat no way, will I consider countenancing being a breaker of books. If your tattered copy purchase is already in pieces, with an incomplete text, and the plates are salable as such, so be it. Put them on acid-free cardboard covered with Pliofilm and sell them in order to pick up cash to buy the better copy you have just found. But do not break up a book for the sake of making money if you want to call yourself a true collector.

‖ THE COLLECTING NETWORK AS A DEVELOPMENT RESOURCE

How best to interact with other collectors in the interest of collection development again depends on the primary variables of price, time, and place and other specifics discussed in Chapter 5. Now it is time to fine-tune established relationships and consider the specifics of your psyche's extrovert-introvert ratio. Other general book collectors are potential friends. Collectors in precisely your current collecting area are identified competitors, which honesty must translate as "enemy." Battle briefings stress knowing our opponents' strengths, strategies, and whereabouts. The browsing extrovert glides knowingly from some feature of book-in-hand into collegial conversation. We do it all the time. This can take us where we will. Introvert strategies for creating collecting connections may be to look up at the right time or, for those who are shy, to compile desired intelligence by keeping eyes and ears open.

The pioneering efforts of Billie M. Levy have produced a giant jump in the opportunities for networking. A Connecticut librarian turned serious children's book collector and advocate, she has organized the first American children's book collectors club, the American Book Collectors of Children's Literature in West Hartford, Connecticut. Beginning in 1986 with just eight members, that group has grown to thirty-five, with other chapters at the University of Southern Mississippi, where the famous de Grummond Collection is located, and in Northern California. Another is projected for Massachusetts, to be sponsored by members of the American Antiquarian Society. To become the organizer of a chapter would be time-intensive to begin, but network-intensive once in place.

Levy gave her own collection of 5,000 illustrated volumes to the Northeastern Children's Literature Collections housed in the Special Collections Department of the Homer Babbidge Library at the University of Connecticut at Storrs. That collection is burgeoning, with two 1991 gifts being the personal collections of artists Barry Moser and Natalie Babbitt. In a phone interview, Levy expressed her conviction that such artists are now coming to realize how important their archives are to the history of children's literature. "Yes, I can understand why artists sell originals. They have to make a living. But the true value of preliminary drawings, dummies, and the like lies in their ability to demonstrate the development of an idea. Therefore they should be kept available to scholars."

How one woman became a dealer is the story that concludes this chapter. The distinguished Gaithersburg, Maryland dealer Doris Frohnsdorff shares her experience in this anecdote that adds an almost anthropomorphic children's literature voice to a discussion of collection maintenance and development. In 1992, Doris celebrated twenty-five years of dealership, and before that she was—naturally—a collector of illustrated books, such as those by Beatrix Potter and Ernest Shepard.

> Part of the process that moved me from collecting to dealing occurred thus. If I found another "good" copy of a title I'd only recently acquired, the urge to rescue it from an unappreciative purchaser or the molesting hand of the next browser became overwhelming. One place I haunted then was the Long Beach, California, shop, Acres of Books, a place that had a large volume of modestly priced books. It was regularly visited by mothers and children in search of fresh

reading to share. I began finding second copies—ones I didn't want to own, but clearly in need of rescuing from the harm that might come in the next moment. The unknowing mishandling of a subsequent browser might crack its spine or tear its dust jacket, thus negating its years of patient waiting for someone to recognize and properly value its pristine survival. The urge to honor this by trying to find a good home for it gradually pushed me into dealership. Once this threshold was crossed, there was no uncertainty in my mind as to the correctness of my rescuing it then, rather than worrying what might happen before I could reconsider and return for it. Yes, of course, children's books are primarily for children, but those that survive their first ownership in fine condition are artifacts too special to be subjected to the moods of another juvenile first owner. And it is again equally "of course" that those beyond "mint" children's books do produce an element of sadness in those of us who are lucky enough to be able to buy them at fair or better prices because, clearly, that particular copy has not really been "read" and loved. Crayons and children go together, but crayons, non-coloring books, and children do not. Willful destruction does not signify use, but flagrant misuse—of anything.

7

The boy stares at the flat circle.
Big hand, little hand, says his mother.
Tick, tick. Like this. You see? Around and
around it measures . . .
He knows Now is a minute with fifty-nine
brothers . . .
Now he will live by ticks.
Out of the drift, the frightening flow.
Sheltered, enclosed, caged.
                              —Vesle Fenstermaker,
             "One Moment," from *Transparencies*

Turnover: Rotating and Disposing of Your Collection

In any of life's enterprises, knowledge of "where we go from here" is dangerous to ignore. But in a guide to doing, should we discuss undoing? Is there value in looking ahead to the end of an affair before its pleasures have been exhausted? All experienced lovers recognize "Yes" as the correct answer. For book lovers, the route to joy has several way stations. Collection development demands both continuous inquiry into any doubts you might have about the identity of the next purchase and continuous assessment of the overall goal. Collection management sees further afield and assumes collection destination. It has several components: the continuing worth of the project; the amount of space needed to house it; the length of time left in which to change direction before goals are reached; and a detailed plan for the potential temporary or decisive end of acquisition. It holds traps and temptations that imagination recognizes as war between our good and bad guiding angels.

Questions about continuing a project signal the need to discover and master the processes inherent in turnover. Foreseeable shortfalls in budget or storage space create questions. The moment change bells sound, the issue of valuation arises anew. If there is no alarm, you probably are wisest to keep what you now own, and valuation for present holdings in your collection becomes a moot point. Conventional wisdom advises that prices will continue to rise, but the 1991–92 recession has shown that when the economy falters, steady and increasing value will be chiefly limited to the impeccable collectibles. If you are a collector who personally and methodically keeps abreast of market prices, that knowledge should be sufficient to guide your weeding. If not, you need to price what you plan to dispose of. If this data is available in published price guides, dealers' catalogs, or shelves, you can gather it. If not, professional appraisal is indicated. Where should you turn for a satisfactory appraisal?

‖ APPRAISAL

If you've used an appraiser to keep your homeowner's insurance policy up-to-date with special items such as your book collection, as recommended in Chapter 6, you simply need to go back and obtain an update. Otherwise, a dealer is your next port of call. Allen Ahearn of Bethesda, Maryland's bookshop, Quill and Brush, set down this advice distilled from a quarter-century of experience:

> A seasoned seller's first reaction to this topic is that most appraisal requests are ploys by the item's owner to obtain for free a current value for something they want to sell. Remember that as a dealer I'm a business person and, therefore, my time is a service for which money changes hands. Furthermore, because of the firm rule—for your protection and scrupulously followed by scrupulous dealers—against an appraiser buying what he or she has appraised, such a piece of nonbusiness has deprived them of both remuneration and the ethical right to buy the item under discussion. If your collection has been purchased over time from just a few dealers, each will appraise books they have sold for what today is a nominal amount—$25 to $50. Otherwise, the best and cheapest way to get your collection accurately valued is to give the dealer your inventory, making sure that condition notes take into account any recent, unfortunate, accidental changes. His clock, then, need only be running to go over your list and update price. Without an inventory—heaven forbid—an appraiser must make a "house call," which necessitates at least two hours at a going rate of around $100 per hour for someone whose credentials—and thus signature—are adequate to meet potential Internal Revenue scrutiny.

‖ UPGRADING AND PRICE

There are two facets to the concept of a "better" collection: better design and better items that embody design. Upgrading concerns the latter. This quotation from A. Edward Newton's *The Amenities of Book Collecting and Kindred Affections* puts the process into literary language. Newton is describing Harry Elkins Widener, killed at the age of twenty-seven with the sinking of the

Titanic, whose brief life and splendid collection were memorialized by his mother in her gift of the Widener Library to Harvard University.

> Indeed, in all his books, the utmost care was taken to secure the copy which would have the greatest human interest: an ordinary presentation copy of the first issue of the first edition would serve his purpose only if he were sure that the dedication copy was unobtainable. His Boswell's *Life of Johnson* was the dedication copy to Sir Joshua Reynolds, with an inscription in the author's hand. (p. 347)

Successful attention to turnover keeps shelves in order, books off the floor, and the bank balance in black, not red ink. Price knowledge surely qualifies as a primary component of the business part of collecting. Successful collection upgrading depends upon continuous, accurate collection valuation. Unless you "buy down" there is no need to "trade up." But most collectors, at least occasionally, have such a need, perhaps because a fine copy cannot be found, rather than one being unaffordable. For reading copies in your collection, except for very scarce items, the value probably is too low for individual pricing. Five dollars a volume is a generally accepted tax-form figure for hardcover donations. For very good or better copies, establishing price ensures fair return to you in turnover. Upgrading always makes sense— unless you've changed direction.

‖ SPATIAL LIMITS AS SIGNALS

To realize that your collection storage has space limitations that have now just been reached signals a problem perhaps more expensive and complex than a financial crunch. If some rearrangement or procurement of new shelving or other storage units will provide escape, you are safe. There, then, is no present need to move to a new house, give up some of your treasure, or brainwash a spouse. To solve this shortage, consult a librarian in your network or study your collection of library furniture catalogs. In collecting books there is a limiting factor not present for devotees of lighter treasures—weight. Your room or rooms may hold the needed new book storage, but will the floor joists support the added weight? If not, then either your present dwelling must go, be added to, or supplemented with rented space, or some books must go.

‖ THE DECISION TO QUIT

Will you tire of book collecting? Just plain run out of ideas and want to exchange its excitement and pleasure for some new fling at *Wind in the Willows* Toadishness? Or will other more ordinary circumstances set you to considering disposing of your collection? Ellen Wells, chief of the Special Collections Branch of the Smithsonian Institution Libraries, author, and collector, answers: "It's a combination of running out of room, gathering everything I can afford to buy and just feeling that it's finished. Sometimes that can take years." Her long fascination with horses led to a collection that related to *Black Beauty*—220 editions of the book, including translations, shortened versions, pop-ups, and recordings. This led to the writing, with Anne Grimshaw, of a 1989 annotated version of *Black Beauty*. "With that project behind me, I donated that collection to the University of Minnesota." She adds, firmly: "I know how it feels to acquire a treasured collection. It's thrilling. And to give it up is every bit as thrilling."

‖ TIME TO STOP—BY GIFT?

To experience such a clear "out" signal as did Wells is rare, but whatever the presenting symptom, decision-making divides quickly into two main choices: gift or sale. These subdivide into gift to a person or an institution, gift or sale en bloc or in part, and sale either private, through a dealer, or at auction. If your choice is gift, you need to ask, "Who wants it?" The answer requires a definition of your purpose in collecting. This will probably indicate at least a suitable class of recipients. For those collectors with children, the impetus to bequeath children's books to one's own or other beloved children may seem overpowering. But again, "Who wants it—for what purpose?" That answer, of course, is to-the-bone personal. It is clear that rare, out-of-print, or antiquarian children's books belong appropriately only to adult children whose interest in them matches that of the collector. That does not describe just any adult child. What has been raised is the sticky, but necessary, wicket of proper care, which in turn breaks down into space, atmospheric correctness, preservation, and conservation. This, in turn, necessitates money. Which, in its turn, brings us back again to desire. Who really wants it—enough?

Friends, relatives, and counselors of all psychological stripes are credentialed advisers if your disposition choice is a personal gift. I would support a discussion of institutional giving, even though that also involves highly personal preferences. Without permission from heart and spirit, there can be no gift. Beyond these, the problem is to match your collection's content, format, and condition to the purpose and the "care" resources of institutions being considered as recipients. Only a special collection facility can provide suitably secure lodging and accessibility for a collection in better than "good" condition. If the artifact—the physical book—is to be preserved, even a "laboratory" (noncirculating) designation in a facility such as a graduate library school or a children's literature collection in a school of education won't do. The purpose of these institutions necessitates handling that will sooner, or not too much later, condemn the physical object to discard or continuous, expensive repair. Many of these libraries have special collections, but that designation has to be specified if the collection you are offering requires it.

The allure of making a gift hides a trap for the unwary donor. Almost anyone will take anything that's free, so it behooves the giver to request and carefully read the policy for retention of accepted gifts for any institution under consideration. Perhaps only an E. K. Lilly, the wealthy businessman who gave the library that bears his name to the University of Indiana, could write a deed of gift that left no loopholes for later de-accessioning, but the wise donor seeks professional help in writing his or her deed of gift. The institution being considered may possess life eternal, but the humans who administer it have a shorter worldly tenure. Currently the famous Ruth Baldwin Collection at the University of Florida is experiencing just such a shift in administrative commitment. It takes both library and field research to evaluate prospective recipients satisfactorily, and that takes time and ingenuity. Anonymous visits to possible special collection beneficiaries and perusal of professional journals such as *American Libraries, AB Bookman's Weekly, Publishers Weekly, Yellowback Library*, Martha Rasmussen's *Kid Lit*, etc., are ways to gather accurate, current information. A regular reader of the daily newspaper cannot help but know that most educational, nonprofit, and public institutions are short of budgetary satisfaction. Our treasured volumes are especially demanding of library resources that are scarce almost everywhere. The term "special collection" infers adequately trained personnel to administer the security precautions that, sadly, grow more necessary each day, as well as to catalog and conserve each volume in the collection. The demand for loose plates to be sold for art prints and their ballooning prices join to produce an epidemic of library vandalism, as the Library of Congress is now unhappily discovering. As these forces grow, there will be increasing pressure upon dealers to break up illustrated books, which will in turn increase both the value of fine, unbroken copies and the threat to library collections.

Logic, it would seem, can be invoked to support the value of keeping your collection together as a unit. Your original collecting goal was to design a unitary whole and secure each projected piece of it. This is not an absolute directive, of course. Sensible, scholarly deviation from it relates to both size and purpose. If your collection contains several units, connected or related to each other, but clearly discrete, separating them does not present a Solomon-like challenge. A collection of Maurice Sendak's books, posters, and reference material could be divided into these sections. If consideration were being given to a special collection within a graduate library school library, it might make sense to donate the books there and put the posters and reference material into a collection designed for use by artists and art historians. Examples could be produced *ad infinitum* but you, the designer of your collection, are the one to assess how it might best be used to further your original desires in an institutional setting.

Some of us do have a mental picture of both the beginning and the end of our collecting life. Should you be of such a mind, with your chosen finale an institution, here is some counsel to serve both your questing spirit and your pocketbook. Selecting the recipient institution as early as feasible has several benefits. One is the questing pleasure to be derived from interacting with professional book people, other than dealers. Creating a team effort should give you seasoned guidance, relaxed access to their reference resources, and the fun of being part of work in progress. Another plus is that such a partnership cannot help but enhance collection design and ensure good value for dollars spent. For the wealthy, the joys of being a patron of the arts come running with any checkbook flourish. For the rest of us, having less disposable income does not have to mean getting less "beep" for our buck.

‖ TIME TO STOP—BY SALE?

Selling a collection involves many of the same caveats as donating. The prime difference is the desire to be rewarded with money rather than with a tax write-off or dramatic gratitude from friends, relatives, or an institution. Those who sell, but not out of the need to replenish funds, generally declare that they do so in order to allow others to have the fun of the treasure hunt and the satisfaction of treasure bagged. Such dispersals are dream stuff for dealers, auction hype for sales of important collections, and network gossip for small-scale collectors. They, of course, provide important, to-be-kept-track-of opportunities for collection upgrading. Which once more reinforces the value of establishing and maintaining knowledge of your collecting competitors and pursuing all relevant, incipient, or about-to-be-published bibliographies and related technical journals.

The topic of selling divides into important and small-scale collections. For the former, dealers and auction houses will be pursuing you with wine, contracts, and roses. For the latter, Cinderella before the fairy godmother is your story. If you consider selling at auction, return to Chapter 5 and reread what Dr. Sorenson has to say on the subject. Selling at auction is the flip side of buying there. Selling to a dealer means that what you have bought at retail you are selling wholesale. Knowing that dealers routinely give other dealers either a 10 or a 20 percent discount can help you compute this markup. Since a high percentage of the sales at antiquarian book fairs come from interdealer selling and a dealer's normal buying price from nondealers is a half to a third of what he will then price the book, it becomes clear that these 20 percent discount purchases imply either filling in a personal collection or having a buyer waiting in the wings.

‖ CAN WE MAKE A QUICK PROFIT?

Is there a place in this discussion for thoughts of quick profitability? Why not! Especially for those who do win lotteries—or at least door prizes. The lottery ads say, "You have to buy to win." I counter with, "To win, you have to shop hard and well, strive mightily to train your bookish eye, and almost of necessity, have a mind adept at storing and retrieving a mass of detailed data." To test this point, open a copy of Van Allen Bradley's *The Book Collector's Handbook of Values* and study his entry for something you collect. Bradley writes:

> Basic bibliographical works I have consulted range upwards into the thousands of books . . . About $50,000 worth of reference books is a good beginning for anyone contemplating running a rare book shop . . . Beyond his little corner, there are vast libraries where, if one looks long enough and hard enough, he may perhaps find all the answers. (p. xi)

Each book is a wondrous, highly detailed physical artifact. Our ability to make a quick profit by buying truly cheap something that can be sold at a fairly high price demands knowledge to use and time to spend. How we accumulate the first and dispense the second controls our success at rotating, upgrading, and disposing of our collection. In spite of evidence to the contrary, rarely are collectibles considered sound investment strategy. Milton Reissman of New York's Victoria Book Shop published figures on a twenty-year (1960s to 1989) gain in antiquarian children's book prices that might seem to refute this opinion. As a total, the 168 titles he listed in his catalog, "Children's Books and Illustrated Books," rose in price from $9,865 to $58,000. This gain does command attention. Yet reflect a moment upon the performance of real estate or investment-quality precious stones over this same time period.

Does this rapid swing through the market give us useful guidance for planning the end of our collecting? I believe that it does, if only because it fits nicely between lines already written by Reisler, Stockham, Frohnsdorff, and Sorenson. *Webster's* defines "hobby" as "something a person likes to do in his spare time; a favorite pastime or avocation." A. Edward Newton will have our last word:

> The advice given by *Punch* to those about to marry—"Don't"—seems, then, to be the best advice to a man who is tempted to buy by the hope of making a profit out of his books; but I observe that this short and ugly word deters very few from following their inclinations in the matter of marriage . . . I do not recommend the purchase of rare books as an investment . . . in spite of the handsome profits many collectors have made from books they have sold. . . . While a man may do much worse than buy rare books. . . . He should be satisfied to eat his cake and have it. . . . The possession of rare books is a delight best understood by the owners of them. They are not called upon to explain. (Newton, p. 120)

Victorian silversmiths used their media to market the icons of Kate Greenaway's children, giving us a whole collectible universe of realia. Pictured is a cranberry glass pickle castor and a napkin ring—together forming a Greenaway ring-around-the-rosy. *(Collection of Karen Garner Gross.)*

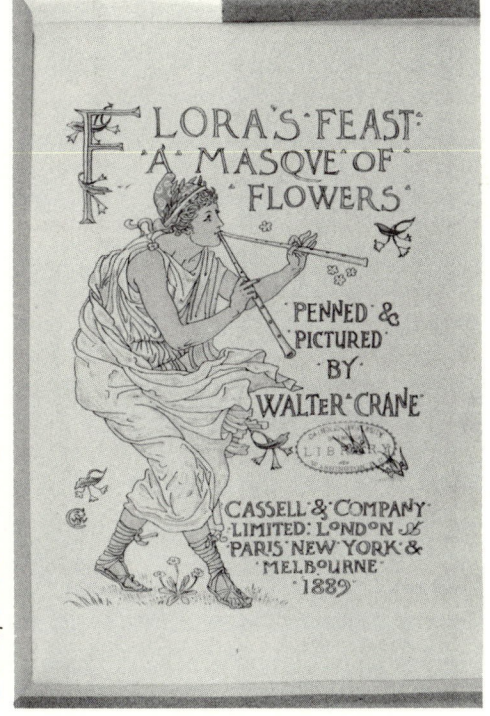

In contrast to Greenaway's fondness for the white, blank page look, Walter Crane, designer, decorator, and colleague of William Morris, preferred a well-filled page. An uncommon Crane, *Flora's' Feast* would seem a natural base for a calendar. *(Courtesy of the School of Library and Information Science, Catholic University of America.)*

Which line of a poem an artist chooses to illustrate is among the collecting variants possible within the 120 editions of Robert Louis Stevenson's *Child's Garden of Verses* listed in *Fiction, Folklore, Fantasy and Poetry for Children*, 1876–1985. Here are two for the poem "Foreign Children": *left*, E. Mars and M. H. Squire (1900) and *right*, Jessie Wilcox Smith (1905). *(Author's collection.)*

"Don't you wish that you were me?"

Frontispiece from my 1902 *Child's Garden* in William Morris style by Charles Robinson (*left*). The first (1895) edition was not illustrated. Stevenson caught childhood, as opposed to the adult sentimentality of the 1835 *Original Poems for Infant Minds* by the Taylor family (*right*). (*Courtesy of the School of Library and Information Science, Catholic University of America.*)

Bookseller Jim Presgraves advised me to try a new collection as research for this book. I chose an imprint, P. F. Volland & Co., only to realize later that, without a bibliography, unity is a dream. After *Animal Children* by Edith Brown Kirkwood (1913), I found *Flower Children*, *Mother Earth's Children*, and *Bird Children* by E. Gordon. M. T. Ross illustrated them all. (*Author's collection.*)

A double-page spread from *Tuesday*, the 1991 Caldecott Medal winner by David Wiesner. I bought an autographed first edition "ahead" for a niece frog-collector at the 1991 American Library Association meeting. By 1992, standers-in-line at ALA got the later, Medal edition. Illustration copyright © 1991 by David Wiesner. All rights reserved. *(Reprinted by permission of Clarion Books/Houghton Mifflin, and courtesy of the artist.)*

Having Trina Schart Hyman's visual voice represented seems a natural way to enlarge upon the sentiments in her letter on page 143. This cat and Christmas tree village from *Christmas Poems* by Myra Cohn Livingston illustrate four collecting connections: anthologist, artist, subject, and genre. Illustration copyright © 1984 by Trina Schart Hyman. (*Reprinted by permission of Holiday House, Inc., and courtesy of the artist.*)

8

Little of all we value here
Wakes on the morn of its hundreth year
Without both feeling and looking queer.
In fact, there's nothing that keeps its youth
So far as I know, but a tree and truth.
—Oliver Wendell Holmes,
The Deacon's Masterpiece

Current Trends
in Children's Book Collecting

Consideration of current trends in children's literature recalls the story of Janus. The Roman god of doorways and beginnings, Janus gazed in two directions—the past and the future. Our hobby encourages us to look backward for past treasures and forward to acquisitions in tomorrow's marketplace. "Trend" implies both change and direction. In our market-oriented society, it is the correct word to use for discussing what genre or type of collectible is being avidly sought, bought, worn, eaten, drunk, displayed, or lived in or with. How, then, should this dual aspect affect our collecting plans? How can we use it to help us fetch the future?

Your own collecting agenda now rests at some pre- and self-determined intersection of time, money, and place. How should you relate that to trendiness? Each of us owns a truth of purpose. Collecting nostalgia mandates a Janus-like passage from rememory to a here-and-now collecting plan while honoring the child of our first memory. Purchase by purchase, how we link the historic and psychological insights about fairy tales in Bettelheim's *The Uses of Enchantment* to the trends we choose to follow or influence affects both our collecting pleasure and the movement of the marketplace.

In the *Washington Post's Book World,* a newspaper editor, Alberto Manguel, writes of his Argentinian childhood:

> I was 7 years old when Peron was ousted . . . Between grade one and my last year of high school, Argentina had six presidents. In a country where civil values were eroded daily by corrupt politics, the only examples of a better world were to be found, for a child, in children's books . . . books in which the world made sense, even though it was inhabited by pirates, talking animals, wily adventurers, creatures from outer space, and sometimes even real people. (November 5, 1989)

Manguel speaks to the capacity of children's literature to harmonize personal development with the impersonal events of the society in which we grow up. This explains why monitoring the evolution of "story" keeps us abreast of our hobby's longest-running trend: the use by children of the comfort of literature's universality to mitigate the discomforts of history's particularities. Children use books to make inner sense of the world—and today's sense becomes tomorrow's collectible book. Christina Hardyment in *Heidi's Alp* writes:

> But we may well ask ourselves why Wilhelm [Grimm] chose one version of a tale rather than another for publication, why he played down some elements, and emphasized others. At any one time, people will be drawn to the stories which express the mood of that time the best. What Wilhelm chose to dwell on undoubtedly reflected on his own very happy childhood, his later experience of war and uncertainty, and his subsequent concerns for order and authority. (p. 144)

Just plain living constantly illustrates the unique potency of story as our collectible mega-genre. Human beings of all ages love stories and use them in many ways. "What's the story?" is a standard way of asking "What happened?" Flashes of beloved stories from our childhood arise to reassure and comfort us at odd and unpredictable moments: in the sleepless dark, in a moment of fear or of poignant humor. The countless stories one has heard in childhood and throughout life serve to illuminate, to give dimension to circumstance. Like Grimm, we too know what to include and what to omit in the stories we tell, and which of the stories heard in childhood we wish to hear again. This makes each collector one unit of a hobby and a trend.

|| FUTURISM AND MONETARY VALUE

For collectors, as for Alice, looking forward can function as a form of running to stay in place. What current events reliably forecast future value? If one of your collecting aims is resale value this is particularly relevant. At a spring 1989 seminar at the Boston Public Library, I heard Anita Silvey, editor of *The Horn Book Magazine,* describe children's literature as "the largest growing part of literature with three authors on the *New York Times* best-seller list— Sendak, Macaulay, and Van Allsburg." In 1990 Dr. Seuss captured that distinction with *Oh, the Places You'll Go!* An observation from Joseph Connolly's 1989 *Children's Modern First Editions* also addresses this point:

> Collecting children's modern first editions will prove to be enormous fun and not nearly as expensive as you might have imagined; perhaps more to the point, I believe it to be so undervalued and little explored a field as to be poised upon becoming the great growth area of book collecting into the 1990s. (p. 6)

The shelves of out-of-print and used book dealers, not rare ones, provide the best place I know to study the movement from current to collectible. Taken together, the content, chronology, and price of what you choose to collect determine your interest in trendiness. No announced timely movement supersedes the personal truth of your collecting path; yet, since you are spending money, to ignore the marketplace puts you in peril of eventual embarrassment.

|| THE BORDERLINE WHERE THE PRESENT BECOMES THE PAST

To understand that children's book collecting encompasses both the current and out of print or historic, one needs to understand the borderline where the present becomes the past. Look at a few numbers. The 1990 *Statistical Abstract of the United States* tells us how many children America counted in 1988: ages five to nine, 18 million; ages ten to fourteen, 16 million; and ages fifteen to nineteen, 18 million. Then relate this data to statistics in the *Bowker Annual Library and Book Trade Almanac*, 36th edition (1991) for the number of juvenile books published. The latest available figures for the year 1988 show a final count of 4,954 for published juvenile books (hardcover, trade paperback, and reprints); and for 1989, 5,413. Preliminary figures for 1990 put the same group of juveniles at 4,711. The average retail price for a hardback in 1992 was $15. Were literacy to become universal, publishing could become the growth industry. One of my bookstore-owner sources validated the decline in number of titles from 1989 to 1990 by saying, "Publishers are deliberately cutting their lists. As conglomerates swallowed established imprints, the collected lists got just too large."

The Horn Book reviewed 417 titles in 1989 and 404 in 1990; *School Library Journal*, 2,841 and 2,963; *The Bulletin of the Center for Children's Books* 832 and 770; and *Booklist* 2,014 and 2,148. Ponder this against a round figure for children's books published in 1991 of 5,000. In magnitude, current fluctuations in children's reading preferences account for many times more money changing hands than does the total out-of-print children's book market. This fact affects our hobby because the type of books being sought now should logically be the ones with which these children, when grown, will begin their own children's book collecting. Can't we conclude, then, that if the cream does come to the reviewing top, lapping that up will be productive?

Another bit of futurism signals the increase in multicultural awareness among publishers. From telephone interviews with local children's bookstore owners we hear that the outpouring has reached bandwagon proportions, a healthy sign for our country's changing demographics. Because these people strongly voice the feeling that learning the facts of life from myths and legends is one of the oldest and most international of educations, they enthusiastically welcome these new cultural windows.

‖ A ROLE FOR CHILDREN'S BOOKSHOPS

Many bookstores now have a children's department, and the number of specialized children's bookstores is growing. Three of America's first were the Children's Book and Record Shop in Santa Monica, California, the Owl and the Pussy Cat in Lexington, Kentucky, and The Cheshire Cat in Washington, D.C. Now there are ten in the D.C. metropolitan area alone. Within the six years from its founding until 1991, membership in the Association of Booksellers for Children (ABC) has gone from 30 to 750. Several societal forces encourage this, fueled by disposable income in some hands. Among these forces are educational pressure generated by older, affluent, two-career parents, and grandparents who properly value reading aloud. The owners of specialized stores offer collectors a real resource. They know what is selling, and to whom. Many owners publish annotated catalogs, and they seem more generous in retaining nonbuyers on their mailing lists than do antiquarian merchants. Being on the mailing list of local bookstores ensures access to book signings and other artist/author-involved programs that help assure continual awareness of this now-to-then borderline.

A partnership with these knowledgeable book professionals not only helps you learn about books with a future, but it provides one of the best ways to acquire first editions of Newbery and Caldecott Medal books, which are automatically worth double the price of the second or third printings. A medal book can be issued any time in the publishing year for which it is honored, and the awards are announced the following year during the early January midwinter conference of the American Library Association. This timetable means that normal sales have already taken place: for example, The Cheshire Cat had just four copies of the 1989 Caldecott winner, *Lon Po Po*, when the announcement was made. Once the medal dust has settled, your best hope of buying a first edition is to locate a small shop where there aren't likely to be collecting customers. Or, if your taste mirrors that of the medal award committee, and you've taken advantage of a pre-medal signing to obtain a first edition, you have just acquired a $50 book.

Your access to quality children's book departments or bookstores is another element of geographic location. Shopping the telephone book when you travel is one way to widen the field. If there isn't time for a bookstore visit, a telephone call should put you on the dealer's catalog list. Some of these merchants are listed in the toll-free telephone directories.

‖ MASTERING THE IN-PRINT PUBLISHING SCENE

Without further computations, the common sense inherent in buying tomorrow's gems today readily appears. From the universe of year-by-year publishing, we can skim the top, as "glowers." Within the current market there is another accepted demarcation. What children choose and what book reviewers and connoisseurs prefer are almost traditionally not the same thing. What can be of value to collectors is the linkage between today's in-print sales and tomorrow's out-of-print collectibility. To comprehend this you need to discover and decipher the forecasting connection between what books reviewers praise and what are bought and read. Can some attention to the former put us ahead in the latter?

My answer is yes—because tomorrow's collectors are among today's children and, by establishing what titles seem most likely to endure, you can build a collection of the very best and become a "future" collector. If the future seems too far away, remember that in these days the next decade or the next presidential term is the future. Successful forecasting allows one to acquire mint firsts in dust jacket at regular and discount bookstores. Limited editions are the most regularly offered examples of dramatic price rises for current books. These are not normally put out by specialized houses, but by the same publisher as the trade edition. The limited edition of Sendak's *The Nutcracker*, with an extra print, published in 1984 in an edition of about 250 at $250, was going for about $700 in mid-1991. Nonillustrated titles become limited editions also. Sendak's *Caldecott & Co.* came out in a trade edition at $18.95 and a limited edition at $75.50, and the fourth in Madeleine L'Engle's sci-fi series, *Many Waters*, also came out in a limited edition. Some dealers will special-order these for a client, but their usual practice is to store such books until their profit has reached a growth limit. In the case of books by illustrators whose fame is currently judged to be beyond "trend," storage won't be prolonged. Otherwise, your stockpile must be allowed to ripen until today's children become tomorrow's collectors. If your collecting instinct agrees that collecting can be extended beyond o.p. books, you will need to become knowledgeable about the current market in children's books.

‖ TODAY'S CHILDREN AS CASE STUDY RESEARCH

For active parents or grandparents, family children offer the obvious starting point for in-house research. If each child represents the taste of many, we have the same relative margin of statistical security as accrues to the Harris pollsters. Beware, though, of not properly respecting the trust implicit in such a mutual interest and activity.

Shared reading—whether carried on by one who can read to one who cannot read at all, or to one who cannot read well enough to handle what is being read, or by simultaneous individual reading and exchange of literary views—should be treated as the priceless spiritual bridge that it is. If you are an active parent or other caregiver or child sharer, and your child audience is properly respectful of a fine book, you might purchase one suitable for current pleasure, remove the dust jacket to a safe place, and entrust the book to the child's careful enjoyment. Ask for an informal, personal book review. Any child old enough to have favorite books is old enough to tell you why.

‖ REVIEWING PERIODICALS

To put your domestic observations into a broader context requires outside information sources. In addition to children's book departments and book-stores there are specialized juvenile book reviewing journals. Reading these will help you develop sound judgment to guide your collecting. The journals are standard, professional tools used by librarians for book selection. Unless you live outside the range of any public library large enough to purchase them for the use of their acquisition librarian, or unless your collecting budget has a sizeable amount for reference materials, there are only two I suggest for personal subscriptions. One is *The Horn Book Magazine*, honored for its publication of quality articles and major reviews. Founded in Boston in 1924 by its first editor, the distinguished Bertha Mahony, it grew from the lists of recommended books that she compiled with her assistant, Elinor Whitney, and distributed at their Boston Bookshop for Boys and Girls. *The Oxford Companion to Children's Literature* praises it as being "from its inception the leading periodical of its kind in the United States" (p. 261). The other magazine is *School Library Journal*, vital because it is the only one said to review the total juvenile publishing output. Information about other important reviewing journals can be found in Chapter 10. Not all libraries put these acquisition tools out on general display. If you don't see them, ask a children's librarian.

‖ TODAY'S SCENE IN NONFICTION

It seems that childhood books about "how things are" are not remembered with enough pleasure to be widely sought for repossession by adults. Such downplaying of nonfiction is highly visible in the antiquarian market. This should not surprise, because it supports the theory that books destined to become collectible are chiefly imaginative inventions. Common sense has explanations for this. Science describes process, and the large volume of information for the writer to simplify accurately as he describes complex processes—biological, technological, and electronic—is daunting. The speed with which scientific and technological information now becomes dated is also daunting. Scientist and children's book's author Franklyn M. Branley expressed this when he commented that only when he must explain a subject to children does he realize that he doesn't understand it at all. To relate your explanation of any physical process—how to turn a hem or build a bow and arrow, let alone describe tree growth or what a star is—to the knowledge that a child possesses requires the knowing the whole "story", and being able to reduce it to its essentials, step-by-step. Children are quick to sense information gaps and turn away from connections that don't connect.

Among the out-of-print items that are still collected are those that provide practical craft information. There were articles tucked between adventure stories in the Victorian annuals and contemporary books, the domestic availability of materials, and long-known, simple technology allowed these explanations to serve as practical handicraft teachers. In an English boys' annual (1883) I found a full-color plate on kilts, another on the design of ship's hulls, and a diagrammatic article on how to make a violin. These transmitted information, practical for its time, in full, clear illustrations done in chromolithography and wood engraving.

Beyond such few survivors as the Story series by Maud and Miska Petersham, exceptions seem to be cookbooks, school readers, membership handbooks such as those for the Boy or Girl Scouts, and those juveniles valued for professional endeavors beyond teaching children's literature. Without a deliberate plan, I've accumulated a personal collection of bibliographic "how-to's" with colorful, diagrammatic visuals for use in teaching library literacy. These, however, are not my rememberers.

Since about 1960 there has been fresh American impetus to enhance the place of nonfiction or informative books within children's literature. In the eighties, the author and academician Jo Ann Carr became a very effective voice for this cause. In *Beyond Fact: Nonfiction for Children and Young People* she sets forth some facts:

> Only six nonfiction books have won the Newbery Award since it was founded in 1922, and five of these were biographies. Children's literature courses give very little attention to the evaluation of nonfiction. Teachers rarely read nonfiction aloud to their classes or encourage children to read factual books for their personal enjoyment . . . Even the most literate parents never think to read a nonfiction book to their children at bedtime. (p. ix)

Margery Fisher made this case for the English audience in *Matters of Fact*, as did Virginia Haviland in the sections on nonfiction in *Children's Literature Views and Reviews*, and Beverly Kobrin in *Eye Openers* in 1988.

Whether through these efforts or new developments in illustrative technology or the appearance of noteworthy author/illustrators, memorably visual "books about" have been arriving in increasing numbers. The artist/author David Macaulay is a case in point. In 1977, the Children's Book Guild (CBG) of Washington, D.C. established an award for a body of nonfiction writing, and in 1983 the *Washington Post* became a cosponsor. Macaulay won the first award of a cash prize and an inscribed crystal paperweight. From his first book, *Cathedral*, to his bestseller for all ages, *The Way Things Work*, and now his 1991 Caldecott winner, *Black and White*, Macaulay's books are memorable.

The considerable output of Leonard Everett Fisher, who won the 1989 CBG nonfiction award, also fits this now-and-future collectible category. Among his 300 illustrated books is *The White House*, which gained a place on the 1989 "50 Notable Books List" of *School Library Journal*. At the Children's Book Week luncheon in Washington honoring him, he shared the teaching methods of his own parents. During his elementary school years, Fisher's mother read him the entire twenty-six volumes of *Compton's Encyclopedia*, A to Z, while his nautical engineer father made his points with handmade, illustrated, technical flash cards! Russell Freedman's *Lincoln: A Photobiography* won the Newbery Award in 1988. This renewed prominence for nonfiction might be termed a trend if the 1989 Newbery winner *Joyful Noise: Poems for Two Voices* by Paul Fleischman can be considered an insect tale.

By 1991, what has resulted is an enormous outpouring of nonfiction books, described by one children's bookstore owner in quantitative terms thus: "When we opened twelve years ago we allotted them half of our space and filled it by buying lots from England. Now we can fill the space with American books." "Why?" I asked. "Is it a reaction to the push for holistic reading instruction?" She replied firmly, "No. Publishers have learned that parents will buy them."

|| NONBOOK COLLECTIBLES

Looking ahead, into what category should we put nonbook juvenile collectibles such as comics and baseball cards? Should we welcome the challenge of extrapolating from today to tomorrow and buy now? Can we say that there exists an ongoing, rapidly changing print equivalent of the hula-hoop? Being a collector who can latch on to such fads should reward you with some real money before too long. For collectors whose tastes run thus, market research suggests observing the habits of a real child or watching the daily press.

An ad in the *Washington Post Magazine* brought me to John Scott, a collector/dealer in Silver Spring, Maryland, who supplied this telephone précis on baseball cards:

Beginning about 1975, when nostalgia turned the baby boomers who had collected as children into adult enthusiasts, it is now the third largest U.S. hobby, measured in dollars and participants. It is a good hobby because it has accurate price guides that are available in the same shops as the cards, and a wide variety of prices to appeal to child and adult collector alike. The most expensive card ever sold is the 1910 Honus Wagner. It was issued in a pack of cigarettes and Wagner, an ardent nonsmoker, forced the company to discontinue the practice. Only twenty-one copies are known to exist in the U.S., one selling for $125,000 in 1989 and another for $415,000 in 1991. The original artwork for the 1953 Mickey Mantle card was recently purchased for $125,000 by a corporation, which has printed an edition of 2,000 copies from it to sell at $1,000 each.

I asked, didn't I? And I am shocked at such prices. Harry Saul, proprietor of Pleasant Street books in Woodstock, Vermont, has found that profit to be made from the sale of baseball cards will now support his antiquarian book business. Sales seem steady in cards from all available time periods. For any of you who are current followers of the game, he suggests buying cards in the current pack format and putting away those for players whose star you deem to be rising. The entry of basketball and football cards into this market is another lead. Payoff has been sure, and not slow. This puts book collecting into a very different financial perspective, doesn't it?

‖ COLLECTING BOOK "GROUPS"

What can be termed "groups," or lists, of books (to separate them from the series genre) now form a limited but important segment of trendy o.p. collecting, especially for beginners. By proclaiming a finite universe of books to acquire, the back cover title list gives collectors an easy route to success. Little Golden Books, the popular, inexpensive picture books of the 1940s, lead the field. To listen to one avid collector: "I'm really hooked. And I hate to get the last one, because then I'll have to find something else to collect that I can also afford." Catalog prices for these now show $3 to $5 for ordinary titles and $7 to $25 for rare ones in mint condition. A January 1991 dealer's catalog offered *The Shy Little Kitten* in dust jacket for $19. Beyond the literary value of original titles such as *The Little House in the Woods*, content of some represents a nostalgia for early television in stories about such favorites as the Flintstones, Romper Room, Howdy Doody, Miss Frances of Ding Dong School, and the Lone Ranger. Another such set was the Wonder Books, which announced itself as having "24 and 4 to be published." The one volume that I could inspect in the rare book library of the University of Maryland was its version of *Mother Goose*. The back cover described the set as "a series of books for young children handsomely and lavishly illustrated by well-known artists. Bound in durable Durasheen and printed on paper of excellent quality, these attractive volumes are a wonderful value."

‖ AGE-GROUP TRENDS

A New York State dealer, Lee Temares, reports several trends from differing age groups. Eight-to-twelve-year-olds are themselves collecting material relating to current favorites they choose from TV, video, and movies. A succession ranges over *ET* and *Star Wars*, *Beauty and the Beast*, and *The Little Mermaid*. Children of the fifties and sixties are seeking out the series books of their childhood. They collect Kathy Martin, Josephine James, and the Peggy Lane Theater Stories such as *Peggy Goes Straw Hat* by Virginia Hughes, illustrated by Sergio Leone. Collectors of any age have responded avidly to the publishing hype generated by the fiftieth anniversary of Disney's *Snow White*, Mickey himself, Babar, and Little Golden Books. Sharp collecting sense decrees pursuing the fullest range of related items—posters, special edition books, toys, crockery (we all know the prices of Shirley Temple glassware), and, possibly, videos. Picture books of the forties are much in demand, generating a plethora of requests for out-of-print searching. The current crop of fifty-year-olds seeks to replace personal favorites lost or thrown out when they (or their parents) moved or divorced.

‖ CHANGES THAT INFLUENCE THE MARKETPLACE FOR ILLUSTRATED BOOKS

Maybe it's beyond either study or crystal ball to predict accurately which of the current group of top illustrators will stay so over time and go on to be important, but doing it successfully will ring the cash register. Doris Frohnsdorff, among other dealers, reports that the price wave for Rackham and Dulac appears to have crested and flattened. At the 1990 Washington, D.C., Beltway Show, Bob McCullum of Cottermole Books in Newbury, Ohio, a shop specializing in 20th-century children's books, proposed a theory linking modern art and children's book illustration. He told me:

> All it takes is money to buy 'fine' 19th-century children's books by Rackham and Dulac, Johnny Gruelle, or Jessie Wilcox Smith, but there was not a Caldecott Medal book in comparable condition for sale at this book fair. Invariably, modern art is not popular since it prefigures the taste of the future. When that future arrives, however, the modern art of the past becomes popular, so the children's books which can be expected to become important will be those which most closely parallel developments in modern art.

As examples, McCullum pulled out copies of the work of Wanda Gag and Elizabeth Enright and pointed to their lively, modern style. "These were done fifty years ago! The modernist Gustaf Tenggren's prices have jumped. I see Tasha Tudor as an example of an artist working in a traditional style whose books have peaked as collectibles and Tenggren as one on the way up." Put together, these comments seem to suggest that it is worthwhile for trend watchers to look for book art even among great artists that is just one generation behind the current or modern art of popular culture.

Overcollecting is another market force. McCullum considers Sendak as possibly "peaked," because of such overcollecting. "I've just sold all my Sendak. He did two great books, *The Wild Things* and *The Nutshell Library*. *Wild Things* has reached the wild price of $5,000. When prices become that high, peaking results because the combination of demand that produces scarcity buys bare market's cupboard for that artist and to collect him or her becomes almost impossibly difficult and expensive."

A book text's popularity is another factor in the relationship between illustrator/written and illustrator/illustrated books. Sometimes there is a seemingly perfect match between the two media and Michael Dirda, Children's Book Editor of the *Washington Post Book World*, accords this to Chris Van Allsburg for *The Polar Express* (1985). "It sold well at Christmas 1989 in a presentation set containing the book, a tape read by William Hurt, and the recipient's own silver bell, and now seems an established seasonal classic." Size of print run is another market variable that bears collecting attention. Some credentialed voices doubt the collectible value of the Helprin/Van Allsburg *Swan Lake*, predicting that it will require five years to double in price because of the huge print run. Garnering a Caldecott Honor Book Award as Jerry Pinkney did for his *The Talking Egg* (1989) assures only a base level of collecting value for all his books. Book by book, demand and thus collecting value will vary as it has for Van Allsburg. Knowledgeable Pinkney cross-collectors will surely move to acquire items connected to his service on the U.S. Postal Service Citizens' Stamp Advisory Committee and ponder whether critics will judge him an inheritor of the Brandywine School of artist/authors or not.

The awards produce important consequences worth evaluating. Two places to monitor are *The Horn Book Magazine* for the acceptance speeches and *Publishers Weekly* for trendy market forces. By extending your interest and observation to the total art world and finding dealers who will conjecture with you should enable you to anticipate trends and thus collect fine illustrated books at prices way ahead of a ripened market.

‖ ORIGINAL BOOK ART

There are four main markets in which to buy this: children's book dealers who represent particular artists; general art galleries that handle children's book art, usually without the related books; galleries that specialize and often include related books; auction galleries, and charity auctions featuring the work of children's book artists. Moment by moment, though, this art glides swiftly into the storage bins and onto the walls of the art galleries. Trying to examine this subject objectively produces the usual pros and cons. From Gloria Kamen, a Washington artist/author, comes this perspective: "When contacted directly, most artists will likely sell. Ninety percent of children's book artists don't make a living wage. While some like Robert McCloskey can live on the revenue from a few books, most gross between $5,000 to $15,000 a year."

The first price breakdown separates three ways: a one-of-a-kind original; an artist's print, printed in multiple copies; and a photo-reproduced print or poster. Not every artist's work is available in all these formats, though. If your definition of affordable is $1,000, you can still buy work by Johnny Gruelle, Harrison Cady, and Ernest Shepard (but not from *Winnie-the-Pooh*). Dealer Jo Ann Reisler adds the distinction of "important"—which accounts for the price differential between her Gruelle pieces, which range from $200 to $2,500, to estimates for *Winnie-the-Pooh* subjects, which run from $10,000 to $30,000. Kamen names the Bush Gallery of Boston and Carmel, California, as one that has been specializing in children's book original art over the long term. From mid-America comes word of the Elizabeth Stone Gallery, which opened in Detroit in September 1990. This gallery sells both the children's books themselves and original art from them. Stone, a collector and former school librarian, carries signed lithographs priced from $25 to $225. She comments: "Many original illustrations are available and very affordable, which is a strong selling point in the current art market, where prices are generally out of sight."

For the artist, retention of the originals is an important contract negotiating point. Gloria Kamen observes: "Now, as always, good publishers routinely return the originals, but in the past it was common practice for mass production publishers such as Golden Books to keep and reuse them— over and over." (Trina Schart Hyman's daughter mentioned this happening to her mother in an article by her that *The Horn Book* published along with Hyman's Caldecott acceptance speech in the July/August 1985 issue.) Like many artists, Kamen responds generously to requests for donations for fundraisers, exemplified in her case by the annual auction of Vermont Educational Television. In October 1989 "The Art of Childhood," billed in its catalog as "[Connecticut's] first-ever charity auction of fine original illustrations by children's artists," raised $150,000 for its sponsor, the Hartford chapter of Ronald McDonald Children's Charities. For any of you who collect original art, this practice offers a public-spirited, possibly bargain collecting source to add to your resource file.

Within the children's book dealership, the major entry of dealers not otherwise associated with the children's book field is viewed with disfavor. Prices will surely rise. The owners of trendy New York galleries obviously welcome this new market and income source. The recent New York five-figure auction prices for "cels," or original art on celluloid, from Disney films will not discourage them from seeking to enlarge their holdings in the world of art for youth. Steven Spielberg and George Lucas were among the buyers at that sale. Another negative possibility is that at least some of the scholarship, gentility, and just plain "belief" that identifies children's book collectors will disappear should the market in original juvenile art lose its bridge with the books that gave it life. The advantage I see would be money in the pockets of those now holding a considerable collection of these true treasures.

As I stood in an ALA convention autographing line that snaked its way toward Trina Schart Hyman, I experienced one of those white balloons that comic artists use to indicate the birth of an idea. What, I thought, is it like to have become collectible in your own time? The knowledge that her important originals are priced at $5,000 to $6,000, added to the respect implied by the book-buying multitude, surely validated her collectibility. So, when my turn came, I put the question. Her first reaction was surprise. Then she offered to reply, and did so promptly by letter:

> If you want to know, the idea of my being "collectible" is astonishing to me. I am a book illustrator simply because I am the sort of artist who loves stories, and needs to have a story in my pictures. But I'm an artist first, an illustrator second, and I consider myself a half-baked artist and a technically rather primitive one at that. All the beautiful stuff that I see other illustrators accomplishing makes me sad because I know I'll never be able to do it, technically. All I have on my side is a knowledge of and love for human feelings and for the power of nature. I'll never be able to successfully draw or paint that knowledge. Partly from lack of talent, partly because I'm a slow learner, and mostly because I guess I'm afraid to. And people saying, "Oh, you're the best!" only makes me confused, because of course it's lovely to hear and it makes me feel good in a way, but I know it's just not true. (I'm not the worst, of course—and I know that I'm good at a certain kind of drawing. And I'm always proud of what I've done. If I weren't, I wouldn't let it be printed.) I'm just an artist in transition, and I'll never be good enough to achieve on paper or canvas the life or strength or beauty of the visions in my mind's eye. But, of course, I'll never stop trying. That's what being an artist is all about.

‖ DOCUMENTING SOME OF THE RISE
IN BOOK PRICES

Milton Reissman of New York's Victoria Book Shop has given permission to include the following preface from his fall 1989 catalog:

> We see no reason not to have a little fun after the ordeal of preparing a catalogue. The last five pages herein contain a list of prices from our catalogues of the 1960s compared with their present values. Screams of joy, yes. Floods of tears, no. Calls will be accepted from the yessers only.

Copies were in fine to good condition. Here are excerpts for book prices that demand my handkerchief:

Baum: *The Lost Princess of Oz*, first issue, $50—$375; *The Patchwork Girl of Oz*, $45—$375. Burroughs: *Tarzan of the Apes*, first issue, No DJ, $50—$2,000. Cox: *The Brownies in the Philippines*, $17.50—$100. Field: *Hitty, Her First Hundred Years*, $17.50—$125. Henty: *At the Point of the Bayonet*, first, $10—$50. Hoffman: *Der Strawwelpeter*, c. 1890, $12.50—$45. Kipling: *Just So Stories*, $65—$225. Leaf: *The Story of Ferdinand*, first, Lawson plates, $25—$150. Lofting: *The Story of Doctor Dolittle*, first, $45—$175. Movable books: a collection of 10 choice early items plus forty 20th-century pop-ups, $2,750—$9,000. Pogany: *The Story of Hiawatha*, folding panorama, first, $25—$175. Nesbit: *The Book of Dragons*, first, $10—$90. Newell: *The Rocket Book*, first, $30—$125. Nicholson: *The Velveteen Rabbit*, first, $25—$600. Otis: *Toby Tyler, or Ten Weeks With a Circus*, first, $40—$350. Porter: *Pollyanna*, first, very fine, $50—$250. Rackham: *Rip Van Winkle*, first trade, $55—$225. Ruth Plumly Thompson: *The Silver Princess in Oz*, fine in DJ, $8—$200.

However, there is no guarantee that the next twenty years will see the same changes.

‖ SERIES COLLECTING UPDATE

In the opinion of most specialists, series collecting is on the upswing with mounting, almost hard-to-believe, prices at the top. In 1989, the Baltimore dealer E. Christian Mattson showed me four titles from the Iron Boys' series by James Mears that he had just sold for $200, with some of the Dave Dashaway series priced at $75 each. In 1990, when I asked again for his view of the rarest series titles, his first thought was the 1915 title by Gilbert Patten, *Cliff Stirling, Sophomore at Stormbridge* (of which only two copies are known to exist), at $400, and second was Rick Brant's 1967 *Danger Below* at $250. An amazing price for a collection of The Hardy Boys, firsts in the red binding, numbers one to eleven, 1922–32, was $3,000. Says Mattson: "Prices for the girls' series, which men as well as women collect, are firmly on the rise, with Dana Girls from the 1930s, fine firsts in dust wrappers, at $40, and a group of fine firsts of Nancy Drews, numbers one to six, at $200 each." This creates only a curtain raiser to dealer Peter Baughman's words to me in 1990 on the popularity of the Tarzan series. A fine first of *Tarzan and the Apes* (1914) without dust jacket was going for $1,000 and the jacket, in mint condition, with or without the book, for $15,000. I asked, "Who'd be willing to pay that price." He replied, "With the word spread among the right people, I'd have five takers." Perspective and validation can be heard in this pricing update from dealer Lee Temares during Washington's 1991 Beltway Book Fair. "Yes, the recession has hit us all—or at least those of us whose greatest volume [of sales] is in the middle price range. For these customers, book purchases are luxuries, firmly tied to fluctuating disposable income. There does not seem to be a corresponding slump in the market for the very expensive, mint rareties, especially the illustrated 'glowers.' " What this suggests to me is a window for sage collectors to use to fill collection gaps in the middle range where prices may drop or be negotiable.

‖ INFLUENCE OF MAJOR EXHIBITS

Attention paid to major exhibits repays the collector who seeks to benefit from trends. Though impact varies with importance, they inherently indicate market flow, demonstrate pricing, and produce definite hype. A single author or illustrator show generates the most intensive collecting response. The most notable recent American show was put on by the Pierpont Morgan Library in New York to exhibit the works of Beatrix Potter. Titled "Beatrix Potter: Artist and Storyteller," it ran from May 12 to August 21, 1988. Included were twenty-two watercolor paintings from *The Tailor of Gloucester* lent by London's Tate Gallery; original illustrations from *Peter Rabbit, Mrs. Tiggy-Winkle, Jemima Puddle-Duck,* and *Squirrel Nutkin*; and literary manuscripts. Ford Motors was the corporate sponsor and a catalog was published: *Beatrix Potter—1866–1943, The Artist and Her World: A Companion to the Exhibition.* The Boston Public Library mounted "A Goodly Heritage: Children's Literature in New England, 1850–1950; An Exhibition from the Alice M. Jordan Collection of the Boston Public Library in Observance of the Year of the Young Reader, May 1989" with a catalog prepared by the curator, Linda Murphy. Two recent shows have fine catalogs. *Read Me a Story: Show Me a Book* documents a late 1991 exhibit of material from the collection of Betsy Beinecke Shirley at Yale's Beinecke Library, and *A Child's Garden of Dreams* does the same for a 1990 show at the Brandywine Library at Chadd's Ford, Pennsylvania. These catalogs are an available-by-mail resource for those unable to attend the shows. Though not inexpensive, they are worthwhile acquisitions because they provide valuable bibliographic information and specifics for travel planning. Because catalogs are usually small printings and thus scarce, they represent a "now" purchase that should produce a "then" profit.

‖ TRENDINESS AND TODAY'S FAST-FORWARD WORLD

In summary: What about trends? Sylvia Ashton-Warner's work with the Maori children of New Zealand has metamorphosed into a new educational wrinkle termed "holistic literacy." This translates into treating all instruction—math, history, science, etc.—as part of learning to read and write, and into replacing textbooks with trade books. It affects us as a trend because any increase in the number of children touched by good literature should directly affect the number of not-too-distant collectors. To give serious attention to new stories and pictures requires a conscious connection to the "rememory" that invoked our hobby. Not everyone finds comfort or pleasure in new books. At the least, keeping abreast can be fun. At the most, you'll be a future collector. In between can be the enjoyment of such pleasures as sharing today's books with kindred or just friendly children; allowing prominent and becoming-prominent authors and illustrators to expose you to their creative mystique and thus widen and deepen your expertise; and owning treasures because you got there just ahead of the everybodies. But only do it if your own story remains true, undistorted by the voices of institutions and media. Remember that *remember* joins *re* and *member*—to put parts back together again by creating tomorrow from today and yesterday.

9

The jar will long retain the fragrance with which it was steeped when new.
—Horace, *Epistles, Book I*

Glimpses of the
Collecting Life

Dictionaries begin their explanations of "collecting" with "gathering" and "assembling." This unsigned article in *The Times* (London) for August 12, 1910, adds some philosophy to those primary descriptions:

> The collector's instinct seems to be a curious by-product of the human mind; and not only of the human mind, for monkeys, magpies and even dogs have it. When a dog makes a store of bones, old and entirely fleshless, he is like the collector who keeps things because they are obsolete. A used postage stamp is to a man what a bone without flesh is to a dog, but the collector of postage stamps goes further than the dog, in that he prefers an old postage stamp to a new one, while no dog, however ardent a collector of bones without flesh, would not rather have a bone with flesh on it. There is more method in the human collector, however, since he always has before him the ideal of a complete collection, whereas no dog probably ever dreamed of acquiring specimens of all the different kinds of bones that there are in the world. The ideal of the complete collection is the usual spur of the human collector. . . . But there is also the spur of rivalry, and, because of that, there are not many collections of things that no one else collects. (Johnston, pp. 13–14)

Reading about the collecting life presupposes an interest in vicarious associations with fellow hobbyists with the thought of using them as a

147

psychological litmus test for oneself. This chapter is an account of a variety of collectors met in print and in person. In a 1983 lecture, "Book Collecting: Personal Rewards and Public Benefits," for the Center for the Book at The Library of Congress collector William P. Barlow, Jr., expressed amazement that books by collectors are written at all—because each collecting experience is so intensely personal. As hobbyists, we are first of all collectors, and then collectors of books. The rare book dealer and the scholar have the same thirst, but the former is satisfied with temporary possession of the book and the application of his knowledge to enhance its value and see it properly placed; and the latter is satisfied with institutional ownership of the objects he wishes to study. Briefly one might say that the dealer knows about a book and seeks temporary ownership; the purchaser becomes a more permanent owner, and the collector both owns and understands. The urge for acquisition and possession and the passion for knowledge produce the true collector. Barlow gives Lessing J. Rosenwald, the greatest donor of rare books to The Library of Congress, as his authority for these opinions on connoiseurship.

Another collector/author, Bamber Gascoigne, has separated collectors into "classifiers" and "hoarders:" "The classifier finds ever greater beauty in objects just because they precisely fill a gap predicted by the process of classification. The hoarder enshrines what comes to hand." Gascoigne illustrates this with a parable of the good hoarder and the bad. His bad hoarder is a charming and somewhat dotty old man who devoted one entire wall of his living room to enshrining stacks of identical empty cigarette packs, tied in bundles of ten. When asked what use he had for them, he replied, "To tell the truth. . . . I haven't found much use for them yet" (Johnston, p. 11). The moral is that a bad hoard is one that would never mutate into a collection.

The good hoarder in Gascoigne's parable was a gentleman loner in Clapham, England. When his house became so lifeless as to attract neighborhood attention, the entering police found paper-stuffed rooms. "For nearly half a century, the man had subscribed to magazines and journals, throwing none of them away and so accidentally providing complete runs of by now very rare material. Most interesting of all were the glossy fashion magazines because from one of these each week he had ordered an expensive pair of high heeled ladies' shoes, as advertised. The shoes had been taken out of their boxes, worn perhaps once or twice around the house, and then replaced in mint condition. Here was a hoard which was instantly transmogrified, by the mere light of day, into a costume collection of extreme importance. It has gone to a larger home where it is more widely appreciated—London's Victoria and Albert Museum" (Johnston, p. 11). What made this latter hoard a collection was the relationships among the items. Value judgment calls a hoard good when it becomes a unity with historical importance. Most collectors fit somewhere between these extremes.

What characterizes the collectors of children's books? For many, it is a pull from a personal past. A pull distilled into the book's blending of message and medium.

Children's books tell stories of love, nature, and relationships through recourse to the imagination. These universal themes are brought home through poetry, pictures, metaphor, dreams. The elements of these dreams and poetry are the literal details, the basic mental furniture of the child's primary "hands on" experience. As these are built and the child grows in experience, connections can be built to the grammar of story which provides a structure through which the child can make personal sense of the confusion of the visible and apprehensible world. Story offers the child a key to the understanding of the universe that stretches in time and space beyond the child's own experience. For grown-ups, this is also true. The second time around, the language of story still provides the best means with which to order our own chaos.

In the preface to his retelling of *The Sleeping Beauty and Other Fairy Tales*, Sir Arthur Quiller-Couch (1863–1944) describes how this shaping occurs.

> In taking each of these liberties I have the warrant of tradition which, in the treatment of fairy tales, speaks with a voice more authoritative than the original author's, for it speaks with the united voices of many thousands of children, his audience and best critics. As the children have decreed that in [Robert] Southey's [1774–1843] tale of *The Three Bears* the heroine shall be a little girl, and not, as Southey invented her, a good-for-nothing old woman, so they have decreed *The Story of Sleeping Beauty* to end with the Prince's kiss, and that of *Beauty and the Beast* with the Beast's transformation. And as *Beauty and the Beast* is really but a variant of the immortal fable of Cupid and Psyche, I might—had I room to spare—attempt to prove to you that the children's taste is here, as usually, right and classical. (p. xiv–xv)

Grown-up collectors may be drawn to these stories because their endings, having been shaped by generations of children, represent ideal solutions to the life quandries in each story. As grown-up collectors of children's literature, we return to the person we were when, as a child, we read a given book. When children are allowed to select their own books, they are empowered to see and satisfy their own needs. In collecting, the adult identifies what is meaningful a second time. The resultant collections form a kind of psychohistory of our double relationships with specific remembered books. Our shelves of "captured" volumes approximate a rough but unique psychoanalysis.

What kind of people tend to be children's book collectors? In researching this book I categorized collectors I met. One definable group consisted of people who are involved with today's children. These people have a memory of children's books from their childhood—their own time-locked reservoir of message, language, and image. At the same time, they are experiencing the literature of contemporary children. Parents, grandparents, teachers, publishers of juveniles, librarians, booksellers, and dealers fall into this category. Many inhabit the dual generationality through reading aloud, which creates an immediately shared exposure to life's common thread. Children who re-read books heard at story hour demonstrate greater comprehension than for books not previously read aloud. Testimony to this comes in the writings of Jim Trelease, lecturer and author of *The New Read-Aloud Handbook* (1989).

Just as grown-ups enjoy this dual generationality, so do children. Mary Ann Brown, a collector and teacher in Alexandria, Virginia, described to me how, for the past three years, her second-grade students have been bringing their parents' books to share in class. One boy came to class holding a book high, saying, "This belongs to my mother. We must take good care of it." These shared copies of *Babar* and E. B. White often bear inscriptions to the child's parent, the first owner of the book. Similarly, a young woman who lives in her grandmother's house which still holds the children's books of her mother, her grandmother, and herself—a seventy-six year span from 1894—has told me of her pride in being inheritor and custodian of these generational memories. She reinforces Mary Ann Brown's experience with the schoolchildren of today.

Sharing children's books can create special bonds among generations. One family of Londoners introduced me to the picture book, *Struwwelpeter*, (*Slovenly Peter*), a collection of cautionary tales in verse by Dr. Heinrich Hoffmann (1809–94). The author's own illustrations, bringing to life his tale of a naughty, wild-haired, nail-biting child whose thumb is colorfully severed by a scissor-man, helped to popularize chromolithography in English children's books. Published first in German in 1845, and in an anonymous English translation printed in Leipzig in 1848, this bestseller made a vivid impression on each generation of that family. At their luncheon table I had asked, "What childhood books do you especially remember?" Stephen, the forty-five-year-old father, answered, *"Struwwelpeter,"* describing a pictured man "with giant scissors coming to cut your thumb off if you sucked it after your parents had gone out." He recalled reading his father's copy, and shuddering with "terrible fear at seeing its bright red blood dripping onto the floor. I would search my soul for possible similar, or related, sins." The ninety-three-year-old grandfather remembered it but claimed, "It didn't frighten me." Stephen's practical wife jumped in: "When I saw it, I couldn't believe there could be such a children's book. I hid it away before my sons could be frightened." The eldest grandson volunteered to extend the family saga "if Mom finds our copy by the time I can add the fourth generation."

Hoffmann was correct when he wrote, "The child does not reason abstractly and one tale or fable would impress him more than hundreds of general warnings" (Carpenter, p. 502).

Another intriguing example of children's book collecting among the generations is the collecting team. I have met a number of mother-son teams. For some the shared hobby was adult-fueled didactic—an educational or other child-improvement motive. For others it seemed to be driven by the mother's pleasure in remembering certain books. Occasionally the mother was the supernumerary and the son was clearly a separate collector. One joint case history features a determined Hague and Sendak addict, now seventeen, who began his collecting at age nine. He was silent at first, just grinning all over, but when asked, he replied: "I buy what catches my eye." At that moment this was the $75 *Fantasy Sketches* by Sendak. His mother spent $15 for the P. L. Travers Little Golden Book, *Sketches from Mary Poppins* (1942). She wanted it because "its pictures are glued in my head, possibly because I read it over and over to my little sister." I hoped to find generations of fathers and sons industriously questing together, but I have not yet seen it. A dealer explained this by saying, "Men do build collections for sons—who seldom want them, because the collecting quest wasn't shared. Many of our customers are settled family men, with established careers, pursuing their version of inherited bookishness. But when they spot a dad-related volume the response is negative—'Oh, my father had that'—and they walk away."

Michael Dirda, children's book editor of the *Washington Post's Book World*, plays an uncommon mix of actively child-connected roles: parent, critic of juvenile books, and collector. Remembering May Lamberton Becker's remarks quoted in Chapter 1 about Mary Mapes Dodge's child-shared *St. Nicholas* editorship, I asked him whether his children had reviewing input. The answer was yes. He continued: "No one in my family read. The grocery store shelves of Golden Books got me started. Library browsing located biographies, *Big Red*, *Hound of the Baskervilles*, and the thrill of discovering *Brave Irene*, until in seventh grade I read that thriller *Crime and Punishment*, which, you could say, ended children's books and started a Ph.D. in comparative lit." Once at the *Post*, the imminent arrival of a first child and editorial turnover resulted in his editorship of the children's book entries that comprise 10 percent of *Book World*. As a collector, he is unenthusiastic about investment and one-author collecting, feeling they become linked when "you buy titles you probably don't like and won't read. Paul Galdone, Van Allsburg, and, yes, Steig, are among my collecting choices."

Gender is another broadly discernible differential among hobbyists. I first became aware of sex-related reading preferences in library work, tested this data in social situations, and had it reinforced in interviewing and researching for this book. All of that distills into a few, broad, case study conclusions.

Women read more fiction than men and favor stories of human relationships in domestic settings. Men choose adventure in tales of pirates, war, ships, and the like. Peter Stockham observed this too. "I knew one male collector, a professor of economics and sociology who, like Henty, ran away to sea and extends that experience by collecting all Henty editions—obsessively." Speaking at a seminar at Montgomery College in Maryland, Jill Paton Walsh, the English author, offered one explanation of this in terms of the masque that the writer adopts in creating fiction.

> I equate the masque, the narrator's point of view, with the divine valuation of events—a personal set of "commandments." One cannot write without values; there is no blinkered view. In a work of fiction, this masque creates the sympathy which can be in two places because one cannot make a character that is completely unsympathetic. Women connect with the author's persona at the center of the novel. Men are not good at wearing masques. They prefer history's plain "why" and novels from the genre of adventure which the airplane now shrinks to toy dimension.

Distilling many dealer interviews into a generic response I've been told: "The serious male collector goes all out, without hesitation. But many a woman will choose a favorite to purchase, then hesitate and return with her husband before she will buy. Yes, it's partly economic. Men still control money. But the deference goes beyond that in its consistency and force."

A tall, decisive male customer of Jo Ann Reisler's was "Fishing" for teddy bear books. Notebook out, I saw a variant on the collecting male. No, indeed, he wasn't charmed by cuddliness. That was his wife. He was pursuing the historic aspect of the Roosevelt Bears, a connection created by a Clifton Berryman cartoon in the November 18, 1902, *Washington Evening Star* that depicted President Theodore Roosevelt refusing to shoot a small bear. The caption read DRAWING THE LINE IN MISSISSIPPI, referring to a boundary dispute between Mississippi and Louisiana. "Teddy Bear," too catchy to avoid being attached to the President, generated a new line of bears that established the Ideal Toy Corporation and increased the demand for the Steiff bear "Friend Petz" once it was renamed "Teddy." My interviewee termed his wife the book collector. Her proudest acquisitions were the series by Seymour Eaton (1859–1916): *The Roosevelt Bears* (Abroad; *Go to Washington; Their Travel and Adventures;* and *Visit Limerick: an Account of Their Possible Experiences on Such a Trip*). He served the team as scout and historian, citing his authorship of an article in the *Teddy Bears and Friends Magazine* (circulation 60,000) and information that prices for rare bears had reached $10,000 to $12,000. Recently, during a charity appraisal session, a *Roosevelt Bears* book emerged from the briefcase of a gentleman and a near riot ensued. Only the rule against appraisers and event staff buying any of the books halted actual bloodshed. "I'd kill for this" was actually heard.

Most collectors belong to the verso of the child-connected group. We are our own child guides. Even in the august halls of the Library of Congress we play out our scenes. Picture a fairy-tale request by a princesslike seeker at the Children's Literature Center which I observed. At closing time a picture-pretty, mink-wrapped, blond baby boomer breathlessly sought help. "Please, oh please, can you help me find my lost *Cinderella*? I'm just in town for a one-day meeting and couldn't get here till now." These are irresistible circumstances to a reference librarian. Margaret N. Coughlan, Reference Specialist in Children's Literature, came to the rescue, translating the plea into bibliographic terms. "My *Cinderella* is big [oversized] and she is on the cover wearing a misty green pleated chiffon dress surrounded by pink and blue flowers. Yes, she went to three balls [another identifier of versions]. I remember it from when I was four." Coughlan's instant answer was, "It sounds like the Little Golden Book version, but do give me your address so I can research and reply."

Over the years from 1988 to 1991, at the London bookshop Marchpane, I had the fun of interviewing as a make-believe bookseller, while the actual one interpreted when necessary. The first year, when Peter Stockham was my ally, I collected this story. A young woman entered with a plea, as plaintive as the *Cinderella*-seeker's. Her home had been burglarized and, amazingly, the thief had taken some books, one of which she desperately sought. She told us what she knew about the book—its indelible story. Its American origin, making it hard for Stockham to place, was the only piece of known bibliographic information. What finally made it retrievable for the seeker was the database link between Peggy Coughlan's brain and the Library of Congress's children's literature collection. I quote from Coughlan's letter to her:

> We list below the bibliographic details for *Star People*, a book Carolyn Michaels told us that you were interested in finding: Dewey, Katherine Fay, *Star People*. With illustrations by Francis B. Comstock. Boston: Houghton Mifflin Co., 1910. Your memory is fine: the story does concern the princess, not a real one, and three others—Prudence, Pat, and the Kitten—who listen to the stories the princess makes up about the stars. Since the book is out of print, we enclose a list of dealers in out-of-print materials, one of whom may be able to locate a copy for you.

In the shadow of bookseller Kenneth Fuller, I "waited on" a thirtyish gentleman. After the breakup of his parent's old home, their children's books had "oozed away." He sought the American Sara Cone Bryant's *Epaminondas and His Auntie* (1938), illustrated by Inez Hogan, which he wanted to republish. That line came up empty. A second fifties-generation patron had been collecting for about eight years, adding to a favorite set, begun at eleven. Her "Fish" was for a school story genre title, "one I still laugh over," from the fifty-nine-title Chalet School series, which began with *The School at the*

Chalet (1925). Elinor M. Brent-Dyer (1895–1969) set them in an international school in the Tyrol. Said our customer, "Confronted with the need to become instantly tri-lingual, the character got in some awful scrapes. The central character is Joey Bettany, an English girl who becomes head of the school and, in later books, a writer of girl's stories. I just need to get ten more titles."

Dr. H. Biemann Othersen, Jr., offers another instance of collecting focus: that which is related to work. A distinguished pediatric surgeon, Medical Director of the Children's Hospital of the Medical University of South Carolina, he uses informational books in a field other than children's literature. "How did you begin to collect?" I asked.

> About 1970, in several successive monthly issues, the editor of the medical journal *Pediatrics* published excerpts from the 1830 children's book *Book of Accidents: Designed For Young Children*. Each issue contained one selection from *Accidents* with a total of fifteen or sixteen different categories of injury that might befall an English child of that day. The section "Being Tossed by a Bull" is the only topic not useful in a city practice. My wife favors the one on "Troubling the Cook"—admonitions to avoid being underfoot and receiving burns from scalding liquids. I'd always been interested in children's books, since my work concerns child life and health. But I hadn't been a collector until *Book of Accidents* came to my attention.

At that juncture, he handed me a photocopy of "Cardiothoracic Injuries," an article he had written that used text and illustrations from *Accidents* as both literary and historic reference. This collector has seen, shrewdly, how the timelessness of an old children's book reinforces the message of the universality of accidents to children and thus increases the success of his efforts to prevent, as well as heal, such juvenile physical trauma. Now, when Dr. Othersen travels, visits to antiquarian bookshops come second only to work.

So far our tales have been glimpses of hobbyists at pleasure from which I've drawn some nonscientific conclusions. For these final stories, I shift to the professionals, those institutional managers and collection builders who serve our enlightened self-interest. My summary features two individuals who are personal collectors as well. These women live and work surrounded by collections they have participated in building over years of time and careers. One is a national, even international figure sitting at the center of a national commitment to children's literature. The other's current domain typifies a resource available to most of America—the children's room of a public library. Though different, both possess the generic requisites of long service, which turns good minds into voluminous, subject-specific databases; excellent networking skills; consummate dedication; and responsive interest in this book. Margaret N. Coughlan is one and Barbara Widem the other.

Peggy Coughlan is the person who, now that Virginia Haviland is gone, stores in her head America's largest databank of both critical and research knowledge of children's literature and its organizations and institutions. When asked for the rationale behind the contents of her office shelves, which held few glowers, her answer was, "To corral and protect single copies that would otherwise be shelved in the general stack area." I pulled out *Dollikin's Party* by Frances Louise Heroy (New York: Cupples & Leon, 1900) tied together with archival red cord and marked "Microfilm Entire." Another protectee was *The Chinese Mother Goose*, translated and illustrated by Isaac Taylor Headland of Peking University (New York: Fleming Revell Co., 1909). Being used in her work of answering research queries was the one glower I found, a first edition of Arnold Lobel's *The Book of Pigericks* (Harper & Row, 1983). A selection of Tom Swift and Carolyn Keene titles represented her personal collecting choices.

A *New Yorker* cartoon (August 13, 1984) tacked above Coughlan's computer gave a visual metaphor for her work. It pictures a door marked JUVENILE BOOKS and a secretary announcing to the editor, "A Mr. Squirrel Nutkin and a Mrs. Tiggy Winkle are here to see you." This is how Coughlan described her career at the Library of Congress to me:

> Over the years I assisted Virginia Haviland with such publications as *Children's Literature: A Guide to Prose, Poetry and Pictures*, and compiled bibliographies such as *From Africa to the United States*, contributed to Brian Alderson's *Penguin Companion to Children's Literature*, and acted as consultant for D. L. Kirkpatrick's *Twentieth Century Children's Writers* and for Carpenter and Prichard's *Oxford Companion to Children's Literature* and the fifth volume of *Junior Authors*.

Reached by a storybook circular staircase, Coughlan's office and that for Dr. Sybille A. Jagusch, Chief of the Children's Literature Center, are now to be found in a spectacular new temporary location. Balconies ring the newly decorated Main Reading Room and the Center perches on the top balcony under the painted and gilded 125-foot-high domed ceiling. Anyone subject to vertigo—beware! There are no glass walls. The almost-overtaken-by-books offices hold that part of the subject collection deemed to be "desk reference", a selection of trade books used in compiling their "best books" lists, and ephemera such as dealers' catalogs. The rest of the collection is shelved in the general stack area, and rareties are to be found in the Rare Book Division.

Nine months after *American Libraries* had published my request for information from collectors and collection managers, Barbara Widem telephoned me and launched into impassioned details of her 160-piece collection of Noah's Ark items. "Where are you?" I countered, and heard that she was head of children's services in the Kensington Park branch of the Montgomery County Public Library—the branch nearest to my home in Maryland. Now I had before me the example of a wanting-to-be-counted, active-plus collector, in a management position in a public library children's room—and near enough to interview in person! We began with her passion for Noah's Ark. Part of the fun is that the uninitiated have no idea of the volume and breadth of formats available to the collector. The genre's charm combines the power of the Bible story with the endless appeal of illustrations of the creatures— two by two. Widem's enthusiastic detailing went back into history with medieval carved arks and forward with a set by Tupperware and toys by Discovery Toys. A friend had recalled a Noah's Ark carving on the end of one of the stalls in the choir of the Washington National Cathedral, which I now had as an item to give to Widem, who immediately planned to ask permission to cast it from the wood carving or at least use high-tech photography.

Now I felt I could ask questions about her role as a children's librarian. Did fellow collectors really use her branch collection in their collecting research? Yes, indeed. And because she is a hobbyist herself, what librarians term a "reference interview"—finding out what the patron really wants to know—proceeds without impediment. I asked what people have come to research. One example she gave me concerned Laura Ingalls Wilder collectors who knew only the Garth Williams illustrations and fell upon early copies with the original art by Helen Sewell. Her branch collection held early editions of Marguerite De Angeli's now out-of-print Pennsylvania Dutch country books that provided answers to De Angeli collectors. Widem made sure that the children's literature reference collection fared well in her acquisition budget, too. She mentioned the early editions of *Children and Books* (Arbuthnot) and all issues and publications of *The Horn Book Magazine* as being in demand by researching collectors, and beyond the resources at Kensington Park, available through the network of branches in the Montgomery County Public Library System.

In addition to being professionally attuned to the current needs of all users, Widem brings forty-three years in professional children's librarianship to her work. By the old-fashioned measure of thirty-three years, that's over a generation, and, by one current measure—the four years of one presidential term—it's ten generations of accumulated children's literature lore and one-on-one experience. During those years Widem has found innumerable ways to make personal collecting serve professional life. Parts of her collection travel to give substance to show-and-tell events within both the library and the community. At one presentation to a senior citizen's group, she used the "Only Connect" theme of *Mary Poppins* author Pamela Travers as a common language, and the grandparents grasped it. They understood how their memories—either made tangible in toys and books, or in recollections of such—could serve to create generational connections to enrich the lives of actual or "adopted" grandchildren. Others, with bookish interests, learned ways that these thought-to-be-past parts of their lives could activate a satisfying collecting hobby whose other connections would be the pleasure of new friendships.

Each unit of our collection tells two stories—that depicted in the book by its author or illustrator; and the one that describes how we came to make it part of our collecting design. Each philosophic musing or collector's portrait holds one verity of the unknown and unknowable story that history will tell whole as *Children's Book Collecting*. To begin her essay in *Celebrating Children's Books*, Paula Fox writes: "Literature is the province of imagination, and stories, in whatever guise, are meditations on life. Goethe wrote that supreme imagining is the effort to grasp truth through imagination. It does not consist in making things different but in trying to discover them as they are" (Hearne, p. 24). I hope that these glimpses of the conflicts of choice, the satisfactions of unities assembled, and the rainbows of treasured human connections have fashioned a true tale—of collecting joy.

10

Human beings pay very little attention to what is told them unless they know something about it already.
—Christopher Morley, *The Haunted Bookshop*

Printed Helpers:
A Directory of Resources

Network and scholarship will always be prime tools for avoiding regrettable rediscovery of the collecting wheel. In serving as a guide to published scholarly resources, this chapter re-states and particularizes the value of reliance on the help to be found within both library reference departments and children's rooms and the dealer community. Precious time, money, and shelf space can be saved. Geographic specifics determine how well those libraries and dealers near you can meet your information needs—in person or by using the telephone reference service most libraries provide. What this chapter provides is a place to begin your research. Armed with it, you are prepared to have these book people assist you.

How can dealers help? They must maintain personal collections of reference sources to support their business. How they will view sharing these depends upon your dealer-customer relationship. But, barring a bazaar bargain, dealers are your best source for purchasing an out-of-print reference book and also for hearing about the newest author or illustrator bibliography.

This chapter is organized to follow the arrangement of information on a library record—card or computer. It aims to be representative, not exhaustive, and lists both standards and new works. Where the sources will most likely be used within the reference department of a public, academic, or special library and are familiar to reference librarians, only the title is given. That is all that is needed to locate a book through a card or online catalog and thus obtain shelf position and full bibliographic information. The know-how of reference librarians will help you widen or deepen your search. For other books, author (or editor or compiler), publisher, and date of publication are given; enough for you to borrow from a library or buy from a bookseller.

There is enough substantial help for you in the specialized, subject-classified reference sources with comprehensive coverage throughout the field of children's literature to recommend purchase. The best known of these were prepared by Virginia Haviland and published by the Library of Congress in three volumes: *Children's Literature: A Guide to Reference Sources*, 1966, with supplements in 1972 and 1977. *Books in Print 1992* shows one for 1982 and all as available, but this is not correct. The first volume, known as the "blue" one, is available free to "qualified" persons who address their request to the Center for the Book, Library of Congress, Washington, D.C. 20540. The "red" (1972) and "green" (1977) volumes are out of print and the 1982 update never got beyond printer's proofs. These are still available in libraries, and the red and green volumes are worth seeking on the o.p. market. Another reliable example is *Children's Literature: An Annotated Bibliography of History and Criticism*, edited by Suzanne Rahn (Garland Publishing, 1981).

Substantial help waits for you in an often underrated source, a general encyclopedia. Do use its articles on children's literature and the bibliographies at the end of the articles. More personal assistance awaits you in *Children and Books, 8th edition* (1991), edited by Zena Sutherland and May Hill Arbuthnot and published by Scott, Foresman; *Children's Literature in the Elementary School, 4th edition*, edited by Charlotte S. Huck, Susan Hepler, and Janet Hickman, (Holt, Rinehart and Winston, 1979); and, for most recent titles, "Reference Roundup," an occasional list in *School Library Journal*, and "Of Interest to Adults" in *The Horn Book Magazine*.

• To find concise biographical data on authors and illustrators consult the children's literature volumes from *The Dictionary of Literary Biography* (Gale Research): Volume 42, *American Writers for Children Before 1900* (1985); Volume 52, *American Writers for Children Since 1960: Fiction* (1986); and Volume 61, *American Writers for Children Since 1960: Poets, Illustrators, and Non-Fiction Authors* (1987); *Twentieth Century Children's Writers* (St. James Press, 1989); *Something About the Author; Junior Authors and Illustrators*; and *The Art of Art for Children's Books* by Diana Klemin (Crown, 1966).

• For in-depth knowledge of an author or illustrator look for biographies such as: *Margaret Wise Brown: Awakened by the Moon* by Leonard S. Marcus

(Beacon, 1992); *Arthur Rackham: A Biography* by James Hamilton (Little, Brown, 1990); *Beatrix Potter's Art* by Anne Stevenson Hobbs (Warne, 1990); *Dr. Seuss* by Ruth MacDonald (Twayne, 1989); *Jessie Wilcox Smith: American Illustrator* by Edward D. Nudelman (Pelican, 1990); and *The Illustrators of Alice in Wonderland and Through the Looking Glass* by Graham Ovenden (St. Martin's, 1972). Other biographies are *The Brandywine Tradition* by Henry C. Pitz (Houghton Mifflin, 1969); *Arnold Lobel* by George Shannon (Twayne, 1990); and *The Art of Babar: The Work of Jean and Laurent de Brunhoff* by Nicholas Fox Weber (Abrams, 1989). Walck published a worthwhile monograph series on major authors and illustrators, each by a different author, such as *Howard Pyle* by E. Nesbit, 1966; *C. S. Lewis* (1963), *J. M. Barrie* (1960) and *Andrew Lang* (1962) by Roger Lancelyn Green; and *Lucy Boston* by Jasper Rose, 1965.

Bibliographies for individual authors seem slow to be published. If you become an expert, at least "desktop" publish your information. *Jessie Wilcox Smith: A Bibliography* by Edward D. Nudelman (Pelican, 1989), is proof of what time, bibliographic scholarship, and money can produce. *Thornton W. Burgess: A Book, Magazine and Newspaper Bibliography* by Michael W. Dowhan, Jr. (Carleton, 1990) is a fully detailed, lightly illustrated bibliography by a dedicated Burgess scholar.

• To read speeches of medalists look for the series published by *The Horn Book* that began in 1955. The latest is the *1986 Newbery and Caldecott Medal Books*, edited by Lee Kingman. *The Horn Book* publishes these speeches each year.

• To find out more about a book for which you know author and/or title there are two lines of access—online and print. Many libraries offer patrons access to OCLC, an acronym that originally stood for Ohio College Library Center and now for Online Computer Library Center. This electronic database holds cataloging records (and locations of libraries) for over 25 million items. It is strongest in material prior to 1970. For help in print, try first *Fiction, Folklore, Fantasy and Poetry for Children, 1876–1985*; *Books in Print, 1948–*, an author-title-subject catalog; *Cumulative Book Index, 1898–*, a world list of books in English; *The National Union Catalog*, an author catalog of the holdings of the Library of Congress, especially valuable for older titles; *Publisher's Trade List Annual, 1873–*, a listing of active titles and forthcoming publications of 2,000 American and some Canadian publishers.

• The following are the great bibliographies plus some personal preferences: *A Bibliography of American Children's Books Printed Prior to 1820* compiled by d'Alte Welch (American Antiquarian Society and Barre Publishers, 1972); *From Peter Parley to Penrod* by Jacob Blanck (Mark Press, 1974); *Les Livres de L'Enfance du XV au XIX Siècle* compiled by K. A. Gumachian (Gumachian et Compagnie, Paris, 1931, 2 volumes); *The Osborne Collection of Early Children's Books, 1566–1910* compiled by Judith St. John (Toronto Public Library, 1958, 1975); *Early American Children's Books* compiled by A. S. W. Rosenbach (Southworth Press, 1933, reprinted by Kraus in 1966); H. W. Wilson's *Children's Catalog*; *They Wrote for Children Too: An Annotated Bibliography of Children's Literature by Famous Writers for Adults* compiled by Marilyn Fain Apseloff (Greenwood, 1989).

• If you are collecting by subject, these will help: *Subject Guide to Books in Print, 1957—; American History in Juvenile Books* by Seymour Metzner (Wilson, 1966); *A to Zoo: Subject Access to Children's Books* by Carolyn W. and John A. Lima (Bowker, 1989).

• To learn more about your collecting focus or genre consult books like these: *Index to Fairy Tales: Including Folklore, Legends and Myths in Collections,* compiled by Norma Olin Ireland (Faxon, 1973–77); *A Reference Guide to Historical Fiction for Children and Young Adults* by Lynda G. Adamson (Greenwood, 1987); *American Picturebooks: From Noah's Ark to the Beast Within* by Barbara Bader (Macmillan, 1976); *Anatomy of Wonder: A Critical Guide to Science Fiction* by Neil Barron (Bowker, 1981); *The Fantasy Tradition in American Literature from Irvin to LeGuin* by Brian Atterbery (Indiana, 1980); *Children of the Series and How They Grew, or, A Century of Heroines and Heroes, Romantic, Comic and Moral* by Faye Kensinger (Bowling Green, 1987); *Stratemeyer Pseudonyms and Series Books: An Annotated Checklist of Stratemeyer and Stratemeyer Syndicate Publications,* compiled and edited by Deidre Johnson (Greenwood, 1982); *You're A Brick, Angela! A New Look at Girls' Fiction from 1830 to 1975* by Mary Cadogan and Patricia Craig (Gollancz, 1976); *Beyond the Looking Glass: Extraordinary Works of Fairy Tales and Fantasy* by Jonathan Cott (Stonehill/Bowker, 1973); *The Bright Face of Danger* by Margery Fisher (Horn Book, 1986); *Nonsense Literature for Children: Aesop to Seuss* by Celia Anderson and Marilyn Fain Apseloff (LPP/Shoe String, 1989); *Horse Stories: An Annotated Bibliography of Books for All Ages* by Terri A. Wear (Scarecrow, 1987); *The Encyclopedia of American Comics: From 1897 to the Present,* edited by Ron Goulart (Facts on File, 1991); *The Prydain Companion: A Reference Guide to Lloyd Alexander's Prydain Chronicles* by Michael O. Tunnell (Greenwood, 1988); *Before Oz: Juvenile Fantasy Stories from Nineteenth Century America* edited by Mark I. West (Archon/Shoe String, 1989).

• If you are collecting Little Golden Books, these will help: *Bibliography of Little Golden Books* compiled by Dolores B. Jones (Greenwood, 1989); and *Collecting Little Golden Books* by Steve Santi (Books Americana, 1989).

• To find information about the characters in children's books consult *Children's Books: A Treasury of the Familiar Characters of Childhood* by

Margery Fisher (Holt, Rinehart and Winston, 1975). For the *Oz* series, see *Who's Who in Oz* by Jack Snow in collaboration with Professor H. M. Woggelbug, Dean of the Royal College of Oz (Reilly & Lee, 1954).

• To locate special collections consult *The American Library Directory*, which is published annually in two volumes. Volume 2 has useful sections in its backmatter on library information networks, library schools (which notes courses in children's literature), and state library systems; and *Subject Collections* compiled by Lee Ash (William G. Miller, 1985). Also use *Subject Collections in Children's Literature* (Bowker, 1969) and *Special Collections in Children's Literature* (American Library Association, 1982), both edited by Carolyn W. Field. Online you can search the DIALOG database with a key subject or subjects (i.e., "Children") and retrieve the names of libraries listing relevant special collections in *The American Library Directory*. These will give you the names and addresses to write to for collection hours, requirements, and title availability for any planned visits.

• To increase your knowledge of one particular title there are annotated editions such as *The Annotated Mother Goose* by William S. and Ceil Baring-Gould (Clarkson N. Potter, 1962); *The Annotated Black Beauty* by Ellen B. Wells (J. Allen, 1989); and *The Annotated Alice* by Lewis Carroll with introduction and notes by Martin Gardner (Clarkson Potter, 1960).

• To locate periodical information use an index with subject breakdowns, such as *Ulrich's International Periodicals Directory*, that can help you find a specialized journal in order to subscribe or write for a particular issue. These three periodicals are representative of those for juvenile book collectors: *Martha's Kidlit Newsletter*, P.O. Box 1488, Ames, IA 50010; *The Mystery and Adventure Series Review*, Box 3488, Tucson, AZ 85722; and *The Yellowback Library* (also devoted to series collecting), P.O. Box 36172, Des Moines, IA 50315.

• For access to articles in periodicals search the general *Reader's Guide to Periodical Literature*, 1900–, *Library Literature*, 1921–, compiled by Serena Day; and *The Horn Book Index, 1924–1989* (Oryx Press, 1990).

• To find and learn more about book reviews consult *Book Review Digest*, 1905– for general coverage with excerpts; *Children's Book Review Index—Master Cumulation 1969–1981*, edited by Gary C. Tarbert (Gale, 1985); *Children's Literature Review: Excerpts from Critical Commentaries on Juvenile and Young People's Authors and Their Books*, Volume 1, edited by Gerard J. Senick (Gale, 1976); *The Horn Book Guide to Children's and Young Adult's Books* (which has a subject index); *The Rise of Children's Book Reviewing in America, 1865–1881* by Richard L. Darling (Bowker, 1968); and reviewing media such as *Booklist*, *The Bulletin of the Center for Children's Books*, *The Horn Book Magazine*, *School Library Journal*, *Library Journal*, *Kirkus Re-*

views, *Publishers Weekly*, *Voice of Youth Advocates* (VOYA), *Library Talk*, *The Book Report*, and others. Back files of these magazines can possibly be found in public libraries, and certainly in specialized collections such as graduate library schools and schools of education. Current addresses are in *Ulrich's*.

• For current pricing consult the following books, but do test published data with personal observation. *Price List for Children's and Illustrated Books for the Years 1880–1940* is a 1990 publication, computer-produced and sorted both by artist and author. It is available from the compiler, E. Lee Baumgarten, Rt. 2, Box 216, Martinsburg, VA 25401. His figures come from dealer's catalogs and auction "prices realized." The introductory text is clear and relevant. For England, see *Children's Modern First Editions: Their Value to Collectors* by Joseph Connolly (Macdonald Orbis, 1988). Otherwise, there are the general "standards": *American Book Prices Current*, *The Used Book Price Guide* by Mildred S. Mandeville; *The Book Collector's Handbook of Values* by Van Allen Bradley (Putnam, 1982), and its successor, *Collected Books: The Guide to Values* by Allen and Patricia Ahearn (Putnam, 1991); as well as dealers' catalogs. Price guides should give full edition description.

• To find first edition identification by publisher use *A Pocket Guide to the Identification of First Editions* by Bill McBride (McBride, 1985); or *A First Edition?* by Edward N. Zempel and Linda A. Verkler (Spoon River, 1985).

• To keep abreast of current publishing see the magazine *Publishers Weekly* (1872–) for news about titles, trends, companies, and persons in all areas of the business and profession of books. *PW* features extensive listings and reviews of forthcoming books.

• To learn more about historical context consult the "Children's Literature" articles in general encyclopedias which are often underrated as starting points. Also try *Written for Children* by John Rowe Townsend (Lippincott, 1974); *The Oxford Companion to Children's Literature* by Humphrey Carpenter and Mari Prichard (Oxford, 1987); *Masterworks of Children's Literature, Volumes 1 and 2, 1550–c.1739: The Early Years* by Francelia Butler (Stonehill/Chelsea House, 1983), (Volumes 3–8 cover up to the 20th century).

• To learn more about the relationship between childhood and books, try *Centuries of Childhood* by Philippe Ariès (Jonathan Cape, 1962); *The New Republic of Childhood: A Critical Guide to Canadian Children's Literature in English* by Sheila Egoff and Judith Saltman (Oxford, 1990); *A Moral Tale: Children's Fiction and American Culture 1820–1860* by Anne Scott MacLeod (Archon/Shoe String, 1975); *Books Are by People: Interviews with 104 Authors and Illustrators of Books for Young Children* by Lee Bennett Hopkins (Citation, 1969); *From Dr. Mather to Dr. Seuss: 200 Years of American Books for Children* by Mary Lystad (G.K. Hall, 1980); and *Engines of Destruction,*

Mischief and Magic: Children's Literature in England from Its Beginning to 1839 by Mary V. Jackson (Nebraska, 1990), the first in a projected series.

• To find dealer information consult: *American Book Trade Directory*; *AB Bookman's Weekly*, especially the annual November Special Children's Books issue; *AB 1990–91 Bookman's Yearbook: Book Dealers in North America* (P.O. Box AB, Clifton, NJ 07015); *Antiquarian Booksellers Association of America Membership Directory* (Antiquarian Booksellers Association of America, 40 Rockefeller Plaza, New York, NY 10020). ABAA also issues regional directories, and state directories put out by state associations can be had through a dealer in the desired state. Occasional lists are published by *Book Source Monthly*, (P.O. Box 567, Cazenovia, NY 13035-0567) and most trade publications. All antiquarian book trade and book collecting journals include some ads for children's book dealers.

• To find the best lists of firms holding book and manuscript sales consult the various annual volumes of *American Book Prices Current, Book Auction Records, American Book Trade Directory*, and trade journals such as *AB Bookman's Weekly* and *Book Source Monthly*. A good account of American book auctions is to be found in George L. McKay's *American Book Auction Catalogues, 1713–1934: A Union List* (New York Public Library, 1937).

• To learn more about juvenile illustration, consult such titles as *Ways of the Illustrator: Visual Communications in Children's Literature* by Joseph H. Schwarcz (American Library Association, 1992); *Writing with Pictures: How to Write and Illustrate Children's Books* by Uri Shulevitz (Watson-Guptill, 1985); and *American Picturebooks: From Noah's Ark to the Beast Within* by Barbara Bader (Macmillan, 1976).

• For help with preservation write to Ellen Wells, Smithsonian Institution Libraries, Washington, D.C. 20560 for the 24-page, free *Book Collecting and Care of Books*.

• For poetry help use *Granger's Index to Poetry*, a general index. Sutherland and Arbuthnot and Huck et al. will be very helpful, as will *Climb Into the Bell Tower: Essays on Poetry* by Myra Cohn Livingston (HarperCollins, 1990), and *Pass the Poetry Please* by Lee Bennett Hopkins (Harper, 1987).

• To join fellow book collectors write to: American Book Collectors of Children's Literature, c/o Billie Levy, 7 Craigmoor Road, West Hartford, CT 06107; or National Book Collector's Society, Suite 349, 65 High Ridge Road, Stamford, CT 06905.

• To obtain library supply catalogs to buy storage furniture, book covers, etc., write to these firms: Demco, P.O. Box 7488, Madison, WI 5307-7488; Gaylord Brothers, Box 4902, Syracuse, NY 13221-4901; and Highsmith

Company, W5527, Highway 106, P.O. Box 800, Fort Atkinson, WI 53538-0800.

• To find trade show information consult *Antiquarian Book Fair and Paper Show Directory 1991*, compiled by James A. Visbeck (Isaiah Thomas Books, 1991). Its calendar lists trade, bookseller, and collector association shows for the U.S. and Canada. All general and specialized book journals carry some of this information.

• To plan ahead to attend *American Library Association Conferences* note these:

	Midwinter Conference	Annual Conference
1993	Denver, January 23–26	New Orleans, June 26–29
1994	Los Angeles, January 15–18	Miami, June 25–28
1995	Cincinnati, January 21–24	Chicago, June 24–27
1996	San Antonio, January 20–23	Orlando, June 22–25
1997	New Orleans, January 11–14	San Francisco, June 28–July 1
1998	Denver, January 24–27	Washington, D.C., June 27–30

I hope that this help will increase your joy in biblio-love—the second time around!

Appendix Guidelines for Cataloging Children's Books

Children's books in general, and early children's books in particular, have certain characteristics that distinguish them from the majority of adult books. In the first place, they are usually better known by their titles than by their authors—at least to their readers. In the second place, they were all too frequently issued without date of publication. Anyone cataloging a collection with a subject specialization wants to bring out the details that make that collection of books special, and most cataloging codes are meant for general application.

These considerations can make identification and recording very difficult for the nonprofessional—the person who needs to analyze and record her own collection to bring out hidden facts or relationships useful to herself and fellow collectors.

Cataloging is the making of a record of a collection, item by item. Its simplest form could be just a list of titles, and it may be expanded to include detailed facts about each book's physical attributes (points) until the catalog becomes a bibliography.

First decide on the type of catalog to be produced:

1. An author catalog. All entries made under the name of the author.
2. A subject catalog. All entries made under the subject of the book.
3. A title catalog. All entries made under the title of the book.
4. A combination of all three—like an index. This is known as a dictionary catalog.

5. A chronological catalog. All entries made by date of publication. Purchase date would be a useful addition.

The entry should contain the following:

1. Heading
2. Transcription of the title page
3. Collation
4. Name of series
5. Binding
6. Notes

Such entries may be on cards, slips, or computer. PROCITE is an example of a computer program designed for cataloging use. In the following examples an author catalog is described:

I. Heading
   This will consist of the name of the author (surname first). The author is the person, or corporate body responsible for the book. If only the initials of the first names are given, full names should be ascertained, if possible, and given in the heading. If no author for the book can be ascertained, the main entry should be under the first word of the title other than "A," "An," or "The." To differentiate between authors having the same surnames, add the author's title or dates of birth and/or death. Some special cases:
   A. Joint authorship. Enter under the name of the first author mentioned on the title page, and make cross-references for the others if there are not more than two.
   B. Pseudonyms. Books written under pen names or pseudonyms should be entered under the author's real name if this is known. If the pseudonym is better known it should be used for the main entry, with a cross-reference to whichever name is not used, e.g., CARROLL, Lewis, with reference to DODGSON, Charles Lutwidge.
   C. Change of name. Where a change of name takes place, for instance upon marriage, it is still desirable to keep the person's works together in the catalog. The choice should be made between the earliest, the best known, or the latest name. Once this decision is made all that person's works should be entered in the one place. A cross-reference should be made to the form of the name not used.

II. Transcription of the title page. This should record exactly what appears on the title page. The following chart provides an example.

	Entry	*Example*
A.	Title	*Hans Brinker*
B.	Subtitle or alternative title	or, *The Silver Skates,* A Story of Life in Holland
C.	Authorship	by Mary Mapes Dodge
	Single author or joint authors, editor, joint editors, or translator.	
D.	Illustrator	Illustrated by F. O. C. Darley and Thomas Nast
E.	Edition statement	None
F.	Imprint	Place of Publication: New York
		Name of publisher:
		James O'Kane
		Date of publication: 1865

III. Collation
- A. Pagination. Notes of plates, illustrations, maps, plans, etc.
  1. A publication with leaves printed on both sides is described in terms of pages, e.g., 64p.
  2. A publication with leaves printed on one side only is described in terms of leaves, e.g., 32ll.
  3. Whenever pagination includes unnumbered pages or leaves, record these in square brackets e.g., [64]p.
  4. Always draw a distinction between the notation for printed leaves or pages in a book, and leaves of plates, etc.

  This can present a variety of difficulties related to the detail with which the cataloger desires to record the collection, as noted below.
- B. Plates. A plate is a page that does not form part of either the preliminary or main sequence of pages, physically or in enumeration. It is usually, though not always, made of a different type of paper from that in the rest of the publication. In the catalog entry the number of plates is given at the end of the sequence of pagination. *Front.* is an abbreviation for frontispiece; *port.* for portrait:

  64p., front. 3 plates

  64p., front. (port.), 3 plates

  64 p., front. (map), 3 plates
  1. Colored plates should be so described:

     64p., 3 col. plates

     64p., col. front., 3 col. plates
  2. Folded plates (or occasionally folded leaves) should also be described.

C. Illustrations
   1. The abbreviation "ill." is used to describe all types of illustrative matter in the text pages, unless particular types in the work are considered important enough to be specifically designated. In the latter case they are designated by specific terms, in alphabetical order, e.g., diagrs., maps, plans, ports., etc.
   2. Specify types of illustrations where this can be ascertained, e.g., engravings, woodcuts, hand-col. engravings, etc.
   3. The number of illustrations may be recorded.
D. Size. Record in centimeters to the next full centimeter, giving height first and then width.

IV. Series
The series statement gives the information that a work is part of a series of publications. The name of the series is usually enclosed in parentheses, e.g., (Golden Book Series).

V. Binding
The binding of children's books should be regarded as an integral part of their description, first because the binding was often devised to give a particular impression to the purchaser, and second because a careful description may give help toward dating the book or relating it to other editions. Without doubt, through, description of bindings—whether leather, cloth, or paper—presents many difficulties not possible to describe in an introductory explanation. It is best, however, to be sure of one's facts before recording descriptions.

VI. Notes
These are made to assist in identification, especially of anonymous and pseudonymous authors and in dating. Many children's books carry no date, and therefore evidence for dating may need to be cited from other sources (e.g., "inscription dated 1882," "Lippincott was at this address from — to — ," etc.).

Notes may relate to all or any of the following: the title (e.g., variant titles); author; edition; imprint; the collation (e.g., if plates are dated or missing); the relationship with other publications (e.g., "based on . . ."); date of original publication; nature, scope, language, or literary form of the work; contents, including the presence (and pagination) of bound-in publisher's catalogs.

‖ EXAMPLE OF A CATALOG ENTRY

Here is an example of a catalog entry by author name in card format for a Victorian gift book using separate paragraphs for each part of the catalog description. Within each paragraph punctuate as for sentences. Make separate cards with heading for second author, title, etc., if desired.

(Header)	KIRBY, Mary, 1817–1893
(Title page)	*The Talking bird; or, the little girl who knew what was going to happen.* By Mary and Elizabeth Kirby, Authors of "The Discontented Children," "Stories from the Classics," etc. With illustrations by Hablot K. Browne [Phiz.] London: Grant and Griffith. . . Corner of St. Paul's Churchyard. 1856
(Collation and size)	[5] 6–96pp., front., 3 pl. by N. T. Green after H. K. Browne. 16.7 x 12 cm.
(Binding)	Dark green honeycomb-grain cloth blocked in blind and gilt, the diamond-shaped pictorial title design in gilt on the front board is signed J[ohn] L[eighton].
(Notes)	Copy lacks front free endpaper. Bound in at the end is a 32-page catalog of the "Original Juvenile Library . . . New and Popular Works principally for the young," published by Griffith and Farran. Both book and catalog are printed by Wertheimer & Co., Circus Place, Finsbury Circus. See Osborne Catalog p. 992, where Mary Kirby is given her married name of Gregg, and where the engraver's name has been misread as "Galen" and only two plates are noted.

No real problems are encountered here. Purists may argue that details about the publisher's catalog and the printer should, if included, go in the collation and not the note. The reference to the Osborne copy of the book shows the value of recording information about further copies of apparently identical editions. (The Osborne decision to catalog the book under "Gregg"—even though Mary Kirby did not marry until 1860—arises from its cataloging policy as a whole and the detailed knowledge it often has of the names of married and pseudonymous authors.)

Glossary

What follows is a practical guide to the terminology most useful to collectors of children's books, based on *The Bookman's Glossary*. The most complete list is contained in John Carter's *ABC for Book Collectors*.

ABA. Antiquarian Booksellers' Association (England); also the American Booksellers' Association, the major association for the retail book trade in this country.

ABAA. Antiquarian Bookseller's Association of America.

ADDED ENTRY. In cataloging, a secondary access point. Where author is used as main entry, there may be added entries for title, subject, series, editor, translator, etc.

ADDENDA. (sing. addendum). Brief additional data added to a book at the back or on a separate sheet laid in. *See also* Appendix; Errata.

ADHESIVE BINDING. The fastening of pages into a book, and the cover onto a book, by means of a layer of glue along the spine. Also called perfect binding. In such bindings, only the glue holds the book together.

ADVANCE COPY. A copy for booksellers and reviewers, either bound in paperwraps or a copy of the trade edition with a review slip laid in.

THE AMERICAN LIBRARY ASSOCIATION, ALA. The largest professional association of librarians and others interested in the educational and cultural responsibilities of libraries. Founded in 1876.

ALS. Autographed Letter Signed, all in the author's hand.

ALTERNATIVE TITLE. Subtitle introduced by "or" or its equivalent, e.g., *Hans Brinker, or The Silver Skates*. *See also* Subtitle.

AMS. Autographed Manuscript Signed, all in the author's hand.

ANNOTATION. A note accompanying an entry in a bibliography or catalog, intended to describe or evaluate the work cited.

ANTIQUARIAN BOOKS. A loose term implying collectible books rather than used books. Refers to old, rare, and out of print, which covers the waterfront.

APPENDIX. Part of the back matter. Supplementary material to illustrate, enlarge on, or otherwise support the text proper.

AQUATINT. An intaglio process of etching on copper or steel plates to which acid-resistant granules have first been evenly adhered. Soft, water color effects thus become possible, alone or in combination with the line effect that characterizes etchings (q.v.).

AS ISSUED. Used to emphasize original condition or to highlight something a little unusual, such as recent books without dust wrappers.

ASSOCIATION COPY. A book that belonged to the author or that the author gave to another person with whom he was associated. The book contains some tangible identifying evidence, such as inscriptions, signatures, bookplates, letters, or photographs laid in or tipped in.

AS USUAL. A favorite term to describe defects that occur only on copies of the book the particular dealer handles, such as "lacks endpapers, as usual" or "lacks title page, as usual."

AUTHOR. The original writer or composer of a book, treatise, or document, as distinguished from an editor, compiler, or translator.

AUTHOR'S COPIES. The complimentary contractual copies, usually six or more, of the finished book given to the author by the publisher.

AUTOGRAPH. 1. In the rare book trade, letters, documents, cards, etc., written or signed with a person's own hand. 2. In the new book trade, an autographing session is a publicity device whereby an author signs copies of his book for customers in a bookshop.

BACK MATTER. The material that follows the text proper of a book. This can consist of reference matter, appendixes, addenda, author's notes, a glossary, a bibliography, or an index.

BACKSTRIP. The spine of a book.

BATTLEDORE. A form of a child's reading textbook made of varnished cardboard or paper folded or put onto a wooden "paddle" that gradually replaced the hornbook.

BIBLIO–. A combining form from Greek *biblion*, "book." Some examples are *biblioclast*, a destroyer or mutilator of books; *bibliomania*, a passion for acquiring books; and *bibliophile*, a lover of books.

BIBLIOGRAPHY. 1. The art or science of the description and history of books (their physical makeup, authorship, editions, printing, publications, etc.). 2. Loosely, the science of books; bibliology. 3. A list of works on a given subject or by a given author; the literature of a subject.

BINDING. 1. The structural materials such as thread and glue holding a book together, plus the attached cover of a book or pamphlet, which may be cloth, leather, boards, paper, or other material. 2. In book manufacturing, the process of assembling the finished book, which includes folding, gathering, collating, sewing, tipping, gluing off, trimming, rounding and backing, lining up, casing in, and, finally, jacketing.

BLIND STAMPED. Die-stamped impressions in the bindings of books that are not colored.

BLURB. 1. A laudatory comment from a review (often by another author) printed on the dust wrapper of a book, covers of a proof copy, or on a wraparound band. 2. The publisher's "selling talk" used on the jacket of a book or in an advertisement for it. Coined by Gelett Burgess in 1907 as a descriptive term for puffing one's own wares.

BOARDS. The front and back covers of the book. "In boards" describes books that have boards covered in paper rather than cloth or leather.

BOOK. "A non-periodical literary publication containing forty-nine or more pages, not counting covers" (UNESCO recommendation adopted in 1964). Broadly, any collection of leaves or pages, bound or unbound, in manuscript, reproduction, scroll, or codex form, inscribed in clay or on stone; or in many currently appearing printed forms.

BOOK CLOTH. Specially prepared cloth material used to make covers for books, probably either starch-filled, plastic-impregnated, or plastic-coated (or imitation leather). Its quality is based on number of threads per inch and their tensile strength.

BOOK COLLECTORS' CLUB. In the English-speaking world the oldest and most exclusive book collectors' club is the Roxburghe Club of London founded in 1812. The Grolier Club of New York is the oldest existing American club, founded in 1884. Most of the clubs had purposes resembling that set forth for the Grolier in its constitution: "the literary study and promotion of the arts pertaining to the production of books, including the occasional publication of books designed to illustrate, promote and encourage those arts." It was followed by the Club of Odd Volumes (Boston, 1886); the Rowfant Club (Cleveland, 1892); the Philobiblon Club (Philadelphia, 1893); the Caxton Club (Chicago, 1895); the Dibdin Club (New York, 1897). In the 20th century there was the Franklin Club of St. Louis, the Carteret Club of Newark; the Book Club of California; the Zamorano Club of Los Angeles, and so on. The Hroswitha Club, of women collectors, bibliographers, and others interested in the book arts (New York, 1944), was named for Hroswitha, a Saxon nun of the 10th century, who was a dramatist, poet (probably a book collector), and canoness of the Abbey of Gandersheim, Saxony. For us there is the American Book Collector's Club of Children's Literature. Contact at: ABC. 7 Craigmoor Rd., West Hartford, CT. 06107.

BOOK FAIR. 1. An exhibition of books and related materials, along with talks by authors and illustrators and other events. 2. A trading center for the sale of books and rights and the making of publishing and copublishing arrangements, or for the presentation of books available for sale or resale. The fairs began in the early 16th century in Frankfurt, Germany, and the major annual international one continues to be the Frankfurt Book Fair. The Bologna Book Fair in Bologna, Italy, is devoted to children's books alone.

BOOKPLATE. A label placed in a book to identify ownership. Bookplates of famous people or collections enhance a book's value. They are collected for artistic, association, or historic interest.

BOOK SCOUT. A person who travels, visiting book, antique, and collectible shops, buying items that he believes are desired by dealers, librarians, and collectors, and that he can turn over profitably.

BOOK SIZE. In the book trade designation of size was originally based on its relationship to a sheet of paper measuring about 19 x 25 inches. The rare book trade still uses a measure in inches, while present trade practice usually refers to the binding, not leaf height and library practice follows—both using centimeters.

BOOK SIZES. Standard book sizes are named as follows, with approximate heights, given in inches: Double Elephant folio, 50"; Atlas folio, 25"; Folio, 15"; Quarto (4to), 12"; Octavo (8vo), 9¾"; Duodecimo (12mo), 7¾"; Sixteenmo (16mo), 6¾";

Twenty-fourmo (24mo), 5¾"; Thirty-twomo (32mo), 5"; Forty-eightmo (48mo), 4"; Sixty-fourmo (64mo), 3".

BOOK WEEK. In the United States, usually a contraction for National Children's Book Week, a special book promotion event held annually since 1919, usually in early November. It is sponsored by the Children's Book Council, which provides posters and other promotional material for the cooperating schools, bookstores, and libraries. Several countries hold simultaneous Book Weeks. Those in England are held in library children's rooms under the sponsorship of the National Book League.

BOWDLERIZED. The text of a book altered by the expurgation of words or passages considered offensive or indelicate (by the bowdlerizer). The term stems from Dr. Thomas Bowdler (1754–1825), whose name has been associated with various such works, the most famous being *The Family Shakespeare*, first seen in Bath, England, in 1807.

BREAKER. Someone who breaks up books to sell the plates individually, or the book itself when the covers are so bad that it either has to be rebound or broken up.

BROADSIDE. A single sheet printed on one side only.

BUCKRAM. A coarse linen binding cloth.

CALLIGRAPHY. From the Greek, literally "beautiful handwriting"; handwriting as graphic art. The letter forms are both inspired and limited by the writing tool— ordinarily the broad-point pen, but also the Spencerian pen, the brush (as in oriental writing), and the crayon.

CANCEL. Literally any printed-matter change to any part of a book, but most commonly it refers to one or more pages that are substituted for existing pages in a book that has already been bound. If or when an error is found, a new, corrected page is printed (cancel, or cancel leaf), and the original page is cut out of the book, leaving a stub upon which the cancel page is glued.

CASE. A preassembled hard cover for a book that comprises the front and back covers and connecting material across the spine, and wraps around the inside pages. Case binding is hardcover binding.

CHAPBOOK. From the Anglo-Saxon root *ceap*, "trade." Small, cheap book in a paper binding, popular in England and the American colonies in the 17th and 18th centuries, containing tales, ballads, lives, tracts, and topical material. Sold by chapman, i.e., peddlers, hawkers.

CHILDREN'S BOOK WEEK. Originated through the efforts of the Boy Scouts of America. Franklin K. Mathiews, chief scout librarian, launched a campaign in a speech to the American Booksellers Association in 1913 and continued his efforts after World War I. Frederick Melcher proposed the creation of a National Book Week for Boys and Girls to ABA, and the first was held November 10 to 15 in 1919 and now is an annual early-November event.

CHIPPED. Usually used to describe the fact that small pieces on the edge of the book's paper dust wrapper have been torn off (chipped away).

CLASSFIED CATALOG. One arranged by a numeric or alphabetic notation according to subject content.

CLOTH. Describes a book's binding when the boards are cloth-covered.

COLLATE. 1. For books, to compare one copy of a book with another to see if it is the same, and also to check each page and plate to ensure that the book is complete, which is a required collecting step even with modern books. Knowledge of how books are made helps determine a book's completeness. Many bibliographies furnish enough physical information to determine completeness and edition. 2. In cataloging, "collation" describes pagination and illustration.

COLOPHON. Derived from the Greek, "finishing touch." Traditionally put on the last page to provide facts about production, author, title, date, etc. Both sides of the title page have generally superseded the colophon as an information source. In modern limited editions the colophon page describes the page that lists the type of paper, printer, and number of copies, and bears the author's signature. Colophon is also incorrectly used to mean a publisher's identifying symbol.

CONTEMPORARY. Used to describe bindings and hand-colored plates (generally of the period when the book was published) and author inscription (dated the year of publication, preferably close to publication date).

COPYRIGHT. Legal registration process that offers literary, dramatic, artistic, and musical property protection as authorized by the United States Consitution, securing for authors the exclusive right to their respective writings for stated limited time periods.

COVERS. The book's binding, most particularly the front and back panels.

COVERS BOUND IN. Original cloth covers included as pages at the end of the book or as endpapers when a new binding is made.

CREDIT LINE. A statement giving the name of the photographer, artist, author, agency, or publication responsible for the picture, photograph, article, or quotation being used.

CROSS-REFERENCE. A reference made between parts of a book or between catalog entries.

CUMULATIVE INDEX. An index in periodical form that combines successively the entries of earlier issues or volumes into a single index.

CUT EDGES. Page edges machine-trimmed, as opposed to leaving them roughly cut or totally uncut.

CUTS. Sometimes used to mean any printed illustrations.

CWO. Check or cash with order.

DECKLE EDGE. The rough edge on a sheet of paper where the pulp flowed under the frame while still liquid. These rough edges are often left untrimmed in the making of books from handmade paper. In machine-made paper, deckle is not obtainable on four sides, but a deckle effect can be imitated.

DEDICATION. A copy of a book with the author's presentation inscription to the person or persons to whom the book was dedicated.

DEWEY DECIMAL CLASSIFICATION. A system of book classification with a decimal basis, devised by Melvil Dewey in 1876 and much used in public and school libraries. The main sections, preceding the decimal point are: 000 General Works; 100 Philosophy; 200 Religion; 300 Social Sciences; 400 Language; 500 Pure Science; 600 Technology; 700 The Arts; 800 Literature; 900 History.

DICTIONARY CATALOG. One in which all entries (e.g., author, title, subject) are arranged in a single alphabetical sequence (in contrast to a classified, or subject-arranged, catalog).

DIME NOVEL. A paper-covered work of sensational American fiction, published in series and sold for a dime.

DUST JACKET. The paper (or acetate) cover folded over a bound book, more to provide a display space for printed and illustrative material that sometimes includes biographical information about the author and short critical notices about the book to promote its visibility and sale than to protect it from dust or other enemies such as light and scratching. This makes "dust" used with "jacket" essentially archaic. Abbreviated "dj." *See also* Jacket band.

DUST WRAPPER. The paper cover, printed or pictorial, issued with the book. Also referred to as dust jacket or dust cover. Abbreviated "d.w."

EDITING. Modification of existing text by adding, deleting, moving, or changing material.

EDITION. 1. All copies of a book printed at the same time (or times). It will stand until changed by the addition of revisions substantial enough to require a notation of a second edition. 2. One of the variant forms in which a literary work is published. Differences between editions can be in text—original, revised, enlarged, corrected, etc., either by the author or a subsequent editor; or format—deluxe, library, trade, limited, paperbound, large print, illustrated, etc.

EDITOR. 1. Person in charge of selecting and organizing material to be published. 2. One who prepares for publication a work or collection of works not his own. 3. An administrator of an editorial department.

ELSE FINE. A condition description that usually follows a list of defects.

ENDPAPERS. Paper, white or colored, printed or plain, placed at the beginning and end of a book, one folded half pasted to the inside of the cover and the other bound to the rest of the pages. They fasten the book to its cover, and are not generally included in a book's pagination. Also termed lining papers and paste-downs.

EPHEMERA. Perishable productions not intended for permanency—pamphlets, posters, broadsides, advertisements, in fact almost anything printed and not readily classified elsewhere.

ERRATA. A printed page or slip of paper tipped or laid in to a book that lists and corrects mistakes and misprints found after binding.

EX LIBRIS. Latin, "from the library." 1. A book discarded from a library's collection with library markings, therefore less valuable as a collectible. 2. The words on a bookplate to indicate ownership.

FACSIMILE EDITION. An exact reproduction of an original work, often published by the institution in possession of the original.

FIRST EDITION. 1. The total number of copies produced in the first impression or printing of a book. 2. A book from this initial printing; often called a "first."

FIRST SEPARATE EDITION. First printing in book form of something published earlier with other matter—usually poems, stories, or essays that previously appeared in magazines, anthologies, or collections of the same author's works. Often termed a "separate."

FIRST THUS. Not a first edition, but something is new. It may be revised, have a new introduction by the author or someone else, be the first publication in paperback form, by another publisher, etc.

FLY LEAF. 1. The blank page following the endpaper. 2. The endpaper itself.

FLY TITLE. *See* Half title.

FOLLOW THE FLAG. If one collects American authors, precedence would be given to American editions, even if the chronological first edition was published in England.

FONT. From the French *fondre*, to cast. A complete assortment of types of one face and size; including capitals, small capitals, lowercase letters, numerals, punctuation marks, etc.

FORE-EDGE PAINTING. A watercolor painting applied to the front page edges of the book, which have been slanted or fanned to expose a greater area. After completion, when the book is closed the painting cannot be seen.

FOREWORD. Prefatory or introductory remarks to a book by someone other than the author. *See also* Preface; Introduction.

FOXING. Discoloration on pages or page edges, usually brown or yellow, resulting from chemical reaction of certain properties in the paper to the atmosphere.

FRONTISPIECE. An illustration at the front of the book, normally facing the title page. Abbreviated as "frontis." or "front."

FRONT MATTER. The pages preceding the text of the book, which usually appear in this order: half title, frontispiece, title, copyright page, dedication, preface or foreword, table of contents, list of illustrations, introduction, acknowledgements.

GALLEY PROOFS. The first appearance of the book in type, these proofs are used for proofreading and design corrections, and are often bound up as advance publicity copies. Also termed galleys or loose galleys. The term came originally from hot-metal typesetting, where newly set type was stored in long shallow trays called galleys, which were just wide enough to hold one column of type about twenty-two inches long. Today's galleys are the result of computer typesetting and are usually divided into pages.

GATHERING. A group of book leaves formed after the printed sheet has been folded to the size of the book for sewing or gluing into the binding. Also called a signature, section, or quire, or "folded and gathered" sheets, abbreviated "f & g's."

GILT EDGES. Page edges that have been trimmed smooth and gilt or gold applied. The abbreviation "g.e." means gilt edges; "a.e.g." means all edges gilt; "g.t." means gilt top; "t.e.g." means top edge tilt.

GLASSINE. A transparent paper dust wrapper that some collectors value highly, but which certainly becomes unattractive and ill-fitting with age.

GOTHIC. 1. A style of lettering dating from the 12th century, the origin of modern black letter. 2. A romantic novel of suspense with a historical or mysterious setting.

GRAVURE. The major commercial use of intaglio printing.

GUTENBERG, JOHANNES (1397?–1468). Printer of Mainz, Germany, considered to be the first in Europe to print from movable type. Best known for his Bible.

HALF CLOTH. Binding with cloth spine and paper-covered boards.

HALF LEATHER. Binding with leather spine and the balance in cloth or paper. Also referred to as three-quarter leather when the corners are also leather-bound.

HALF TITLE. A page preceding the text containing only the title of the book. There are often two—one before (bastard or fly title) and one after the title page.

HALFTONE. A photographic technique for reproducing by optical illusion the different tonal shadings in photographs, drawings, or paintings. The continuous shadings of an original become a series of tiny dots almost invisible to the unaided eye.

HANDMADE PAPER. Paper made one sheet at a time by ladling pulp onto a sieve. The water runs through while the sieve is shaken to mix the fibers thoroughly. The pulp is prevented from running over the edge by a thin frame called the deckle. All paper was so made until about 1800, when a machine with a continuous sieve was perfected. It comes in small sizes and has no grain, and all four sides can be deckled.

HEAD AND TAIL PIECES. Small ornaments or designs printed at the beginning and end of a chapter or other division of a book.

HINGES. The junctions where the front and back covers meet the spine. John Carter's *ABC for Book Collectors* differentiates the inner and outer junctions as hinges and joints, respectively. Book dealers refer to hinges as being "weak" or "starting," which can mean anything from the endpaper starting to split to the cover actually starting to come off. If the copy is also described as "tight" or "still tight," it could be assumed the break in the paper hasn't yet weakened the binding.

HOLOGRAPH. Entirely in the handwriting of the author, used particularly for manuscripts, as the term *autograph* is used for letters. *See* A.L.S.

ILLUMINATED. Embellished with ornamental letters, scrolls, miniatures, and other designs, usually in gold and color. A feature of many ancient manuscripts and early printed books.

IMPRESSION. The copies of an edition printed at one time. For collectors, the first impression is the first edition.

IMPRINT. 1. Originally the person or firm responsible for the actual production of the book. 2. More recently the publisher, place, and date as it appears at the foot of the title page. 3. The printer's or publisher's name on the spine.

INCUNABULA. Latin for "things in the cradle." It refers to books printed from movable type before 1501. *Incunabulum* or *incunable* is used as the singular, with *incunables* as an alternative plural.

INSCRIBED COPY. A copy inscribed by the author for a particular person, not merely autographed by the author. It is often difficult to differentiate between inscribed copies and presentation copies (q.v.), and for the most part the terms seem to be used interchangeably.

INTEGRAL. Refers to a page when it is part of a gathering or signature, rather than a cancel or tipped-in leaf (q.v.).

INTERLEAVED. Condition of a book when blank leaves alternate with the printed leaves or pages.

INTERNATIONAL STANDARD BOOK NUMBER (ISBN). A unique number assigned to a book identifying one title, or edition of a title, from one specific publisher.

INTRODUCTION. A preliminary portion of a book leading up to the main subject matter. It is usually an attempt to define the organization and limits of a work; a preface (q.v.), by contrast, may explain the author's reasons for undertaking the work, his qualifications, and his indebtedness to other authorities.

ISSUE. A form of first impression important for determining edition points (q.v.). A change in issue occurs when textual changes are made after the book has been published and gone on sale. *See also* State.

JACKET. *See* Dust Jacket; Wrappers.

JACKET BAND. A strip wrapped around a book or book jacket for some promotional purpose.

JOINTS. The exterior hinges of books.

LABEL. Book title printed on a piece of other material and affixed to the spine or sides.

LAID IN. A photo, errata slip, autograph, letter, or review slip enclosed in the book but not attached to it.

LAID PAPER. Paper that, when held up to the light, shows fine parallel lines (wire marks) and crosslines (chain marks), produced naturally by the wires of the mold in handmade papers. This can be simulated in machine-made paper.

LAMINATED. Layers of two or more substances glued or adhered together. Book covers and jackets often are laminated to an outer film of clear plastic to protect their printed surfaces.

LARGE-PAPER EDITION. Produced using the same type as the regular edition but printed on larger paper, resulting in larger margins.

LEAF. A piece of paper comprising one page on the front (recto, obverse) and another on the back (verso, reverse).

LIBRARY OF CONGRESS CATALOG CARD. A printed catalog card issued by the Library of Congress for the use of libraries throughout the United States.

LIBRARY OF CONGRESS LIBRARY CLASSIFICATION. An alpha-numeric system for classifying and shelving books developed by the Library of Congress for its collections and widely used in academic and research libraries in the U.S. and abroad.

LIMITED EDITION. An edition that is limited to a small, stated number of copies, usually numbered (or lettered) and signed by the author and/or illustrator. It is not necessarily a first edition and is normally issued in a different binding than the trade edition (q.v.) and in a slipcase, sometimes referred to as a box.

LIMITED EDITIONS CLUB. American subscription book club founded in 1929 by George Macy that specializes in fine design and printing. Through its policy of using the best designers and printers, the club has furthered book arts. By putting its unique volumes into homes it has made many new collectors, both through the parent organization and the Heritage Press, which has unlimited membership.

LINING PAPERS. *See* Endpapers.

MAIN ENTRY. In a catalog or index, the entry under which full information is given, usually that for the author.

MARBLING. A hand or machine process of decorating sheets of paper, cloth, or book edges with a variety of colors in a pattern that resembles marble.

MARGINS. The areas around the edges of a page outside the main body of the printed or written matter.

MASTHEAD. A statement of the name, ownership, staff, etc., of a publication. Usually found at the head of a newspaper's editorial page or on a periodical's editorial or contents page.

MINIATURE BOOKS. A small format produced from the earliest days of printing, and in children's books from the mid-18th century. Its original purpose was practical— to create the most portable and convenient size for the Bible, prayer books, and literature classics. The dimensions vary from less than an inch square to approximately 2 x 1¼ inches.

MODERN FIRST EDITIONS. A category that seems to include all authors whose first editions were published in this century. "Twentieth-century first editions" is a much better term to define the stock of most "modern" first edition dealers.

MOVABLE TYPE. Though its actual invention was probably not that of any one man, in the mid-15th century in Mainz, Germany, Gutenberg developed the apparatus to cast type in metal. After that breakthrough printing became a business and spread throughout the world.

MOUNTED. Describes illustrations that are pasted down or lightly attached to a page. When referring to restoration of a damaged page, it means laid down on or backed with paper, gauze, or linen.

NATIONAL LIBRARY WEEK. A week-long annual promotional effort and focus of a year-round program in support of libraries, launched in 1958 and sponsored originally by the National Book Committee in cooperation with the American Library Association. When the National Book Committee discontinued operations in 1974, the program was taken over solely by the ALA.

NO DATE (N.D.). A catalog notation. In English catalogs, if the date is included on the title or copyright page, introduction, or cover, the dealer will state it: "1960." If the date does not appear in the book but the dealer knows the date, the catalog entry will state "n.d. (1960)." If the date does not appear in the book at all, but is known, the American dealer will follow the English lead and state "n.d. (1960)."

NOM DE PLUME. A pen name; a pseudonym; a writer's assumed name.

OBVERSE. The right-hand page of an open book. More commonly called the recto.

OFFPRINT. A separate printing of a section of a larger publication, generally of composite authorship, in periodicals or books. Offprints are made from the same typesetting and occasionally are given their own pagination. They normally have a separate paper cover and sometimes a special title page. They are of interest because they represent the first separate appearance of the work, although they are not really a first separate edition.

OUT OF PRINT. The publisher no longer has—and will not have—copies of the book.

OUT OF STOCK. The publisher's stock is temporarily exhausted; the book will be reprinted.

PAGE. One side of a leaf.

PAMPHLET. A small separate work issued in paperwraps.

PAPER. A sheet of matted cellulose fibers produced either by hand or machine. Book papers are made from chemically prepared wood pulp or acid-free ingredients. Paper may also be coated or uncoated, sized (for offset printing or to take pen and ink) or unsized, handmade (the only kind that is without grain, i.e., that does not bend or tear more easily in one direction than the other) or machine-made, laid or woven, etc. It is made in a variety of surface finishes from smooth to rough and dull to glossy.

PAPERBACK. A paper-covered book; also termed paperbound.

PAPER BOARDS. As used today, book covers made of stiff cardboard covered in paper.

PARCHMENT. A writing material, also used for bookbinding, made from the inner side of a split sheepskin. It was probably used as early as 1500 B.C.

PARTS. 1. Part isues. 2. Separate monthly installments of novels, published in magazine format, particularly in the 19th century.

PASTEDOWN. That half of the endpaper that lines the inner side of the cover.

PERFECT BINDING. Binding method used in most mass-market paperback books. Now many hardcover trade books are actually perfect-bound. *See also* Adhesive binding.

PICTORIAL. Describes a book with a picture on the cover.

PIRATED EDITION. One published without the consent of the author or copyright owner.

PLATES. Whole-page illustrations printed separately from the text. *See also* Cuts.

POCHOIR. In French, "stencil"; a process similar to silk screen that often uses paper stencils and applies color differently.

POINTS. 1. Anything that distinguishes one edition or state from another, such as illustrations, misprints, textual alterations, binding, advertisements, etc. 2. Measure of type size; about 1/72 of an inch.

PREFACE. A short explanatory note by the author preceding the text of a book and usually touching on the book's purpose, sources, extent, etc. *See also* Foreword; Introduction.

PRESENTATION COPY. This is a copy the author meant to sign for the recipient, usually for some special event or purpose, as opposed to a copy inscribed at the request of the recipient.

PRICE CLIPPED. Notes the fact that the price has been clipped from the corner of the dust jacket flap.

PRINTED COVER. Used to describe a dust jacket or paper cover that is only lettered (without any picture).

PRINTING. An alternative word for impression.

PRIVATELY PUBLISHED. A book that is published not for sale but for distribution by other than the normal commercial channels.

PRIVATE PRESS. A printing establishment whose owners or operators print what they like, rather than what a publisher pays them to print. Print runs are small, with books being sold to the public directly or through a publisher's organization. The motivation is more the creativity required to make a fine book than to make a profit. Some examples would include the Baskerville, Daniel, Kelmscott, Ashendene, Cuala, and Golden Cockerel presses.

PROOFS. Stages of type composition that precede the published book. The normal sequence would be galley proof, uncorrected page proof, and advance reading copy bound in paperwraps.

PROVENANCE. A record of the previous ownership of a particular copy of a book.

PUBLICATION DATE. The date the book is to be put on sale, allowing time for distribution to stores and reviewers after the actual printing is complete.

PUBLISHER. One who issues or causes to be issued books, periodicals, music, maps, software or the like. Publishing as a business apart from bookselling developed about the middle of the 19th century.

The publisher's functions consist of selecting the manuscript; acquiring publishing rights; editing the manuscript; designing the format; having the type set; ordering, purchasing, or leasing the plates; arranging for the purchase of paper and other materials, and for printing and binding; promoting and advertising; distributing; arranging for sales of subsidiary rights; paying royalties to the author; and generally undertaking the ultimate financial risk of the venture as entrepreneur.

RAG PAPER. Paper made from cotton or linen rags.

RARE. Implies the book is extremely scarce, perhaps appearing in the marketplace once every ten years or so. The degrees of rarity include *unique* (no other copy appears in a lifetime); *extremely rare* (examples seen by a specialist but once in a lifetime); *rare* (examples seen by a specialist but once in a decade; and *scarce* (examples turn up but once in a year).

REBACKED. Means the binding has been given a new spine or backstrip.

RECASED. Means the book was loose or out of its covers and it has been resewn or glued back in, usually with new endpapers.

RECTO. The front of a leaf, the right-hand page of an open book. Also called the obverse.

REGISTER. In printing, the correct position on the sheet. Register is essential when using more than one plate in color work. When there is faulty adjustment the printing is said to be "off register" or "out of register."

REISSUE. A reprint of a published work from the type, plates, or film of the original edition.

REJOINTED. Means the book has been repaired preserving the original covers, including the spine.

REMAINDER. Publishers' overstocks of titles offered at a reduced price. In many cases the edges of books sold as remainders are marked with a stamp. Remainder shelves are excellent places to find expensive reference books needed to support personal collecting interests.

REPRINT. A new printing from the same plates, or an edition in cheaper form than the original book and often issued by another publisher who specializes in such editions. Often confused with *reissue* (q.v.).

REVERSE. The back of a leaf or the page on the left of an open book. More commonly called the verso.

ROMAN. A style of lettering developed about 1500, south of the Alps, where early type designers followed the rough, humanistic handwriting of indigenous scribes.

SELF-WRAPPER. A printed or unprinted paper cover of a pamphlet or book. A self-wrapper, as opposed to wrapper or wrappers, is an integral part of the sheet or sheets comprising the body of a publication so bound.

SEWING. The method for holding pages and signatures of a book together by means of thread. The terms *sewing* and *stitching* are sometimes used interchangeably, but the preference today among binders is to use sewing to indicate thread binding and stitching to indicate wire-staple binding.

SHEETS. Printed pages of a book, either flat or folded, but unbound.

SIGNATURE. A folded printed sheet forming one section of a book. A signature commonly has sixteen or thirty-two pages, although any multiple of four is possible. Sometimes called gathering, quire, or section. (*See* Book sizes).

SLEEPER. A trade book for which there is apparently little initial demand, but for which a steady, often wide, market develops later; or a rare book in a catalog or on a dealer's shelves that is marked at a very low price because the seller is unaware of its actual, higher monetary value.

SLIPCASE. A cardboard case usually covered in paper, cloth, or leather to hold a book in order to protect it.

STATE. Variations from an ideal copy created when changes are made during printing or before publication or sale. 1. Intentional or unintentional alterations not affecting page make-up made during printing, such as stop-press corrections; resetting as the result of accidental damage to the type; or resetting of distributed matter following a decision during printing to enlarge the edition quantity. 2. Addition, deletion, or substitution of matter, affecting page make-up, carried out during printing; 3. Changes made after some copies have been sold (not involving a new title page) such as the insertion or cancellation of preliminaries or text pages, or the addition of errata leaves, advertisements, etc. 4. Errors of the arrangement of type pages, or machining. 5. Use of special paper undistinguished typographically from copies on ordinary paper. *See also* Issue.

SUBTITLE. An additional or second title of a book, usually following the title and preceded by a colon. For example, *Bibliophile in the Nursery: A Bookman's Treasury of Collector's Lore on Old and Rare Children's Books.*

SUNNED. Means the covers have been bleached or faded by sunlight.

TIPPED IN. A separate leaf, illustration, or signature added during binding. Known also as *pasted in*. Common for full-page illustrations on special paper.

TISSUE. Very thin papers, almost transparent, used to cover the face of an engraving, an etching, or an important, often tipped-in, illustrative plate to protect both the plate and the text pages.

TRADE EDITION. An edition of a book intended for sale to the general public through bookstores or for general circulation in libraries, as distinct from an edition of the same book intended for some other use (e.g., textbook) or for sale through some other channel (e.g., subscription books).

TYPE. A rectangular block having its face so shaped as to produce, in printing, a letter, figure, or other character, capable of being assembled into text and used in a printing press. The Chinese used these carved from wood from the 8th to the 13th centuries. Cast in metal, they formed the basis of the Western invention of printing. As nonmetallic composition (or photo-offset) has grown, type is being redefined more in terms of its visual properties, e.g., as a standardized design for typeface or typefont.

VANITY PRESS. A designation for a publishing company that specializes in producing books not at its own risk, but at the author's request, risk, and expense.

VARIANT. A book that differs in one or more features from others of the same printing. Variations may occur in the sheets, binding, etc., or in two or more of these. There may be, and sometimes are, two or more variants within a single impression. These variations often make sequence of printing or stamping very difficult to establish. *See also* Issue; *State*.

VELLUM. The skin of a calf, unsplit and specially treated for use in writing, printing, or bookbinding. It is a finer material than parchment, although at one time the word *parchment* was used to mean both parchment and vellum.

WATERMARK. A design faintly apparent when paper is held up to the light. Paper for fine editions is sometimes watermarked with a special design to show that the paper was made specially for that edition.

WRAPPERS. The printed or unprinted cover of a pamphlet or book bound in paper.

Bibliography

This bibliography includes those references that I consulted in preparing the text—background sources—and those books and articles from which I have quoted. Enough data is given for all the hundreds of books mentioned within the text for the reader to be able to obtain complete citations where desired. Chapter 10, "Printed Helpers," tells you how to do this for both in and out-of-print books.

AB Bookman's Weekly: For the Specialist Book World, P.O. Box AB, Clifton, N.J. 07023.

Ahearn, Allen. *Book Collecting: A Comprehensive Guide*. New York: G. P. Putnam, 1989.

Ahearn, Allen and Patricia Ahearn. *Collected Books: The Guide to Values*. New York: G. P. Putnam, 1991.

Allison, June. "Hoosier in Manhattan: Miss Ball's Books Given to New York Library." *The Muncie* [Indiana] *Star*, September 13, 1975.

American Library Association. Association of Library Service to Children, Item 46, Midwinter, 1988.

Arbuthnot, May Hill. *See* Sutherland, Zena.

Avery, Gillian and Julia Briggs, eds. *Children and Their Books: A Celebration of the Work of Iona and Peter Opie*. Oxford: Clarendon Press, 1989.

Bader, Barbara. *American Picturebooks: From Noah's Ark to the Beast Within*. New York: Macmillan, 1976.

Barlow, William P., Jr. "Book Collecting: Personal Rewards and Public Benefits." Viewpoint Series No. 11, Washington, D.C.: The Center for the Book, Library of Congress, 1984.

Bettelheim, Bruno. *The Uses of Enchantment: The Meaning and Importance of Fairy Tales.* New York, Knopf, 1976.

Bradley, Van Allen. *The Book Collector's Handbook of Values,* 1976–1977. New York: G. P. Putnam, 1972.

Carpenter, Humphrey, and Mari Prichard, eds. *The Oxford Companion to Children's Literature.* Oxford: Oxford University Press, 1987.

Carr, Jo Ann. *Beyond Fact: Nonfiction for Children and Young People.* Chicago: American Library Assocation, 1982.

Carter, John. *ABC for Book Collectors.* London: Hart-Davis, MacGibbon, 1974.

Chernofsky, Jacob L. "Children's Books as a Source of Cultural History." *AB Bookman's Weekly,* November 14, 1988.

Chester, Tessa Rose. *Children's Books Research: A Practical Guide to Techniques and Sources.* Oxford: Thimble Press, 1989.

"Childhood Choices: American Pastimes and Everyday Fantasies, 1900–1950." Washington, D.C.: Exhibits Division, Library of Congress, 1986–87, 1988.

Commager, Henry Steele, ed. *The St. Nicholas Anthology.* New York: Random House, 1948.

Connolly, Joseph, ed. *Children's Modern First Editions.* London: Mcdonald Orbis, 1988.

Coughlan, Margaret N. "Individual Collections." In "The Study and Collecting of Historical Children's Books." *Library Trends,* Spring, 1979.

Dalby, Richard. *The Golden Age of Children's Book Illustration.* New York: Gallery Books, 1991.

Delmar, Gloria T. *Louisa M. Alcott and "Little Women."* Jefferson, N.C.: McFarland, 1990.

Delsol, Christine. "A Child's Garden of Storybook Friends." *The Times* (London), December 20, 1986.

deVries, J. Leonard. *A Treasury of Illustrated Children's Books.* New York: Abbeville Press, 1989.

Egoff, Sheila A. *Thursday's Child: Trends and Patterns in Contemporary Children's Literature.* Chicago: American Library Association, 1981.

Encyclopedia Americana: "Children's Literature." New York: Americana, 1986.

Field, Carolyn Wicker, ed. *Special Collections in Children's Literature.* Chicago: American Library Association, 1982.

Fox, Paula. "Some Thoughts on Imagination in Children's Literature." In *Celebrating Children's Books,* edited by Betsy Hearne and Marilyn Kaye. New York: Lothrop, Lee & Shepard, 1981.

Garceau, Oliver. *The Public Library in the Political Process.* New York: Columbia University Press, 1956.

Getlein, Frank and Dorothy Getlein. *The Bite of the Print.* New York: Bramhall House, 1963.

Goldman, Paul. *Looking at Prints, Drawings and Watercolors: A Guide to Technical Terms.* London: British Museum Publications, 1988.

Halsey, Rosalie V. *Forgotten Books of the American Nursery: A History of the Development of the American Story-Book.* Boston: Charles E. Goodspeed, 1911.

Hallstead, William F. "Pages from the SEPIA Years of Hoops and Hobbles." *Maryland,* Vol. 11, no. 2.

Hamilton, Virginia. "Ah, Sweet Rememory." In *Innocence and Experience: Essays and Conversations in Children's Literature,* compiled and edited by Barbara Harrison and Gregory Maguire from programs presented at Simmons College

Center for the Study of Children's Literature, Boston, Mass. New York: Lothrop, Lee & Shepard, 1987.

Hardyment, Christina. *Heidi's Alp: One Family's Search for Storybook Europe*. New York: Atlantic Monthly Press, 1967.

Hawes, Joseph M., and N. Ray Hiner, eds. *American Childhood: A Research Guide and Historical Handbook*. Westport, Conn.: Greenwood Press, 1985.

Hazard, Paul. *Books, Children and Men*. Boston: Horn Book, 1947.

Hirsch, E. D., Jr., Joseph F. Kett, and James Trefil. *The Dictionary of Cultural Literacy: What Every American Needs to Know*. Boston: Houghton Mifflin, 1988.

Hopkins, Lee Bennett. "Letter to the Editor." *The Horn Book Magazine*, July/August 1990.

———. *Pass the Poetry, Please*. New York: Harper & Row, 1987.

Huck, Charlotte S., Susan Hepler, and Janet Hickman, eds. *Children's Literature in the Elementary School*: 4th Edition. Fort Worth: Holt, Rinehart and Winston, 1979.

Huthwaite, Motoko F. "The Library of Congress." In "The Study and Collecting of Historical Children's Books." In *Library Trends*, Spring, 1979.

Ivins, William M., Jr. *Prints and Visual Communication*. Cambridge: Harvard University Press, 1953.

Johnston, Susana and Tim Beddow. *Collecting: The Passionate Pastime*. New York: Harper & Row, 1986.

Livingston, Myra Cohn. *Climb the Bell Tower; Essays on Poetry*. New York: Harper-Collins, 1990.

Macaulay, David. *The Way Things Work*. Boston: Houghton Mifflin, 1988.

MacDonald, George. *The Princess and Curdie*. Illus. by Nora S. Unwin. New York: Macmillan, 1954.

McElderry, Margaret K. "The Best of Times, the Worst of Times: Children's Book Publishing, 1924–1974." *The Horn Book Magazine*, October 1974.

MacNeil, Robert. *Wordstruck: A Memoir*. New York: Viking, 1989.

Manguel, Alberto. "An Argentinian Childhood." *The Washington Post Book World*, November 5, 1989.

Meigs, Cornelia, Anne Thaxter Eaton, Elizabeth Nesbit, and Ruth Hill Viguers. *A Critical History of Children's Literature*. New York: Macmillan, 1959.

Moeser, Vicki. "Ellen Wells—Eclectic Collector Extraordinaire." *The Torch* (Smithsonian Institution staff newsletter), August 1990.

Narahashi, Keiko. *I Have a Friend*. New York: Macmillan, 1987.

Nelson, Karen. "The Kerlan Collection." *Top of the News*, January 1968.

Newton, A. Edward. *The Amenities of Book Collecting: and Kindred Affections*. Boston: Little, Brown, 1929.

Opie, Iona, Robert Opie, and Brian Alderson. *The Treasures of Childhood; Books, Toys and Games from the Opie Collection*. London: Pavilion Books, 1989.

Peters, Jean, ed. *The Bookman's Glossary*. New York: Bowker, 1983.

Pitz, Henry C. *Illustrating Children's Books, History, Technique, Production*. Philadelphia: Watson-Guptill, 1963.

Quayle, Eric. *Early Children's Books: A Collector's Guide*. Totowa, N.J.: Barnes & Noble, 1983.

Quiller-Couch, Sir Arthur. *The Sleeping Beauty and Other Fairy Tales*. Garden City, N.Y.: Garden City Publishing Co., 1930.

St. John, Judith. "The Osborne Collection of Early Children's Books: Highlights in Retrospect." *The Horn Book Magazine*, September/October 1984.

Sayers, Frances Clarke. *Summoned by Books*. Compiled by Marjeanne Jensen Blinn. New York: Macmillan, 1965.

Schiller, Justin G. *The Distinguished Collection of L. Frank Baum and Related Oziana, Including W. W. Denslow, Formed by Justin G. Schiller*. Catalog auction sale #1118. New York: Swann Galleries, 1978.

Sendak, Maurice. *Caldecott & Co.: Notes on Books and Pictures*. New York: Michael di Capua Books, Farrar, Straus & Giroux, 1988.

Sewell, Anna. *The Annotated Black Beauty*. Introduction and annotations by Ellen B. Wells and Anne Grimshaw. London: J.A. Allen, 1989.

Shaw, John MacKay. "Childhood in Poetry." *Top of the News*, November, 1967.

Smith, Lilian. *The Unreluctant Years*. Chicago: American Library Association, 1970.

Stuever, Hank. "Pop Goes the Culture." *The Washington Post*, September 11, 1990.

Stevenson, Robert Louis. *My Shadow*. Illus. by Glenna Lang. Boston: David R. Godine, 1989.

Sutherland, Zena, and May Hill Arbuthnot, eds. *Children and Books*, 8th ed. Chicago: Scott, Foresman, 1991.

Targ, William, ed. *Bibliophile in the Nursery*. Cleveland: World Publishing, 1957.

Townsend, John Rowe. *Written for Children: An Outline of English-Language Children's Literature*. Philadelphia: J.B. Lippincott, 1974.

West, Mark I. *Before Oz: Juvenile Fantasy Stories from Nineteenth-Century America*. Hamden, Conn.: Archon Books, 1989.

Woodworth, Fred. *The Mystery and Adventure Series Review*. Box 3488, Tucson, Ariz. 85722.

Wormell, Christopher. *An Animal Alphabet*. New York: Dial, 1990.

Index

Indexed are authors, illustrators, collectors, bookdealers, librarians, commentators, and other "people of the book"; some book characters that have become icons; book-centered organizations; and selected subjects. Not indexed are the alphabetical collecting genres of chapter 3, and the resources listed in chapter 10.